T0386641

Driven by Desire

The Desiré Wilson story

WWW.VELOCE.CO.UK

First published in September 2011 by Veloce Publishing Limited, Veloce House, Parkway Farm Business Park, Middle Farm Way, Poundbury, Dorchester, Dorset, DT1 3AR, England.
Fax 01305 250479/e-mail info@veloce.co.uk/web www.veloce.co.uk or www.velocebooks.com.

ISBN: 978-1-845843-89-2 UPC: 6-36847-04389-6

Readers with ideas for automotive books, or books on other transport or related hobby subjects, are invited to write to the editorial director of Veloce Publishing at the above address.
British Library Cataloguing in Publication Data – A catalogue record for this book is available from the British Library.
Typesetting, design and page make-up all by Veloce Publishing Ltd on Apple Mac. Printed in India by Replika Press.

Driven by Desire

The Desiré Wilson story

VELOCE PUBLISHING
THE PUBLISHER OF FINE AUTOMOTIVE BOOKS

CONTENTS

FOREWORD BY THE
EARL OF MARCH AND KINRARA

DESIRÉ is a remarkable woman. A loyal supporter of both the Festival of Speed and the Revival at Goodwood, she has become a good friend. Nowadays, of course, she races for fun – but she is and always was a fierce competitor.

She is best known for being the only woman ever to win a Formula 1 race, winning a round of the Aurora series at Brands Hatch in a Wolf WR4, in 1980. A year later she raced a Tyrrell, at Kyalami, back in her homeland of South Africa, where she began racing micro-midgets as a five-year-old child.

Desiré and the Earl of March. (Courtesy Jeff Bloxham)

Later in her career, she took on the challenge of Indycars in the United States – not an activity for the faint-hearted. But there's much more to Desiré than just statistics.

She is full of life, always up for a challenge – as her exploits in a Shelby Cobra in the RAC TT Celebration race at the Revival have proved. Her love of the sport and her knowledge of its history have made her an extremely popular guest at Goodwood events. She would never consider herself 'a woman in a man's world,' just a person who identifies a challenge and takes it in her stride.

When she and her husband, Alan, came to Britain from South Africa, they immediately made their mark, working with John Webb to put Brands Hatch firmly on the international motor racing map. '*Driven by Desire*' is Alan's account of a journey that, over 50 years, saw Desiré become what many consider to be the best woman ever to race cars.

I am delighted to wish her every success with a book which will fascinate all those who know Desiré, as well as those who have not yet had that pleasure.

Fast-foreword
by Derek Bell MBE

I was delighted when Alan and Desiré Wilson asked me to write this foreword, for a number of reasons, but, particularly, because this is a story that needed to be told. During my long career I've raced against a number of women and, without doubt, she is the most versatile, not to say fastest, that I've encountered. Some years ago I even recommended to a certain team owner that he should hire her to race as my team-mate in the States. He turned the idea down simply because she was a woman. This is just one instance, and I believe there have been many more, where her gender has worked against her. People just didn't take her seriously enough as a racing driver.

We're supposed to make our own luck, but, when you look at her career, there are a number of occasions when, through no fault of her own, things simply didn't run her way. Her husband, Alan, has always been a tremendous support to Desiré, and some of the stories I've heard from him over the years are in this book – but there are plenty of other incidents that have never previously been revealed. As a five-times Le Mans winner I particularly enjoyed the chapters relating to her drives with that extraordinary character Alain de Cadenet, as well as the amazing story about the pink Japanese-run Spice at Le Mans. I'm only glad that I didn't have to drive for that particular team.

Many of you know that I've had a lifelong love affair with Goodwood, so it's with particular pleasure that I now see Desiré regularly competing at the great Sussex track. We've even been on the same grid together. She not only enters into the spirit of the occasion, but whatever she drives, she still proves that she's very fast. I think this book will not only prove to be an informative and amusing read, but will also be an inspiration to those women with a driving ambition.

Derek Bell. (Courtesy Jeff Bloxham)

THANKS

THERE'S no way that Desiré and I could have lived the lives we have without the help and support of a number of valued friends and associates. We would like to use this book to thank some of these very important people.

At the top of this list is Charlie Randall. In any other time and world Charlie would have been an internationally recognised rider and engineer, but his lot in life was, instead, to be a mechanic in a small town in South Africa, camouflaging skills and talents that not only helped launch Desiré's career, but also those of many South African motorcycle racing champions. Charlie's engine building skills, his understanding of the true racer's mind, and his devotion to daughter Desiré's racing is the keystone on which her life was built. Maurice Rosenberg, who devoted the time and provided the skills and advice that led to a championship; Jim, Huub, and Loek Vermuelen, the Dutch brothers who made her first year in Europe possible; and the late Roy Thomas, who was a friend in need during tough days in England.

John Webb, the best and most creative race promoter there has ever been, played a crucial role in getting Desiré into Formula 1. Along with Jackie Epstein, Tony Lanfranci, and Brian Jones, he was a wise hand during a fast-moving and maturing period of her life. John's contribution to British racing cannot be underestimated: whether his creative developments of Formula Ford, Formula Ford 2000, Formula 5000, and Sports 2000 – to name just a few of his ideas – or his development of Brands Hatch into the world's leading Grand Prix circuit of the early 1980s. John's belief in Desiré was the single factor that dragged her out of club racing and thrust her into the international limelight.

Nick Challis, who provided Des with cars to race, wholehearted support and friendship, and was a strong believer in her potential; Tom and Sally Bagley, whose invitation to drive at Phoenix, ignited our dream to live in the USA; Alain de Cadenet, the chauvinist who put Des' talents above his own ambitions and earned them both historic World Championship victories. Teddy Yip, who took her to Indy; John Fitzpatrick, the professional's professional, who treated Des with respect, recognised her talents, and provided her with two of the best cars she ever drove – and told her to drive them as hard as she could. Ken Tyrrell, who gave her the best ride of her life, and an offer to race in the full 1981 Formula 1 World Championship. Heather and Norman Carstensen, Porsche fans in South Africa whose financial support at a crucial time launched her into American racing, and a very special drive at Le Mans. Herb and Rose Wysard, Indy fans, whose budgets could never match their best intentions and ambitions, but, who believed and tried so hard; and Arthur Abraham, who reached out from South Africa to arrange support for Des' Indycar and IMSA programs.

To the late Mark Freeman, the mechanic who believed to his bones that Des could do it and worked so damned hard to give her the car she needed, and, at the same time, epitomized all those other mechanics and crewmen who worked long hours with skill and patience on her cars. Mark's type of mechanic is a breed without whom racing could not exist.

Jurgen Barth, the Porsche man and fine driver, who believed in her enough to get her a great drive at Le Mans. Lord Charles March, whose invitations to Desiré to compete at his wonderful Goodwood events opened new horizons, and enabled her to wind-down her racing career in the most pleasant and enjoyable way, and the car owners who made their cars available for her to drive.

Then there are Juliette (Jules) Brindley and Sally French-Griffiths, friends for more than 30 years, whose support and belief have been constant.

And thank you Andrew Marriot, our longtime friend who read, believed in and agreed to edit this book, and made the crucial connection to the team at Veloce, without whom this book would have sat on my computer forever!

There are too many more friends, fans, and acquaintances to name here. If you did anything to contribute to Desiré's success, her happiness, or her life, you know who you are. Thank you.

There are also those who belong on the 'No Thanks' list …

Read on: you, too, are part of the story.

ACKNOWLEDGEMENTS

ALL photos are from the personal collection of Alan Wilson, except where otherwise marked. The author has made every reasonable effort to contact the copyright holder in every case where he believes permission to be required, but in some cases, particularly with older photographs, it hasn't been possible to locate the party concerned. The author would be obliged if those parties, or their agents or heirs, would contact him via Veloce Publishing.

Alan Wilson

Opposite: (Courtesy Wilson Collection (1, 2, 4, 7-13, 15), MA-Torres (3, 14), IMSPhoto (5), and David Hutson (6).

Brock Yates, in his era-defining book, *Against Death and Time*, said of race drivers that they ...

... "come in all shapes and sizes. Yet –° seem to share one characteristic. It is the eyes. Someone had once described them as 'gunfighters eyes,' even and clear, deeply penetrating, unblinking, laser-like at their target" ....

Not all gunfighters were male.

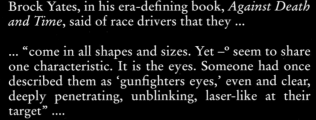

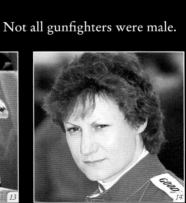

PROLOGUE

No woman has ever raced at the top level of the Formula 1 World Championship, and, in the minds of many, no woman ever will. Yet there's no physical or psychological reason why this shouldn't be possible. After all, even though Grand Prix racing requires a driver to be tremendously fit, is a Grand Prix driver physically fitter than a top female athlete? Even though a modern Formula 1 car takes strength to drive, are female Olympians any weaker than the men who race Formula 1 every second weekend of the summer? Does a male racer have more endurance than a women's marathon gold medallist? Are male Formula 1 drivers really any braver than women who set downhill speed records of nearly 125mph on skis?

What about lady drivers, like rallying's Michelle Mouton and Pat Moss? They won World Championship events against the best drivers in the world during their years on the Audi and BMC factory teams. Maybe they didn't win every time, but they beat their best male competitors in some of the most gruelling events, and they certainly justified the positions they held in the top factory rally teams of their time.

It's a fact that no female race driver has been able to assert herself near the top of Formula 1 racing, even though Lella Lombardi raced in Grand Prix events for two years; Maria Theresa de Filippis drove a Maserati 250F, against the likes of Stirling Moss, in 1958 and 1959, and prewar drivers like Glenda Hawkes and Kay Petrie all raced head-to-head with, and beat, some of the best male drivers of their times. While it's certainly true that very few women have been able to challenge the best male drivers in the top categories of racing, this doesn't mean that no woman will ever be incapable of doing so.

That there haven't been more lady drivers who have raced and won at the highest levels may just be a result of statistics. After all, since professional racing began at the beginning of the 20th Century, there have been hundreds-of-thousands of men around the world, who have taken up the sport with the intention of progressing as far up the ladder of success as they could, compared to, probably, only a few hundred-or-so ladies who have set out on the same path.

While this numerical imbalance is surely a factor, there are other reasons why so few women racers have made the grade. These include lack of opportunity and lack of sufficient grounding in the basics of the sport, as well as a lack of financial support – rationales that have also applied to thousands of male drivers. But there's another factor that's played it's part, unique to the female sex: decisions taken by men that have kept women out of competitive cars – the 'no women is going to drive my car' syndrome.

Motor racing has been called a cruel sport, not only because of the lives it has taken, or the injuries that have been suffered by so many of its participants, but, also, because there were so many drivers who deserved success, but were prevented from achieving their ultimate goals by fates that conspired against them. Drivers like Tony Brise, Roger Williamson, Tom Pryce, and Timmy Mayer, who died before they could reach the stars, and others, like Stephen South and Danny Watts, who suffered grotesque injuries when poised to make the grade into Formula 1; and many, many others who simply couldn't find the cash to fund their way to fame. For sure, there is also someone, somewhere in the world outside of racing, who has had the skills of a Stirling Moss, Jimmy Clark, Ayrton Senna, Michael Schumacher, or Lewis

Hamilton, but whose talents have never been seen on a race track.

One of the great things about racing, though, is that, while many would-be stars fall by the wayside, there always seems to be someone whose career is on the rise; the up-and-coming driver of the future, who the pundits, fans, and the media believe will be the next superstar – the next Alain Prost, Niki Lauda, or Sebastian Vettel.

Why couldn't that someone be a Michelle Schumacher?

This is the story of the one lady driver who came closest to being that female racing superstar; whose flirtation with Formula 1 was recognised by her peers as the most credible approach to a Grand Prix career that's ever been achieved by a woman driver; a woman recognised by many knowledgeable members of the international racing media (always slow to hand out accolades), and by many of her male competitors, as most probably the best woman race driver there's ever been.

While this is the tale of one woman driver who fought her way towards the top, it's in many ways, also, a story that parallels the careers of many talented male drivers, who've also risen from club racing into the world of professional motorsport. Over the years there have been many thousands who have raced at this level. However, of these only a very few have managed to reach the verges of Formula 1, and only five of these have been women; only one of whom was ever seriously considered for a full time ride in a leading Formula 1 team.

This is a story that includes success and failure, patience and perseverance, impatience and opportunity, tragedy and triumph. There's humour and sadness, fear and extreme bravery. It's the story of a struggle against fellow drivers, against financial barriers, against politics, and against prejudice. Above all, it's a tale of a determination to succeed that goes beyond commitment, beyond self belief, beyond expectation, and far beyond the bounds of gender.

It is the story of a lady-in-racing.

It is the story of Desiré Wilson.

❀ ❀ ❀

BEFORE going any further, I would like to clear up the spelling and pronunciation of Desiré's name. It has been an issue ever since she started out in the sport.

First, Desiré is spelt incorrectly. At her baptism, someone forgot the last 'e,' giving baby Desiré Randall a name that, in its true French context, is masculine. Not that it's mattered that much. Except, perhaps, to the two French journalists at Le Mans, in 1980, who tried to paint her as butch – partly because of the name; partly because they wanted to trash the reputation and credibility of the 125lb girl who'd recently won two World Endurance Championship sports car events, and was reckoned to be one of the favourites to win the famous 24-hour race – and, most likely, because a story that questioned her sexuality would sell more newspapers.

'Desiré' has, over the years, been given many different pronunciations. In South Africa, it was 'Desray.' In Holland, 'Daisy-ray;' in England 'Des-ear-ray;' in the USA 'Des-er-ray.' And, by Tony Lanfranchi, 'Deathray.'

I call her Des, Desi (sometimes pronounced Dayz-i), Des-er-ray, or wife.

Alan Wilson

1

"PUT THIS CAR ON ITS WHEELS AND PUSH"

TINA Randall screamed. Charlie Randall and Hughie Cruse dropped everything and ran. Beverley Randall drove her race car into the pits and burst into tears.

Spectators jumped to their feet to watch the blue and yellow race car as it tumbled down the track, finally landing upside down in the fence, the driver hanging in the seat belts, arms frantically waving for help.

Charlie arrived first, dropping to his knees to peer into the cockpit. Hughie Cruse released the driver.

"Dammit, what's the matter with you? Put this car on its wheels and push man, push!"

Five-year-old race car driver Desiré Randall wasn't just unhurt, she was furious. She was no longer leading the race and wanted to get back on the track – fast.

Photos of Desiré taken during her first year of racing show a small, skinny, dark haired, elfin girl, wearing oversized overalls, a helmet that threatened to envelope her entire head, and goggles so big that her piercing, dark-brown eyes could almost see through a single lens. They also show a blue and yellow micro-midget racer at 60mph, hustling around a corner under perfect control, the driver totally focused on her job. They show a little girl, much smaller than the second- and third-placed drivers on either side – smaller even than the trophy she is holding; a Coca Cola in the other hand, and the cocky smile of a winner on her face.

Desiré Randall was already winning races when she was just five years old.

Charlie and Tina Randall had two daughters; Beverley and Desiré, who was the younger by four years. Charlie had been a racer all his life, first riding on the grass and dirt tracks of South Africa's East

Sideways, Slideways and Fearless. Desiré knew how to hustle a race car from her first turn at the wheel. Her determination showed from the very beginning. (Courtesy Wilson Collection)

Rand area, and then, when he had become dominant in that sphere, on the road courses of South Africa. Recognising that he didn't have the financial resources to compete in the 500cc and 350cc National Championships, Charlie used his mechanical skills to create his own 250cc machine. Starting with an older 350 Norton, Charlie made a new connecting rod, cast new crank cases, modified the barrel, and re-engineered the head and valves until, more Randall than Norton, his creation proved to be faster than any other 250cc machine in the country, taking him

Great Things Come In Small Packages. Desiré (far right) was always the smallest girl (or boy) in every race she ran. She made up for size in intensity, courage, and a fierce will to win. (Courtesy Wilson Collection)

to the South African Championship. In fact, the 250 Randall-Norton hybrid was so fast, he competed at the front of the field in many 350cc national races, too.

Charlie continued to race the South African and Rhodesian circuit for several years, before multiple leg injuries from too many racing falls caused his doctors to warn him off motorcycle riding for ever. Not yet ready to quit racing, he bought an F3 Cooper chassis, and inserted one of his Norton engines. But, Charlie was a bike guy and decided that car racing wasn't for him. He was much happier hanging around with the friends who'd helped him through his bike racing days. These friends, too, are part of the Desiré Wilson story.

Hughie Cruse, Fred Van Niekerk, 'Van' van Breda, Uncle Jack Auret, Laurie Zeeman, Benny Scott, and a few others, came from the hard mining towns of the East Rand; Brakpan, Boksburg, Benoni, and Springs. They had grown up together, gone to the same schools, and been bitten by the motorcycle racing bug together. Some became riders, others chose to be mechanics. All supported each other, and everyone enjoyed the travel, the parties, the drinking, and the fun that was an essential part of their sport.

Charlie Randall was by far the best rider of the bunch, so the group of friends rallied around to help him race in the much more competitive world of the South African National Championships. Helping with money, and with mechanical work on the bikes, they were always there, providing moral support and friendship. They helped Charlie win his National Championship; something he didn't forget, and was to repay with interest in the years to follow.

During this period, the men married, settled into steady jobs, and started families, whom they took with them to races. Charlie married Catharina Botha, and became the father of two girls. Beverley was the same age as most of the other friends' kids, while Desiré was a little younger, born on November 26th, 1953. Their children played at each other's homes and in the paddocks of South Africa's race tracks.

Several of the children would later become race stars in their own right, among them future champions Les van Breda, Keith Zeeman, Gilles Cruse, Bobby Scott, Kenny Gray, Roy Klomfass, and Trevor van Rooyen.

As the 1950s progressed, friendships strengthened, and the kids grew, soon becoming old enough to want to race themselves. So, when Charlie's leg injuries forced him to stop, it just seemed natural for everyone to switch their focus from his racing activities, to those of their children. The East Rand bunch moved into micro-midget racing.

Micro-midgets were small, rear-engine, single-seat race cars, powered by modified scooter engines. They featured American sprint car style bodywork, chain drive, coil spring suspension, and narrow scooter wheels and tyres. All were home built, and most could reach 60mph on the short dirt tracks and ovals carved out of the dirt of the Highveld.

Charlie built two cars, one each for Beverley and Desiré. Beverley was quick, maybe even the better driver of the two. She won many races, but didn't have a burning desire to drive, and soon decided that racing wasn't her thing. Desiré won regularly and decided racing was for her.

Desiré's micro-midget career lasted until she was twelve, by which age she had won multiple races and club championships. During this time, she developed into a fast, aggressive, and very uncompromising driver for whom patience wasn't a strong point. Usually racing against older boys, and almost always the smallest driver in the field, she didn't take to others bullying her on the track. Her determination to win was matched by a fierce temper, typified by

13

Doing Girl Things! *During her teens, Desiré focused on her horses and athletics. Racing was not something a young lady should be doing!*
(Courtesy Wilson Collection)

Charlie's Angels. *The Randall girls certainly had their Dad's instincts. They may have looked angelic but they were devils on the track! (Courtesy Wilson Collection)*

one rousing scene where she stood on tiptoe to reach the height of an older driver who had displaced her on the track, pushed her face right up against his, and screamed at the top of her voice;

"If you do that again, I'll kill you, kill you!" This was from a six-year-old girl who was the smallest and youngest driver in the field.

Desiré's temper wasn't confined to the track. Being small, she often found herself ignored, the adults talking over her head, so she developed a technique that quickly gained both their attention, and a nickname she hates to this day. They called her 'Boots,' because the sharp kicks she delivered to the adults' shins always got their attention. She was also

noted for her determination, and her demand to be treated fairly and be recognised as a serious racer.

At one Friday night stock car race, at the Benoni Golden Sands dirt oval, the micro-midgets shared the evening with full-size, adult-driven stock cars. Winning her event, Desiré, now eight, set a lap time that broke the outright track record, faster, even, than the modified sedans could achieve. At the post-event prize giving, in front of the crowded stands, Desiré adamantly refused to accept her trophy because the officials had determined her lap time to be 'unofficial,' and instead recognised the slower time of a full-size stock car as the new track record.

When Desiré was twelve, and raced in the fastest category of micro-midget racing, she competed for the South African Championship, ending the season in Cape Town with the same number of points as 16-year-old Les van Breda. Both drivers had won each of their heats and amassed the same number of points, and were, according to the rules of the competition, equal champions. The organisers, however, decided to settle the championship over five laps, much against Les' will, as he wanted to share the victory with Des, but he was over-ruled and then won the match race by inches.

Whether as a consequence of this, or simply because Des had now grown into a typical 12-year-old girl, who had fallen in love with horses, racing no longer seemed appropriate, and she lost interest in the micro-midget scene. She quit, and concentrated on athletics, winning three Transvaal junior, and two senior Championships. For the next six years, Desiré's interests were shared equally between horses and track and field.

As a rider, she operated out of a family friend's professional racing stable where she spent hours each day riding, training, and generally mucking about with horses, eventually buying and owning several jumpers. She even played a competitive game of polo, again, in unofficial matches, as women weren't allowed to compete in formal club events. At school, although never a top scholar, she was soon recognised for her leadership qualities, and her athletic skills, winning many awards and honours. This culminated in her two final years at school, when she became Victor Ludorum, winning every event in each year-end school sports day, except shot putt, and setting, amongst others, a school hurdles record that was to stand for many years.

Charlie Randall, too, switched his efforts. Now working as competition manager for the South African importer of Suzuki motorcycles, he used both his technical expertise, and his philosophical genius, to develop the skills of the sons of those same friends who had helped him with his career. Among the riders who Charlie took under his wing, coached, and provided with competitive motorcycles, were Freddie van Niekerk, Gilles Cruse, Les van Breda, Keith Zeeman, and Trevor van Rooyen, who, between them, were to win many South African National Championship titles.

Eighteen is the magic age at which South African teenagers were allowed to obtain their car driver's licence. So, very shortly after her eighteenth birthday, Charlie and Desiré arrived at Kyalami, South Africa's famous Grand Prix track, with an old, borrowed race car in tow. Racing was back on Des' agenda. The story was typically Charlie Randall.

A Brakpan garage owner ran a Formula Vee race car for a local driver, so Charlie persuaded him to let Desiré test the car.

Home Built. *With no money to buy a race car, Charlie Randall and Hughie Cruse built their own Formula Vee racer for Des to drive. While not very competitive, it gave the 18-year-old girl the experience she needed to move onwards in racing. (Courtesy Wilson Collection)*

He strapped her in, telling her, "This is the lap record. Get on with it."

Desiré didn't break the record in her first drive in a proper race car, but she did lap significantly faster than the regular driver, earning the use of the car for the rest of the 1972 club racing season.

She accomplished little in her first year on the big tracks, but gained valuable experience, while Charlie soon realised that the borrowed race car was far from competitive. Consequently, with the help of Hughie Cruse and Jack Auret, Desiré was able to start the 1973 race season with a new, but home-made, chassis, and an engine (recovered from a scrap yard) which had been rebuilt to Charlie's exacting standards.

Over the following two seasons, Desiré learned quickly, becoming competitive in what was then a very strong national series. The handicap of running with very little money, using the home-built chassis, and scrap yard engines, was something that the inexperienced driver and team found difficult to overcome, yet by the end of her second full year of driving, she was regularly racing among the leaders, finishing the season in fifth place, and as one of the favourites to challenge for the 1974 National Championships.

At this point, I need to digress from the Desiré story.

My own involvement in racing began while at University, when I first rallied an old MGA, before switching to motorcycle racing on my road-going Yamaha. On graduating at the end of 1969, I joined Ford Motor Company, in Port Elizabeth, as a Graduate Trainee, having been selected to join a fast-track trainee management programme, intended to provide me with a stellar career with the automobile giant. Unbelievably, my first assignment was within the advertising and competitions department. My first year with the company was incredibly exciting. My roles included coordinating Ford's support programs for Group 5 and production-based cars; Ford's involvement in the South Africa Formula One Championship; development of its new rally programme, and responsibility for managing the newly introduced Formula Ford race series. My role in this latter capacity was to develop the series, and ensure it would become an important part of the South African racing world.

Several years before, while still a student at Natal University, in Durban, I had been hired by the *Natal Daily News*, one of South Africa's leading daily newspapers, to write a weekly motor sports column. In October 1968 I wrote a story about a 'Driver to Europe' scheme, to help South Africa's promising drivers to progress into international racing. Now, with the power of Ford behind me, I was able to act on the idea, and under the political guidance, and with help from, journalist Adri Bezuidenhoudt, a programme was established. This was based on a short series of international Formula Ford races that would take place during the South African summer season, in which South African drivers would compete against some of the best European Formula Ford stars. These included the very talented Tony Brise, who was to progress to Formula One before dying in the plane crash that killed his team owner, and ex-world champion, Graham Hill.

The challenge was to ensure that there were sufficient local drivers to provide real competition because, at that time, Formula Ford racing in South Africa was still in its infancy. Here, again, fate was to play its part.

At the time (1970) a young Jody Scheckter was making a name for himself, racing a fast but fragile supercharged Renault R8, pushing Ford's Peter Gough in the factory Escort hard for the saloon car championship. Halfway through the season, Jody approached me and asked to be included in the Ford team – a request I excitedly passed on to my boss, Robin Field, the advertising and competitions manager for Ford. Robin wasn't impressed, turning down the opportunity with a curt response: "He'll never get anywhere, we don't need him."

Still, I believed that Jody had an exceptional talent, so, using my position as the Formula Ford series manager, I offered him the use of a Lola T200 that we had imported to be raced by Doug Serrurier's team, but which lay unused in a workshop in Johannesburg.

Driving a single-seater for the first time, and having missed practice and qualifying, Sheckter's first race in the Lola was astonishing. Starting from the back of the grid, he spun five times in the first six laps, but then flew through the field, knocking more than half a second off the Kyalami lap record, to finish just behind the leaders. A star was born.

Jody went on to finish as the leading South African in the Sunshine Series over the summer holidays, and became the first winner of the South African 'Driver to Europe' award. I was proud of my role in developing the 'Driver to Europe' programme.

My tenure with the Ford Competitions Department ended after one year, with my transfer to another department as part of my graduate training scheme. A year later, I moved, with Ford's blessing, to Canada, returning at the beginning of 1972 to take up a position in the Johannesburg regional office.

Which brings us back to the Desiré story.

Back in Johannesburg, a few weeks after my return from Canada, I received a phone call from Ford's new competition manager, Bernie Marriner.

"Alan," he said, "I want you to go out to the races at Kyalami this weekend and take a look at two girl drivers. We've decided that we need a lady driver in the Formula Ford series to help promote it, so we're going to give one of them a new car, engines and a budget; but we need to know which one to choose." The two drivers to be evaluated were Desiré Randall and Judy Witter.

I knew something of Judy, who was already an established star. She was the National Formula Vee champion, driving a professionally built chassis imported from Germany, as part of a two-car team run by her garage-owning father. Fast, smooth, and experienced Judy portrayed the best possible image. Her team was always immaculately turned out, she was a proven race winner, and she had all the financial and mechanical support she needed to stay at the top of Formula Vee. I knew nothing about Desiré.

I had seen her, once, at a Kyalami open practice day; a girl standing in the cockpit of her race car gesticulating at her crew, obviously very upset about something. Unimpressed, I had walked on.

The following weekend, I went out to the national race meeting at Kyalami, watching from Clubhouse Corner, where I could get a close view of one of the more action packed sections of the famous track.

The Formula Vee championship race started, and the field came into view around Sunset Bend, led by Judy Witter's green and white car. The pack stormed into the braking zone, a mass of swerving, jostling cars fighting for the apex of the tight left-hander. Chaos!

From the middle of the pack, a yellow car suddenly emerged, overtaking at least five others.

Overtaking in the real sense, as Desiré Randall's racer leapt over the top of several cars, flying through the air to land on its nose on the outside of the turn.

It was difficult to see exactly what was happening, given the dust, tyre smoke, and confusion that resulted from this aerial assault, but when everything cleared, I could see the yellow car firmly latched onto the back of the lead pack, as Desiré strove to get back into the fight. The fun, for the spectators at least, didn't stop there. Three times in the next few laps Desiré's car left the track at Clubhouse Corner, each time sliding along the right-hand side guardrail, until the driver wrenched it back onto the track to continue her chase through the field. Obviously damaged from the crash landing on lap one, the car was a handful, yet the young girl at the wheel refused to quit, earning a standing ovation from the knowledgeable fans in the clubhouse for her tenacity and sheer fighting spirit. Judy won the race with ease, Desiré was sixth or seventh.

The following Monday I called Bernie Marriner: "There is only one choice. Ford has to go with Judy. Desiré may ultimately be the faster and harder driver, but right now Judy is more professional, smoother, and a much better image for Ford Motor Company and the series."

So, Judy Witter took delivery of a brand-new Merlyn Mk 25, several spare engines, a tow car, trailer, and perhaps the biggest budget in South African Formula Ford racing.

Desiré Randall towed her bent car back to Brakpan, where Charlie, Hughie, and Uncle Jack cut, welded,

Overtaking In the Real Sense. *Desiré caught Alan's attention with this dramatic overtaking move, on the first lap of the first race that he ever saw her drive. Despite a damaged car, Des continued to run with the lead pack at Kyalami. On Alan's recommendation, she lost her opportunity to be given a fully sponsored car by Ford Motor Company! (Courtesy Wilson Collection)*

straightened, and repainted it for the next event. Desiré raced on for the rest of the season, finishing the year fifth in the National Championship.

Motor racing in South Africa in the early 1970s was both well supported and very competitive. Run under the (sometimes benevolent) dictatorship of Alex Blignaut, who was one of international motorsport's best-ever promoters, it was centered on the famous Kyalami race track, situated between Johannesburg and Pretoria. The National Championship series featured events for: the South Africa Formula 1 Championship (which included Formula 5000 and Formula Two machines); Formula Ford 1600 (as the main single-seater support series); Formula Vee; heavily modified Group 5; and semi-standard, production-based saloon cars – as well as several classes of modified, very quick motorcycles, all running in the same two day events. These regular National Championship events attracted as many as 45,000 fans to Kyalami. Almost as many were attracted to tracks in Natal (Roy Hesketh in Pietermaritzburg), Cape Town (Killarney), and the Aldo Scribante Circuit (in Port Elizabeth in the Cape Province), as well as in Bloemfontein and Welkom, in the Orange Free State.

The different events drew large and competitive fields, and presented exciting, close racing to the fans. The top class – the Formula 1/F5000/F2 series (which was subsequently replaced by Formula Atlantic) – was fiercely fought by drivers who included Dave Charlton, John Love, Sam Tingle, Ian Scheckter, Guy Tunmer, Eddie Keizan, Paddy Driver, Basil Van Rooyen, and Jackie Pretorius. These drivers, who were national sporting heroes and well known throughout South Africa, typically chose to carve their careers in their home country.

The Formula Ford series, however, not only attracted drivers who hoped to rise to the premier South African class, but also those whose goal was to get to Europe, where they could race on the world stage.

Most notable of these was, of course, Jody Scheckter, who used the 1970 Driver to Europe Award to catapult himself through the ranks and eventually became Ferrari's 1979 World Formula One Champion.

Jody was followed, in 1972, by his brother, Ian, who raced for the Rothmans-backed March team, and, in 1973, by Kenny Gray, whose Formula Ford career in the factory Van Dieman came to an abrupt

Winning. (Courtesy Wilson Collection)

end against the catch fences of Silverstone. Then there was Roy Klomfass, who didn't win the South African title, but moved to England where he proved to be very quick in the factory Hawke. His real legacy, however, was bringing Rory Byrne with him: Rory went on to become Ferrari's chassis designer through the Schumacher Championship years. Rad Dougal also failed to win the South African Championship, but joined Royale (and Rory Byrne) to dominate British FF2000 in 1977, before moving on, with the Toleman Group, to win an F2 event at Thruxton. Trevor van Rooyen, who won a South African 250cc motorcycle championship on a Charlie Randall supported works Suzuki, also missed out on a South African FF title. He went to Europe and won many races, becoming one of FF1600's leading engine builders. Other South African FF1600 graduates included Mike White, who starred in British F3, Basil Mann, and Graham Duxbury. They also made their way to England, racing with various levels of success, all proving that the best South African drivers could compete at the highest levels of British national championship competition.

Competing in the South African National Formula Vee and Formula Ford Championships was a crucial element in Desiré's move to a professional racing career. The intense competition, the need to prepare cars to their ultimate potential, the sometimes friendly – and occasionally bitter – relationships with her competitors, the lack of money, and the long hours all provided a base of experience that was to stand her in good stead as her career progressed.

2

SOUTH AFRICAN CHAMPION

DESIRÉ continued in Formula Vee throughout the next few seasons, finishing fifth, then second in the National Championships. Meanwhile, I purchased a Formula Ford Titan MkVI, first racing it in club events before moving up to the national series, at the beginning of 1974. After a hiatus, when all racing was banned as a result of the OPEC fuel crisis, we both resumed competition, often racing at the same events, but never actually meeting. I, in the meantime, had left Ford Motor Company to become general manager for a fabrics company owned by the brother-in-law of my steady girlfriend, working in a building in the south end of Johannesburg.

Coincidently, Desiré worked as an accounts clerk and internal auditor for a large retail motor company headquartered in the same building.

At the end of September 1974 two things happened that were to affect both our lives. My long-time girlfriend wanted the commitment of marriage – but, at 28, I wasn't so keen. While my girlfriend was on a three week holiday, Desiré happened to come into our showroom to order curtains for her manager's office. We immediately recognised each other from the track and started talking. We hit it off immediately, started to date, and fell in love.

When my girlfriend returned from her holiday, I had to tell her that I now did want to get married, but not to her! A few weeks later, on Desiré's 21st birthday, we made it formal, setting a wedding date of May 10th, 1975 – the day after my 29th birthday. It was certainly a whirlwind romance and the date, of course, was on a weekend when there wasn't any racing

Now that we were together, and at Charlie's instigation, we decided it was time for Des to move

More to Life than Racing. During 1976, Des and Alan enjoyed life together, living on a farm just outside Johannesburg, going to college in the evenings, riding motorcycles through the veld, and just having a great time together – the basis for 36 years of marriage. (Courtesy Wilson Collection)

up to the Formula Ford category. Charlie arranged to sell her Vee and replace it with a well used MkVI Titan, similar to mine, with the idea that we would race together in our own team. Consequently, with a little sponsorship from a ladies hair products company, we set out to race in the 1975 South Africa Formula Ford Championship series.

For the first few races I was clearly the quicker and more experienced driver, and it wasn't until the fifth race of the season, just one week before our wedding day, that Desiré beat me for the first time and became a contender to win Formula Ford races. The way she beat me was typical of her approach to racing.

We started the Bloemfontein race with my Titan fifth on the grid, Desiré's in 12th. On the run down to the first turn the cars strung out in a long line, running nose-to-tail with no reasonable opportunity to pass. I looked into my mirror as I lined up to take the first turn to see the yellow and green nose of Desiré's car aimed directly at my front wheel. I flinched, braked hard, and gave her room.

Confident that I would give way to her, and clearly taking advantage of our relationship, she dived into the small gap I opened to the car in front of me, turned the corner, and accelerated alongside the car in front as she tried to take third place. Its driver, the far more experienced competitor Quentin Maine, saw that a mere girl was trying to overtake him, slammed his wheels against hers, and pushed her off the track. Even as she fought for control I saw her looking across at him, and watched from two feet behind as she raised her right hand in a fist, and then threw her car across the asphalt at his, hitting it so hard that he skittered into the grass on the opposite side of the track. He nearly lost control, lost time, and allowed Desiré to draw ahead.

As she pulled away to close-in on the race leaders, I realised that my wife-to-be had a level of determination, courage, and sheer ability that was way beyond mine, and that, while I might be an acceptable race driver, she had the talent to become a star.

Desiré finished the race in third place, taking fastest lap and earning her first Formula Ford podium. Quentin and I 'discussed' the incident afterwards. He apologised. Desiré said nothing, but it was to be the last time that I would ever try to fight her battles for her. Neither he nor I were ever to beat Des again.

By the end of the 1975 season, Des was a regular front-runner, although thanks to her early season learning curve, she was to finish only eighth in the Championships.

We married in May, and, just like any newly wed couple, set out to put a home together, living in a rented bungalow on a farm to the north of Johannesburg. Although important, racing was just one part of our lives, for in every other way we were just an ordinary young couple, with financial concerns, careers to follow, and a new life to live together. At the end of the year we faced an important decision.

We both wanted to race, but it was obvious we couldn't afford to run two cars, especially if we wanted to improve Desiré's chances of winning the FF title. I decided to stop racing and we sold both cars to finance the purchase of a newer car for her. We chose a three-year-old Merlyn Mk 25, identical to the car given to Judy Witter by Ford Motor Company at my instigation. This Merlyn had won the 1975 Championship in the hands of Bobby Scott, a friend against whom Desiré had raced in the micro-midget days.

We expanded our team to include Maurice Rosenberg, the guru of South Africa Formula Ford racing. Well, that's not quite true. Maurice 'adopted' Desiré. A fiercely independent loner, Maurice worked for the Alconi performance equipment company and was a key figure behind the company's strong reputation in South African racing. Working with Alconi's blessing, Maurice also spent countless extra hours each year working, for no pay, with the driver who he believed would be that year's Formula Ford Champion, and had played a significant role in developing the careers of several national champions.

When Maurice, who neither of us knew very well at the time, approached Des and informed her that he would be working with her in 1976, we knew immediately that her chance of success had increased immensely.

Our small team set to work on the car, and with a little sponsorship from Castrol, and, later in the season, from *Fairlady*, South Africa's leading national women's magazine, Desiré set out to race for the South African Championship.

The 1976 racing season began with the South Africa Formula 1 Grand Prix, where FF was a major supporting event. Desiré started from tenth, having run her bearings in qualifying, but, by lap six, had moved into the lead, ahead of a six car bunch that quickly broke away from the rest of the large field. For several laps she held her first ever Formula Ford

Team Mates, Soul Mates. *Des and Alan with the Merlyn before the start of a race at Roy Hesketh Circuit, near Pietermaritzburg. (Courtesy Wilson Collection)*

lead, in front of the 100,000-strong crowd – until John Simpson, who was in sixth place, tried a do-or-die overtaking manoeuvre going into the ultra-quick, right-hand Sunset Bend. With no real chance of making the move, he slammed into the side of Desiré's car, sending her into a spin that dropped her back to 18th place. While her storming drive back up to eighth failed to win her any points, she did set the race's fastest lap, confirming to South Africa's racing world that she would be a genuine championship contender. As so it proved.

Wins at Pietermarizburg, Bloemfontein, and strong finishes at Cape Town, Welkom, and again in Kyalami, saw her take a dominant lead in the Championship from veteran Mike Hoffman. Consequently, with four races of the 11 event series to run, Desiré, needed just a few points to clinch the title. Then, disaster!

During a wet Friday practice session, the day before the final Kyalami event of the season, Desiré slid into the catch fencing on the climb up to Leeukop Bend, severely damaging the Merlyn's chassis. A hasty deal with Richard Marais, to borrow his Van Diemen, enabled Des to gain a last minute fourth place, but also allowed race winner Hoffman to close the points gap. Then, she had two engines blow-up, at Roy Hesketh in Natal, and in Port Elizabeth, leaving her facing the season finale in Cape Town with a six point lead, needing to finish third or higher to clinch the title. If she did not finish in the top three he would still have to win the race to be champion.

The long haul down to Cape Town was tense, not only because we weren't sure that the engine problems had been resolved, but also because the Killarney track was home to a very strong contingent of Cape Town-based drivers, several of whom were

Our Magic Merlyn. *We borrowed the Magic Merlyn nickname from a famous car raced in the UK by Emerson Fittipaldi, Colin Vandervell, and Jody Scheckter, hoping that this championship-winning car (with Bobby Scott) would repeat the magic for Des. Here, Des hustles the Merlyn through Angels Angle at Roy Hesketh circuit, well in the lead of the race. (Courtesy Gavin Stapleton)*

fully capable of taking all the top points-scoring positions. Race weekend was catastrophic.

It started when Desiré had a relatively poor qualifying session, starting from fifth on the grid, although Hoffman was even worse off, having qualified near the back after making the wrong tyre choice on a damp track. Pole position was taken by Briton Mike Needell, against whose brother, Tiff, Desiré was to race in Formula 1 cars later in her career.

Desiré made a good start in the first 18 lap heat, to emerge in third place at the end of the first lap. Mike Hoffman, however, had a great start, and ran just ahead of Des' green Merlyn in second. Des tucked in behind Hoffman, knowing that all she needed was third to clinch the title. Then, unbelievably, as she approached the final corner on the last lap, her car slowed and stopped at the bottom of the uphill climb to the finish line. Des jumped out and started pushing as the field flew past to take the flag.

We watched Des struggle to push the car up the rise to the finish line, knowing that her desperate attempt to finish the race was a waste of time, because there was no way she would be able to make up the lap she was losing during the second heat. Yet, despite the near 100°F heat, the weight of the car, the uphill climb, and her own exhaustion, she refused to quit. Drivers, mechanics, and hangers-on in the pit lane moved to the barrier, encouraging her in her quest, watching her championship hopes fade away. Still she pushed, until the Merlyn finally reached the line, where she collapsed in exhaustion as medical workers rushed to her side.

While Des was being treated in the first aid room, Charlie tore the car apart, trying to get it ready for the second heat. He found that the flywheel bolts had sheared.

As we didn't own a spare engine, there was little option but to bolt the flywheel back on, although we all knew that the elongated bolt holes meant it probably wouldn't stay together for long. Mike Hoffman came to see what was happening and immediately offered Charlie the use of his spare engine, but we had to turn down his sporting offer as there was no longer enough time to change motors before the start of the final heat.

Desiré returned from the first aid centre, obviously washed out, but desperate to get back into the car to try to salvage her pride. But the replaced flywheel shook itself to pieces within the first few laps of the second heat, and she despondently drove into the pits to retire.

Mike Hoffman stormed into the lead ahead of Needell's Crosslé, as the two headed the field for the next few laps. Then, Needell moved to the front while Mike tucked in behind, obviously capable of slipstreaming past at will to win the heat, and with it the race and the Championship. But he didn't pass, and Needell won the race with Mike right behind.

We were astonished. It seemed that Hoffman could have passed whenever he chose, and we couldn't work out why he'd chosen to stay in second place, as that gave Desiré the South Africa Formula Ford Championship.

Both drivers had the same number of points. Both drivers had the same number of race wins and second place finishes. Neither had finished third in any race. Desiré's next best finish was the fourth she earned in the borrowed Van Dieman, at Kyalami. Mike's was a fifth! It was the tie breaker. Desiré was champion. Or so we thought.

That night at the prize giving Desiré was feted as the champion. Formula 1 race winner, Dave Charlton, handed over the award that he had won for his performance in his race to Desiré, as a measure of his respect for both her achievement in winning

Good Friends and Hard Racers. *Desiré and Mike Hoffman dominated the 1976 South African Formula Ford Championships in a season-long battle that saw Des win the championship by the narrowest of margins. (Courtesy Malcolm Sampson)*

the title, and for her determination and courage in pushing her car to the line and her refusal to quit.

Mike Hoffman remained at the track, watching officials tear down Needell's engine, the result of his protest against its eligibility. We now understood why Mike hadn't tried to pass on that last lap: he was convinced that Needell, who had never been a factor in previous races, had used an illegal engine. Three long weeks later, the Automobile Association ruled against Mike's protest and confirmed Desiré as Champion.

She was the first women in world-wide racing history to win a major National single-seater championship. She had won four races, finished second three times, and earned two lap records. She had run fastest race laps eight times, but suffered three engine failures in the 11 race season. She was the acknowledged rising star of South African racing.

3

MEDIA MATTERS

THE 1976 season had been a fun, hard, frustrating, but ultimately successful year. Desiré had shown the beginnings of an exceptional talent, and an ability to compete at a level beyond anyone's expectations. She had learnt a tremendous amount about racing, even though the Formula Ford series consisted of just 11 events.

Father, Charlie, and guru, Maurice Rosenberg, provided the ideal supporting cast. Charlie had taught her how to sense the soul of a motor, how to feel its minutest changes and needs. Maurice taught her chassis dynamics, how to read the road, how to sense the effect of the smallest changes to a car's setup. Both taught her the nuances that are so essential to the development of a modern race driver, and the skills that many otherwise brilliant drivers fail to learn. Together, they taught her tactics, both on and off the track, tried (less successfully) to teach her patience, taught her when to use her natural aggression, and how to win when speed alone was not enough.

Together, they provided the best possible grounding in the art of racing, and gave her a base on which to build her career. Desiré owes an awful lot to Charlie and Maurice.

Thanks to her successes, Des was beginning to be recognised by the South African media, an evolution that several years later culminated in her being named as the 1979 South African 'Newsmaker of the Year.'

Her emergence from club racing brought with it increased exposure in the media, and greater recognition amongst the non-racing public. This media exposure was important because Desiré was competing at national level with no financial resources of her own, and was becoming increasingly dependent on sponsorship. A driver who's unable to fund their first basic steps in racing can never progress, no matter how talented they may later become.

Sponsorship would seem to the average fan to be a basic commodity in racing. After all, signs of sponsorship are everywhere – on the cars, the driver's uniforms, and all around the track. But persuading companies to support a racing career is far more difficult than it might seem. Much of the sponsorship at club and national level is, really, little more than patronage.

Sponsorship is support provided to a driver based on his or her ability to provide a commercial entity with: media exposure or visibility; name or product recognition to race fans and the general public; or the driver's ability to help establish strong commercial connections between the sponsor company and its clients. Few club drivers can do this.

Patronage, however, is support given with no expectation of financial or commercial return from the money provider. Patrons are friends, family, or fans who simply want the driver to succeed. Most successful race drivers have had the support of at least one patron during their career. Without significant private funding, or the support of one or more patrons, no race driver will ever reach the position where his or her talent can justify true sponsor support.

Desiré started the 1976 season with no patron support and no sponsorship. Glyco-Lemon chose not to renew its sponsorship, even though its low level of financial support in 1975 was, most probably, justified by the few newspaper and motoring magazine photos that were published during the year. But this wasn't enough for Glyco-Lemon to continue the programme into 1976. Truthfully, we didn't deserve its ongoing support because we didn't know how to look after a sponsor.

As a result, we faced the challenge of the 1976 season with only the money raised by the sale of my race car and the very limited amount of cash available from Charlie Randall's after-hours work, maintaining delivery motorcycle fleets.

Our first break came as a result of Desiré's performance at the South African Grand Prix meeting, when Castrol came on board with free products, a cheque (which just about paid for four sets of tyres), and a small contingency fund. Then, a few weeks later, we were approached by national women's magazine, *Fairlady*, a *Cosmopolitian*-style glossy that dominated the women's glamour media in South Africa. Its R1000 completed our annual funding. Welcome indeed – but still significantly less than our operating costs.

There's a perception that any woman in racing will garner much more publicity and media exposure than an equivalent male driver, and this was certainly true for Desiré during the 1976 season. Some of the publicity was simply the result of her being a lady in a man's world, some was because she was winning, and some was because we set out to generate as much media attention as we could. Wherever it came from, it was welcome and helpful.

We began our own 'promote Desiré' campaign. Team T-shirts, press releases, and a Castrol-funded printed brochure seemed, at the time, to be very professional and was certainly more than Desiré's competitors were doing. In retrospect, it was all very amateur, but we had no professional media consultants, public relations advisors, or racing media specialists available to advise us. So, we cultivated relationships with key journalists and our media programme worked, to a degree.

Winter in the Heat of Summer. Desiré was featured in a winter clothing story for sponsor Fairlady magazine, although the pictures were taken at Kyalami on the hottest day of the year!
(Courtesy Wilson Collection)

The three leading motor sports writers in Johannesburg were Ewart Van Neikerk, of *The Citizen*, Leicester 'Sy' Symons, of *The Rand Daily Mail*, and Harvey Thomas, of *The Star*.

An Afrikaaner, Ewart was big in both the physical sense and importance, but was genuine, fair, and great fun to be around. He provided balanced, if not extensive, coverage of Desiré's activities. Sy Symons was much older; a gentleman who became very supportive of Desiré, and whose reports recognised her achievements. Harvey Thomas didn't.

Harvey was by far the most important and visible motoring writer in South Africa at the time, and he knew it. His weekly, multi-page motoring supplement in *The Star* was widely read and influential. He had the motor companies eating out of his hand because his car reviews increased or slowed the sale of cars. He was the number one racing journalist, whose reports were eagerly read by every fan. He was a king maker, who could make or break drivers, and he knew it.

While Sy Symonds and Ewart van Neikerk gave fair comment to Des' growing success, *The Star* hardly mentioned it. Harvey usually ignored her.

Soon, his bias became so obvious that, had we not taken it so seriously, we would have laughed. Desiré would win a race and Harvey's report would cover the drivers she beat, with no mention of her name. Any outstanding drive or overtaking manoeuvre would be ignored, covered by reports of lesser activities by the drivers she passed. It was almost as if, in the motorsport pages of *The Star* at least, Desiré simply didn't exist.

At a later stage of her career we might have found Harvey's attitude pathetic, but in 1976, when money was tight and when a mere mention in Harvey's columns could open doors to sponsorship, this deliberate posture hurt, and though our anger and disappointment seems immature in retrospect, at the time we had a factual basis for our frustration.

Des and I had approached a local crash helmet manufacturer for support, hoping to get a small amount of sponsorship. We were well received; Des was given a free helmet, but our approach for sponsor support was turned down by the marketing manager. The reason he gave?

"Harvey really doesn't seem to like you, does he?" No coverage from Harvey, so, no deal!

Several years later, Harvey again showed his colours. We returned to South Africa after Des' first season in the British Formula 1 Championship, where she had truly emerged as a star in the making. Sitting on the plane, just three rows behind us, was Harvey. Despite the opportunity for an in-depth story on a local driver making good, he chose to ignore her throughout the 12 hour flight. For any other South African writer it was the opportunity for a scoop, but not Harvey.

His lack of reaction to Desiré's emergence as a national star ultimately had little real effect on her career, but it was an indication that, while her femininity presented many real advantages, there could also be some disadvantages to being a woman racer.

Another result of Desiré's emergence as the leading driver in the National Formula Ford Championship was the noticeable jealousy that grew among some of her competitors. Whereas, at the beginning of the season, everyone in the paddock seemed to welcome her participation and everyone seemed to be friends, we soon began to feel changes in our relationships with some of the other drivers. Once again, this was unexpected, as we had all raced together for several years and, in the relatively small group of serious competitors, there seemed to exist a real sense of camaraderie. The unpleasantness began with an unsuccessful protest against her engine after the Grand Prix meeting, and continued to grow until, by the end of the year, we felt very isolated in the paddock.

Once again, hindsight has lent some clarity to the situation, but at the time and in our naivety, we didn't recognise the effect that Desiré's success would have on some of her opponents. Whether this was because she was a girl, or just because she was winning, is difficult to tell.

The 1976 season ended with one final race that, while not providing a meaningful track result, proved to be crucial to Desiré's career.

The annual 9 Hours International endurance race at Kyalami was South Africa's second most important racing event. The November event attracted a significant field of international sports car drivers, taking the opportunity to race in the South African sun. More than 60 cars, ranging from Ferraris to Mini-Coopers, would run late into the evening, in front of crowds that often exceeded 100,000 fans, attracted by the overseas stars, interesting cars, South Africa's best drivers, and plenty of beer.

Desiré was asked to join the factory Alfa Romeo team for the 9 Hours, to share an Alfetta with rally star Louis Cloete. Finishing mid-pack and second in class, behind the lead Alfa team of Jan Hettema and Roy Klomfass, was an acceptable achievement for Desiré in only her second-ever saloon car drive, and it was enough to attract the attention of visiting Dutch driver Huub Vermeulen. During the celebrations after the race Huub introduced himself to Desiré.' "I understand that you won the Formula Ford Championship," he said, "and also the 'Driver-to Europe Award.' Well I can help you if you want to race in Holland." Huub and his two brothers, Jim and Loek, were the Dutch importers for Crosslé race cars and Huub's offer was the loan of a chassis for the 1977 season. It was a breakthrough.

Opportunity When Least Expected. *A one-off race in a factory Alfa Romeo, in the Kyalami 9-Hour race with rally star Louis Cloete, led to a meeting that opened the door to a career in Europe.*
(Courtesy Wilson Collection)

4

"IT'S A GIRL!"

WHEN Ford and the AA started the 'Driver to Europe' Award, the programme was intended to provide the most promising race driver in South Africa with substantial help in progressing their career into the international arena – as Jody Scheckter proved.

When Jody arrived in England, courtesy of a free ticket on South African Airways, he had a small cash allowance from Ford, a job waiting for him at Ford's Boreham Competition Department, the use of a road car, and a racing Escort Mexico for the national one make championship. He had the guidance of Ford UK's competition manager, Stuart Turner, and was included in Ford's promotional activities. Ford Motor Company was heavily involved in many forms of racing during this period. It supported its on-track activities with national media, promotional, and trackside activities, all of which heightened the public recognition of its products and its drivers. With this support, enough of his own money to buy a good race car, and his undeniable brilliance, Jody rapidly emerged as the shooting star of the 1971 British club racing scene. The rest is history.

Subsequent winners of the Driver to Europe Award were less fortunate. The winning driver in 1971, Richard Sterne, chose to race in the South Africa Formula 1/Two/5000 Championships and the programme lost its momentum. Subsequent winners, Jody's elder brother, Ian, and two of Des' micro-midget rivals, Kenny Gray and Bobby Scott, each received little more than the airfare and a few thousand rand with which to start their racing in the UK. Ford's enthusiasm for the programme had waned, and the many benefits associated with its support in the UK disappeared.

By the time Desiré won her award it meant little more than a check for R2500, two return air tickets to London, and a cocktail/media party, held in Johannesburg. The award still held significant prestige, and was to become an important factor in Desiré's rapid acceptance in British and European club and national racing. Everything else, including the expectation of matching Jody's success, was left to her.

Although we desperately wanted to take up the award and race in the UK, we realised very quickly that we simply didn't have the funds to compete at this much higher level. As newlyweds we had raced with no resources other than Maurice Rosenberg's and Charlie Randall's skills, which we would have to leave behind in South Africa, plus the proceeds from the sale of our race car, tow truck, a few home furnishings, and a very small bank account.

But even selling our championship-winning Merlyn wasn't that simple. Although we had several potential buyers who offered a good price, we chose to sell it to local Formula Vee driver, Basil Mann. We took the Merlyn to Kyalami for Basil to try out. Des went out first, did a few laps at near lap record speeds, and then gave Basil the opportunity to drive the car. Five laps later he came into the pits, talked with his father, and they excitedly committed to buy the car.

Mr Mann and I went over to his road car to collect the cheque, while Basil returned to the track. Two laps later, Des came running over with the bad news that he had crashed big time.

Only Basil knows exactly what happened (he claimed a wheel fell off), but it seemed that he had simply left his braking too late: at the end of the very fast, one-mile-long straight, he locked up, spun, and hit the catch fencing. The impact tore off all four wheels, the chassis was bent like a banana, and every single piece of bodywork was demolished.

Everything of value, excepting the engine, gearbox, and instrument panel was smashed, crumpled, and destroyed. Basil's dad refused to hand over the money and simply walked away. Our Driver to Europe plans were as crumpled as the race car.

We returned to Brakpan, where Charlie and Hughie Cruse reviewed the remains, deciding that the chassis could be cut, welded, and straightened, but that almost every important element of the suspension, cooling systems, and bodywork would have to be replaced. Des and I looked at our bank account and made the necessary purchases. After several weeks of long hours and hard work the rebuilt car was taken out to the track again, where Des tested it and ran at lap record speeds. But the damage was done. Nobody wanted it anymore and we eventually sold the car to a local garage owner for a fraction of its pre-crash value. After involving a lawyer friend, we were able to persuade Basil to pay us a small sum of money as his contribution to the damages.

It took a while, but we managed to put this disaster behind us and, somehow, rustled up the equivalent of £12,000 to take with us to England, where we arrived at the end of February 1976, to begin the adventure that has consumed the rest of our lives.

February in the UK is cold, windy, and wet – but, to us, England was as exciting as any place on earth. This is where real racing happened. Where the best and most competitive forms of national level competition took place; where the best up-and-coming drivers in the world came to show and develop their skills. Where Desiré could find a good ride with a factory team and where she could win races. England was where all the Formula Ford manufacturers were located, where the fabled 'factory' drive could be bought, career enhancing steps could be taken, and huge amounts of money we didn't have could be spent. Reality soon stood up and punched us between the eyes.

After purchasing a used Ford Transit van we visited the Hawke factory, where designer/owner David Lazenby simply asked us how much money we had. He said he would take all of it, plus several times the same amount again, and would only then consider running Des for the year in his factory team. Alan Cornock, of Royale, was more pleasant, but said much the same.

Despondent, we looked through the adverts for used race cars in *Autosport* magazine, but quickly realised that, even if we did buy a lower priced and less competitive car, we would still only have enough money for about two months of living and racing in England.

Taking stock of our situation, we remembered the offer that Huub Vermuelen had made to Des, after the 9 Hours race at Kyalami a few months before, so we loaded up the Transit and caught the overnight ferry to the Hook of Holland. We drove to The Hague and arrived at the door of the Vermuelen's sports equipment company, Pinguin Sports, early one morning.

The difference between our English experience and the reception we received from the Dutch racing world couldn't have been greater. The Vermuelens welcomed us as if we were old friends. They quickly confirmed that they would be happy to lend Desiré a brand-new Crosslé 33F Formula Ford 2000 chassis for the year; that they would allow us to base ourselves at their race shop; use their transporter when racing at events in Holland, Belgium or Luxembourg, and that they would give us jobs to carry us through until the race season started. They also introduced us to the Dutch Formula Ford 2000 crowd.

Formula Ford 2000 was the next step up the ladder from the 1600cc engined Formula Ford cars that Des had previously raced. Although utilising the same basic chassis, FF2000 cars featured wings, slick racing tyres, and an engine that was 35 per cent more powerful. It was a relatively new series that had begun to catch on, especially in Holland, where a large number of drivers made it a very competitive and aggressive racing category. The Vermeulen brothers were the Dutch importers for the Irish machines and had sold 24 brand-new FF2000 chassis for the 1976 season. Our job was to assemble every single one of them, including the 24th, which was to be ours.

But, we had a month or so to kill before the cars were ready for assembly, so they gave us jobs at their sporting goods distribution company. Des worked at stringing tennis racquets, while I designed artwork for them. Then, we had to convert a dirty, 15-year-old semi-trailer into a race car transporter. After many 14 hour days of rubbing it down by hand, it looked immaculate, which is more than you can say for our hands.

Then we went to Liverpool, to pick up boxes of Crosslé parts. With virtually no skills – and less experience – Desiré and I, usually working alone, assembled the 24 race cars. From the bare chassis and the many piles of parts we added suspensions, wiring, instruments, gearboxes, and engines, and then set up the suspension so that each car left the workshop fully ready to race. It was painstaking work, which proved invaluable to Desiré's understanding of the mechanics of how a race car worked. It was certainly an experience that few race drivers and no other women driver could match.

We started building car No 24 on the Thursday evening before the season opener at Zolder, in Belgium, and loaded it, partially completed, onto our trailer. Once at Zolder, I finished it off, working in inches-deep pools of ice-cold water fed by incessant rain and accompanied by bitterly cold winds. Sunny South Africa seemed a long way away.

There were 28 entrants for this inaugural Belgian FF2000 race. Most were experienced European-based Formula Ford drivers, who knew the track well, while others were experienced competitors from England, intent on getting an early start to the season. All had raced many times in the wet. All went onto the track for the first 15 minute qualifying session, while our car sat in the pits as I struggled to fit the starter motor. Des made it onto the track with just a few minutes remaining in the session, finishing slowest of all. She improved to 12th after the second session.

This was an inauspicious start to her Driver to Europe season, and one which led to many sniggers around the paddock. After all, who was this South African girl who had been given a free car by the Vermeulens? She wasn't even quick.

Despite racing in the rain for the first time in her life, Des passed one car after the other, until, by the beginning of the last lap, she was up to fourth place and chasing Dutch star Artur van Dedum. She drew closer to him and, as they entered the final Esses, she dived alongside in a fair but difficult pass. Van Dedum reacted quickly and pushed her across the track. She retaliated, slamming her wheels into his with a vengeance, forcing him to put two wheels on the dirt as she bullied her way past.

She finished third, ran the slowing down lap, and stopped on the track in front of the victory podium.

Van Dedum turned into the paddock, climbed out, and immediately starting talking animatedly to several other drivers. He looked very upset with Desiré's tactics, and I anxiously waited for the confrontation that was sure to follow.

In the meantime Des climbed from her car onto the podium, and I could hear the track announcer talking enthusiastically about her performance.

He had watched her race through the field and had become increasingly animated as the race progressed. Now, as she climbed out of the car in front of him, he sang the praises of this driver, listed in the programme as D Wilson from The Hague.

Then, she removed her crash helmet and balaclava, allowing her long brown hair to fall to her shoulders.

"It's a girl! She's a lady!" he screamed crazily, "Wilson is a woman!"

I couldn't help but laugh at his excitement. He had been emotional during the race, but now he went completely over the top, especially when he learned that she had also set the fastest race lap.

His reaction, although excessive, was something that was to become quite common as Desiré continued to move up the racing ladder. European and British fans, far more than their American counterparts, both enjoyed and found satisfaction in watching a woman driver compete equally with the best of her male competitors, and they tended to react accordingly. She quickly became a favourite with the Belgian crowds.

When the excitement of the Winners' Circle ceremony ended, I prepared myself for the reception I expected for Des in the paddock, as we had been told that Artur Van Dedum had a reputation for being the toughest and meanest driver in the field. To my amazement Artur welcomed her with an enormous hug, and then promptly told everyone around them that they shouldn't try to push her around on the track, because she would return the complement with interest. A marker had been put down and noted by some of the aggressive young tyros she would be racing in the coming months.

Time and again in 1977, Des proved she might be a lady, but was no push-over, even for the men who simply couldn't stand the thought of being beaten by a mere woman.

The next race in the series was her first at Zandvoort, where she qualified way back in 15th and finished ninth, in a race which started in the dry, changed to rain, and ended in a driving snow storm. The series then returned to Zolder, where she qualified eighth, finished third, and again set fastest lap and a new lap record. After the race there was a message from one of the other competitors, that a man called Jan Bik wanted to sponsor her and to contact his Amsterdam office.

Despite the Vermeulen's help, we were already almost at the end of our cash resources. We had purchased an engine, gear ratios, miscellaneous spares, a trailer, a used Ford Transit van, winter clothes, wood to make a bed, and we had to pay rent for accommodation. We reckoned that we had enough left to last another two months, before we would have to return to South Africa. We were so strapped for money that we were eating a full meal only once every three days, subsisting on the breakfast provided at our boarding house each morning, and fatty sausages purchased from a street vendor for lunch and dinner. We were elated, but when we told Jim Vermeulen, he wasn't impressed.

"You don't want to take sponsorship from Bik," he said, but didn't elaborate. A few weeks passed, during which we received more messages from the mysterious Mr Bik. As we were getting even more concerned at the diminishing funds, we finally decided to follow up on his approaches. We made a visit his office in Amsterdam and, unusually, Des put on a dress for our all important sponsorship meeting. We cleaned and polished the Transit van and drove up to Amsterdam, then worked our way through an intricate maze of streets, until we found ourselves in the docklands of the great city. We found Bik's offices amongst the warehouses, identified by a gloss black glass door with the name Jan Bik EC written in gold leaf scroll.

We were first met at the door by an exceptionally beautiful lady, who greeted me with a smile and Desiré with surprise. When we identified ourselves, she said that Jan Bik was expecting us and showed us upstairs to an ornately decorated bar area, where another eight gorgeous ladies waited. I was fascinated. Desiré wasn't amused. This was no warehouse, it was a whorehouse. EC – Eros Club. The meeting that followed was bizarre.

Small, well mannered, and speaking perfect English, Jan Bik told us that his business was legal prostitution on a nationwide scale. He said he had sponsored various race cars for several years, but had always wanted to support a good female driver. It would, after all, be good recognition for his business. We listened while he answered call after call, during which he matched men with his girls in towns all around Holland. He even offered to 'try out' one potential worker – the leopard skin bed we were sitting on had more than one purpose.

We discussed the possible sponsorship fee. Although Des and I had agreed to ask for ƒ30,000, we spontaneously asked for a ƒ60,000 fee.

Jan Bik blinked, then, with disappointment showing on his face, responded. "I can't afford that. It's a pity, I really would like to sponsor you, but I know someone who can afford it. But I don't know that you should deal with them," he continued, "They run the live sex shows in town and they are Sicilian." We drove home, unsponsored, but much wiser to the ways of Holland.

The next day we received another phone call, this time from Tonio Hildebrand, manager for the F&S Properties team. He told us that F&S would be sponsoring Des for the rest of the year and that it would pay her ƒ25,000. We were to take the car to a paint shop near Zandvoort, to have it ready for that weekend's European Championship event.

We collected the freshly painted, red, white and blue car on Saturday morning, and took it directly to the track, parking it in the paddock where it immediately attracted the amazed stares of Michael Bleekemolen and Maarten Henneman, the two drivers already sponsored by F&S. They had no idea that Desiré was now part of their team. Neither did the two owners of F&S Properties!

We were asked to visit the F&S hospitality suite above pit lane, to meet Mr Fagel and Mr Van der Schluys, co-owners of the company, neither of whom knew anything of the deal, and neither of whom wanted it to happen. They apologised to Des for Hildebrand's unauthorised commitment and offered to pay her a fee for this race only, confirming that there would be no further sponsorship from F&S for her after this race.

We were extremely disappointed and embarrassed, but we returned to the paddock and went about our business of preparing the car for qualifying. Then, determined to impress, Des surprised everyone by putting the car on the pole, well under the lap record. Desiré was still very unfamiliar with the very fast and difficult Zandvoort circuit, while it was home track for most of the FF2000 field. Alongside her on the front row were two similar Crosslés, driven by Bleekemolen and Ross De Salva Giaxa, with Huub Vermeulen lined up behind her.

The race started in pouring rain and Desiré led the first lap, the next two turns, and into the famous, steeply banked left-handed Hunzerug corner, down the middle of which ran a wide stream of water. She hit the water, aquaplaned, and spun around, sliding backwards off the track.

The entire field passed as she tried to restart the

How to Impress a Sponsor. When the two owners of F&S Properties told Des that their team manager should not have signed her into their team, she put the newly-painted Crosslé on the Zandvoort pole, took an early lead, spun, and then drove past their number one driver twice in 15 laps, as she fought her way back to contention. Their reason for following her drive with a season's sponsorship was an eye-opener for the naïve South Africans. (Courtesy Wilson Collection)

car, but the starter motor had failed. She undid her belts, climbed out, and pushed the car back down the hill towards the oncoming traffic, which, by now, had completed another lap. She waited for the entire field to pass by, then pushed, jumped in, and restarted the car, furiously spinning it around to face the right direction, before storming back into the race, now a full lap and a few seconds behind the last car in the field.

Even knowing that she now had no chance of finishing up front in this short 15 lap race didn't make her quit. Instead, she chased after the pack, un-lapped herself from the entire field, and then pulled away from the leaders, passing many drivers, including F&S team leader Bleekemolen for a second time. Although she still finished out of the top ten, she had demonstrated an exceptional ability to drive very fast in the rain, no matter how far behind, and proved her determination.

I was overjoyed at her performance, but gave her hell because, when she pulled into the pits, I saw that she had driven the entire race with her seatbelts undone: she was unable to strap them up by herself when she climbed back into the car after her spin!

Now the F&S directors wanted another meeting, and this time the reception was much friendlier. Now they did want to sponsor her, but not because of any desire for publicity, or to promote their company. They wanted to sponsor her to settle a wager that Fagel made with his partner Van Der Shluys! Fagel believed that Des could beat Michael Bleekemolen at least once during the season, while Van der Schluys said that this could never happen. To make the competition fair, they agreed that Desiré and Michael had to have similar equipment, and consequently they decided that they should sponsor Des to ensure that this would be the case. We had no idea of the size of the bet, but given their extravagance it was obviously quite substantial. Regardless, the F&S sponsorship, together with additional support we obtained later in the season from the Olau Lines ferry company, was to make all the difference, and ensured that we could race through to the end of the season.

Almost as if to confirm Ton Fagel's confidence, Desiré won the very next European Championship race, taking her first victory of the year at Colmar-Berg, in Luxembourg, on one of the worst tracks we had ever seen. The course, which doubled during the week as the European Goodyear tyre test venue, featured a very long and wide straight, and a narrow return road that consisted mainly of never ending sweeps. Des ran off the track early in the race, dropping over a three foot high bank that bent the rear of the chassis and broke an engine mount. So, with a badly handling car, she was forced to defend her lead by blocking the cars behind with some very aggressive moves down the straight. After the race, some of the drivers were quite upset, but when they saw the damage to the car, they all agreed they would have done exactly the same!

The race had been run in near 100° heat and she was so dehydrated by the end that, instead of spraying the champagne, she chose to drink too much of the bottle. By the time she returned to the paddock, she was far too drunk to accept the congratulations that everyone was giving to her!

Bleekemolen dropped out of the race when lying behind Des, so we couldn't honestly claim that she'd beaten him fair and square, so, fortunately the much needed F&S sponsorship continued and helped pay for two bizarre major accidents.

The first happened at Zandvoort when, for tactical reasons relating to new tyres, I waved her off on the warm up lap after the rest of the field. Running as fast as she could to get heat into the tyres, she came across two guys who had stopped and blocked the track while practising their standing starts, just after the Oost Tunnel. Des had to chose between slamming into them at 120mph or swerving off the track. She made an instant decision and swerved into the catch fencing, taking down over 100 metres of posts and chain-link before coming to a stop. Needless to say, the car was very badly damaged, although Des was uninjured, if extremely angry. The sad thing about this episode is that Charlie and Tina Randall had just arrived in Holland to visit, and they lost the opportunity of seeing Des race.

The second major crash of the European season also took place at Zandvoort, near the end of the year. At the end of the long pits straight, hitting 135mph in a nose-to-tail line, the driver in front of Des pulled out to pass Artur Van Dedum, misjudged his move, and hit Artur's right rear wheel, immediately turning his Crosslé sideways into Desiré's path. She swerved to the left, bounced off the guardrail and flew back across the track over Van Dedum, leaving tyre marks on his helmet and landing sideways across the track where she was hit hard by racing journalist Ric von Kempen's similar car. His car's exhaust pipe pierced her cockpit, cutting her wrist, although a chassis spar prevented the gearbox from smashing into her hip.

I witnessed the horrific crash from the pits and ran to the scene, arriving just as Desiré pulled herself from her car. She levered herself out from under Ric's car, in which he was pinned by another car's gearbox that was jammed into his hip. Des ran over to yet another Crosslé, which was on fire, stood across the cockpit, and struggled to pull the unconscious driver from the cockpit by his overalls. I ran across to help, arriving just as yet another car came flying over the top of the dust, heading straight for us. Des and I

Podium Time! Although she and team leader, Michael Bleekemolen, shared the podium several times during the season, it wasn't until the last Zandvoort race that Desiré beat him to win Ton Fagel's bet. (Courtesy Wilson Collection)

both ducked and the car flew right over our heads, missing us by inches, and then slammed into the ground just a few feet behind us.

When the dust settled, we saw that more than 30 cars were involved, 11 of which were severely damaged. Miraculously, only von Kempen, with a broken pelvis, suffered major injuries, but the race had to be cancelled because of the amount of time it took to clean up the mess.

Driving a car borrowed from Loek Vermeulen for the final Zolder race of the season, Des finished fourth, with yet another fastest lap and lap record. We then travelled to England to pick up a new chassis and a large box of spares, and hastily rebuilt our car – just in time to make the start of qualifying for the final Zandvoort race weekend of the season. Des slotted the car into second place on the grid, qualifying just behind Michael, but outraced him into Tarzan Bend and opened a gap that she held to the end, beating him by several seconds. At last, Ton Fagel had won his bet.

Despite the many incidents, our time in Holland was far more than just hard work and accident repairs. It was often exhilarating and exciting. We made some good friends, enjoyed the camaraderie of the Dutch racing world, and loved living in the city of Den Haag. More importantly, Desiré proved herself to be extremely competitive in a very hard fought category of racing. She qualified in the top six eight times, earned one pole position, set several fastest laps, and, by the end of the season, held the lap records at Zolder, and Colmerberg. Despite the accidents, she finished in third place in each of the Dutch, Benelux, and European Championship series.

While our deal with the Vermuelens committed us to these series, we were also able to compete in an additional 13 races in England – where the racing was even more competitive.

5

JEREMY'S SORRY ...
HE WON'T DO IT AGAIN

As competitive as the European Formula Ford 2000 scene had been, the racing wasn't nearly as vicious as it was in the British National Championships. England was home to the world's most competitive club and national racing series.

Competition in the 1960s, '70s, and '80s was unbelievably fierce. The British national scene was the cauldron from which many of the world's most notable Formula 1 drivers had emerged.

While Formula Three was the series that produced most of the Formula 1 stars, it was, even then, extremely expensive, so when Brands Hatch boss, John Webb, created FF2000 in 1975 (which was only marginally slower than F3), he was onto a winner. Two years later, 2000 had become England's most competitive race series, featuring factory entered teams from at least seven manufacturers. Leading drivers at the time included South Africans Kenny Gray and Rad Dougal, whose Royale was engineered by future Ferrari designer Rory Byrne; Adrian Reynard and his team-mate, Jeremy Rossiter; Venezuelan Oscar Notz; Lola's Mike Blanchet; Philip Bullman, in the factory Hawke; Geoff Friswell; David MacPherson; Rob Wilson; Syd Fox, and Frank Sytner. Typically, up to 45 cars entered each race, but as fields were usually limited to 20 to 25 cars, the competition to even make the grid was, itself, incredibly fierce, resulting in fields that were often covered by as little as a second-and-a-half. The short 20 minute practice sessions were always hectic and fiercely fought, as more than half the cars attempting to qualify would be eliminated from the competition before the race even started. With the whole grid often separated by less than a second, every FF2000 race in England was an adventure.

With close racing, intense competition, and drivers with dreams of Formula 1 fame – and a determination to pass the car in front at all costs – crashing was an inevitable consequence of racing in the British FF2000 championships. A driver either pushed too hard, making his own mistakes, or was taken out by someone having their own crash. On occasion, crashing someone else was a deliberate strategy. With large fields of cars racing so close together, race officials had little chance of controlling or preventing the deliberate pushes, nudges, brake tests, wheel slams, and other tactics that were a feature of the intensely competitive series.

The worst place to be was in the middle of the pack, somewhere between tenth and 16th place. Here desperation ruled, incompetence was common, and stupidity was everywhere. Racing in the midfield pack was scary: almost all of Desiré's accidents occurred when she was fighting for position there. There were far fewer crashes among the top six or so, because, generally, the drivers had greater skills.

Whenever Desiré could take a break from racing in Europe, she raced in England. Because of her commitments to race in Europe, she was unable to compete for honours in either of the two British championship series, so, instead, we selected races from both, seeking out the best competition we could find, to prove that she could run with the best of the British-based drivers.

Her first UK race was at the fast, bumpy, and frightening track of Thruxton, in Hampshire. On this difficult to learn circuit, and with no previous track knowledge, Des qualified 18th of 44 cars. It put her at the back of the midfield pack.

The start was a mass of confusion, as she fought for position. She lost five places on the first lap giving way to more aggressive drivers, but then realised that this wasn't going to do her any good. Fighting back, she passed a handful of cars to get up to 13th, and then refused to give way when Frank Bradley tried a late braking pass in his Elden. She felt a big thump at the rear of the car that caused her Crosslé to leave the track, flying several feet in the air before it landed hard, on two wheels, and slid into a concrete block that was lying in the run-off area. She then lost a whole lap when the starter motor refused to work, but eventually continued with weird handling that made the car unpredictable and difficult to drive. Still, she soldiered on with the bent chassis to the finish. Welcome to England!

We towed the car to St Neots, in Bedfordshire, where we'd been offered the use of a workshop by Roy Thomas, owner of Titan Engineering, also known as 'Roy the Weld,' who built the engines that Desiré used. True to his name, he cut and welded the frame, after which I reassembled the car. Roy recognised Des' talent and was always extremely friendly and very helpful.

We then crossed the Channel to Luxembourg, where she won her first European race, returning two weeks later for her first race at Snetterton. At this demanding and very fast Norfolk track, she qualified eighth on a damp circuit. I then made the wrong tyre choice, selecting dry slicks for what turned into

a very wet race, although Des did manage to finish tenth. Disappointed and determined to make the most of our weekend trip to England, we managed to buy a race entry from another driver and drove up to Donington Park that evening for the brand-new circuit's first major race event.

With the track new to everyone Des felt at less of a disadvantage. Qualifying was wet, and she made the most of conditions to put the car fourth on the grid. But she had a major battle with Hawke driver Philip Bullman in the race. Prior to the start, Oscar Notz, the very fast Venezuelan who had become a good friend, warned Des that Bullman had been boasting in the paddock: he was going to take this woman out, teach her a lesson. So, when he slammed his car into the rear of her Crosslé, at Redgate Corner, Des was ready for him. Reacting quickly, she deliberately nosed his rear wheel as he slid past, sending him into a spin. Unfortunately, hampered by the wrong gear ratios, she made a mistake later in the race, allowing him past, but she then set about closing the gap, crossing the line in sixth place – inches behind him, but with the consolation of taking fastest lap and setting Donington Park's first outright lap record.

Several weeks later, after racing at Zandvoort and Luxembourg, we returned to England, making the long trek up to Oulton Park for her first race on this very difficult track. Des qualified 12th, but made a

Nail-biting. Nerves on the grid at a race at Snetterton. (Courtesy Wilson Collection)

Oulton Park … *Scene of the Crime! Des liked Oulton Park from her first run on the difficult track, and quickly moved her Crosslé up through the field. That is, until she came to pass Jeremy Rossiter. The cigarette box on her suspension was not part of any sponsorship deal! (Courtesy Chris Davies)*

First Lap Mayhem! *Racing in England was tough. Here Des spins in front of the pack after being hit by a following car. Competition in the world of FF2000 was extremely fierce and accidents were common.*
(Courtesy Wilson Collection)

great charge through the field to close onto the rear of Jeremy Rossiter's works Reynard, which was lying in fifth place. At Knicker Brook, he gave her a classic 'brake test.' Des braked as hard as she could, but was unable to avoid slamming into his gearbox, while at the same time being hit hard, from behind, by Steve Farthing's Reynard. Des retired to the pits with yet another bent chassis. She climbed out of her car in the paddock, her face black with fury, ignored me, and stormed across to Jeremy as he climbed out of his car. It didn't help matters that he was laughing as he talked to his crew about his race.

She stuck her face into his and, in very clear terms, let him know what he could expect at the next race. He simply shrugged and walked away. Rad Dougal and his father watched, smiling.

We loaded the car and drove straight back to Titan's, where Roy Thomas, again, cut and welded the chassis, after which I prepped the car for the following weekend's race at Snetterton. We were both working on the car in the paddock, when Adrian Reynard approached. He introduced himself to Des.

"Jeremy's sorry," He said. "He's really sorry. He says he won't do that again. Please don't retaliate. He's a nice guy. He's sorry." We were taken aback:

why would Adrian take the time to apologise for Jeremy's actions?

We soon found out. South African Rad Dougal was leading the championship at the time, just a few points ahead of Jeremy, and he and his father had overheard Des' threat to get even with the Reynard driver. Partly in fun and partly to intimidate him, they spoke to Jeremy after the Oulton paddock confrontation. Dad, Dougal, who had been an enthusiastic supporter and organiser of both Formula Vee and Formula Ford racing in South Africa, knew Des very well.

He told Rossiter "Watch out for her, Jeremy, we know her from South Africa. She's completely crazy. She won't forget what you did. She'll drive you right off the track. She won't care a damn if she kills you."

Jeremy Rossiter never beat Desiré in an FF2000 car again. But he wasn't the only driver to try punting Des off the track in 1977. Of the 26 races we took part in that season, she was crashed out by other drivers six times, only once crashing of her own accord. These six races don't include several more where she was put off the track, but managed to continue. It was frustrating and expensive, but part of the learning process.

The Oulton Park race was the first time Desiré broke into the top six in the UK. From then on, she was always racing near the front of the field, usually in the top five or six, at least on those occasions when she wasn't recovering from spins, or accidents caused by other drivers. It was, also, the last time that season that she failed to qualify on the front three rows of the grid, even on tracks she had never seen before.

The trips across the channel weren't kind to Des, as she suffered from sea sickness, so we usually scheduled in a couple of recovery days. We usually stayed in small village pubs, which all seemed to be called 'The Cross Keys,' although, later, our rival and friend, Oscar Notz and his wife, Nazira, provided a place to stay – as did Kenny Gray and his wife, Sheila. Kenny's promising career was later curtailed by a serious accident at Silverstone. Oscar was underrated and helped Desiré with her driving. Had he not been so lazy he could have gone far – but we enjoyed many fun evenings with them and with the Grays.

Our regular cross channel trips also served another purpose – to collect race parts for the Vermuelens, although paying duty for the parts we were importing to Europe wasn't part of the plan. We unwrapped the new parts and mixed them with our own spares. The ploy worked well, because our Olau line sponsors introduced us to the friendly Chief Customs Officer, at the Hook of Holland, with whom we always shared a coffee when we passed through. But we got complacent and stopped unwrapping the parts. One day, we were stopped as we re-entered Holland, told to drive our Transit to the inspection lane, and were gruffly informed by an officer that he had been watching us for months and knew we were smuggling something. We thought we were in big trouble, but the big boss came to the rescue and had a fierce argument with his junior. He motioned us leave and they were still shouting at each other as we disappeared down a Dutch side street.

Racing in the UK was extremely important to Desiré's development as a race driver. Apart from teaching her the sheer ability to race hard, it also taught her other valuable lessons. For example, she learnt how to learn a track incredibly quickly and how to decide what do to make a car work effectively in the shortest possible time. With no budget to test, little practice, and probably a new track to learn, it was a tall order to qualify in the essential top five or six in the single 20 minute session before the race.

So we developed our own qualifying system. We made sure she was always one of the first cars to get onto the track. She would then run for ten minutes, using this time to learn the track and get a feel for the changes she needed me to make to the car. Then, she would come into the pits to tell me what suspension and wing settings she needed. I would then have less than five minutes in which to make all the changes. She would then return to the track with just five minutes left in the session, run one slow lap to look for a gap in the traffic, and then two flat-out runs targeting pole position. It was a valuable experience.

Almost half of the 26 races Des drove in 1977 were run in the rain or, at least, on very slippery tracks and she quickly became a master of wet conditions. Many drivers fear racing in the rain, with its reduced grip, poor visibility, and ever changing surfaces. Desiré thrived on it. Her ultra-smooth driving style, soft braking technique, and split second reactions enabled her to handle the wet better than almost anyone she was ever to race against.

By the end of the 1977 season, Des had run 26 races on ten different tracks. She held lap records at Zolder, Castle Combe, Colmar Berg, and Donington and had qualified at or under lap records at Mallory Park, Castle Coombe, and Brands Hatch. She'd started on the pole and won twice and had set an additional four fastest race laps. Considering that this was just her first year in Europe; that she was driving a car that had no factory support; our lack of financial resources; and my minimal mechanical skills, she had done extremely well.

Her performance was recognised by the South Africa Automobile Association, who announced that she had been awarded her Springbok colours – the most prestigious award that can be made to a South African sports person. They are awarded by the sanctioning authority of each major sport to competitors who have represented South Africa in international competition, either as part of a team (cricket, rugby, etc), or for exceptional performances against international competition. Typically, the AA, who controlled South African motor sports, presented just one or two awards each year, so Desiré was thrilled to hear that she had been awarded her colours, especially as it was an award that her father had also won, many years before.

Further recognition came in the form of a letter, sent by Max Mosley, then Managing Director of March Cars. At the time, March was the dominant force in Formula Three racing and any driver who

Close Racing. *Mallory Park always provided close racing. Here, Des challenges Philip Bullman and Syd Fox through the 180-degree Shaws Hairpin. She had qualified under the lap record in less than ten laps, but was still only fourth on the grid. (Courtesy Jeff Bloxham)*

raced for them was almost certain to reach Formula 1. So we were excited to read that Max wanted to meet Des to discuss the potential of her driving for the March F3 team in 1978.

We arrived at March's Bicester factory one November morning and were immediately ushered into Mosley's office. He made us welcome, telling us how impressed he had been with Desiré's performances during the year and how he thought she would be very successful in F3. Then he asked how much money we had. Des and I looked at each other. We thought he would be offering her money to drive for him!

"Uhmmm. None really," I replied.

"Well, take a look around the factory if you like. It was nice meeting you." With more experience we would have asked him how much he needed, never have let on that we were broke, and would have asked him to give us a letter containing his offer to show potential sponsors. In our naivety, we simply left and closed a door to the potential opportunity behind us.

With no money, no job, and a long cold winter ahead if we stayed on in the UK, we decided that it would be best if we returned to South Africa to try to raise funds for another European campaign, or to return to racing in South Africa. Fortunately, we had resisted the temptation to sell our return air tickets, so we still had the ability to get home, even if we did arrive with little more than the clothes we could carry in one small suitcase.

6

THE CLOSEST RACE

THE two best women race drivers in the world, at the beginning of 1977, were Divina Galica and Lella Lombardi.

31-year-old Divina had been Britain's top downhill ski racer and captain of the Women's Olympic ski team, and was a superb athlete. She'd come into racing much later than most drivers, having been introduced to the sport by John Webb, Managing Director of Motor Circuit Developments, which owned the Brands Hatch, Mallory Park, Oulton Park, and Snetterton race tracks. John invited Divina to drive a Ford Escort in an all-women's Celebrity Race, at Brands Hatch, which she easily won.

Ever on the lookout for a good angle from which to promote his track, John took Divina under his wing, allowing her free use of the Brands Hatch Racing School cars. He entered her in club Formula Ford and FF2000 races, and then arranged for her to drive a very powerful modified Ford Escort in national championship races.

Her fierce aggression and natural athleticism allowed her to race so competitively, John arranged for her to race in the Formula 1/F5000 championship that he organised at the MCD tracks and at England's other major venues. Heavily promoted by the Brands Hatch publicity machine, Divina, who took to the powerful Surtees Formula 1 car with ease, rapidly became one of the best known drivers in the UK.

In 1977, John also arranged for Divi to drive a new Lola in national Sports 2000 championship races, to generate publicity for the new class of racing he had devised. She did more than just race: she won ten races and soon led the championship point standings. She was the undoubted star lady racer in the UK.

Roy Thomas believed that Desiré could beat Divi

and, by beating her, attract John Webb's attention and, hopefully, his support.

Sports 2000 is a closed wheel version of FF2000, using the same Ford engine and similar suspension. The key difference is that, instead of having a single-seat and exposed wheels, the Sports 2000 racer had two seats and streamlined bodywork that covered all four wheels. It too had an open cockpit.

Roy built engines for both FF2000 and S2000, and included among his clients Ted Toleman, who was subsequently to form the Formula 1 team that became Renault. In 1977, he sponsored Rad Dougal in FF2000 and ran a Lola, for himself, in Sports 2000 races. However, while Rad won races, Ted was more often found near the tail of the field.

Ted agreed to loan his car to Desiré and Roy arranged for her to try out the Lola during a test day at Snetterton. Because she'd never driven an S2000 car before, Rad took the car out to bed it in and set a speed target for her. She jumped in, ran one lap and pulled into the pits.

"The right engine mount is broken," she told a mechanic. The crew looked across at Rad.

"There's nothing wrong with the car," he said. "Just get in and drive."

Des persisted but to no avail. Nobody wanted to lift the engine cover to check. After all, Rad said there wasn't anything wrong and he had just driven a pretty fast lap. Eventually, I undid the body clips and raised the cover. A mechanic came over, looked down at the engine, and confirmed Des' diagnosis.

This type of situation was to become a fact of life over the coming years, as Desiré moved from team to team. At almost every one, especially the American teams, the initial reaction of the crew members was to discount any input Desiré tried to offer, convinced, as

Race Queen. *Divina Galica was the fastest lady driver in English racing when Des arrived in the UK, in 1977. Divi won by inches when they raced against each other in Sports 2000 cars at Snetterton.*
(Courtesy Jeff Bloxham)

they were, that no woman could have the mechanical ability to read the condition of the car as well as their male drivers. Inevitably, each team would soon discover that she had an exceptional ability to read and setup a car, but it generally took some time for them to accept her skills.

The race at Snetterton, the following Sunday, was described in the subsequent week's *Motoring News* as the closest and most competitive race ever seen at the Norfolk circuit.

Desiré qualified in the middle of the front row, sharing the same lap time with pole-sitter Chris Alford and just a fraction faster than Divi. She made a great start, immediately jumping into the lead ahead of Divi. Racing nose-to-tail and side by side, with the difference never more than a few feet – most often just an inch or two – the two girls raced away from the field, their cars jinking and diving as Divi

tried desperately to pass, while Desiré did her best to block and hold her position. For 13 laps the two fought as hard as they could, leaving the rest of the field far behind, until, entering the fast right-hand Riches Corner at the beginning of the final lap, the engine mount on Des' Lola broke again, causing the gear linkage to flex and pulling the car out of gear. In the time it took for Des to react and find fourth gear again, Divi, sensing the microscopic opportunity, snuck past and into the lead.

Des will say that she lost the race because of the missed gear; Divi, that she won it by taking advantage of a mistake under pressure. Regardless, it was round one to Divina. But Desiré had made her point; she had clearly shown that she was every bit as fast as the English girl.

We waited for John Webb to call, but heard nothing and we assumed that he had no interest in her.

7

GET THE F**K OUT OF SOUTH AFRICA

Aᴸᴇx Blignaut used profanity as a negotiating strategy. So, when he called me to tell me to take my f*****g wife and get her to f**k off out of South Africa back to f*****g England, my surprise wasn't at the crudeness with which he spoke, but his intensity and the message he was delivering.

Alex Blignaut was the godfather of South African racing. He was the man who conceived Kyalami; laid it out from the back of a tractor; built it into South Africa's premier circuit; invited the world's best drivers to compete on it; updated it, and developed it into one of the world's truly great race tracks. He was the man who made Kyalami the home of the South Africa Formula 1 Grand Prix. At the same time, he was almost single handedly responsible for building South Africa's national racing scene into one of the strongest in the world. He ran Kyalami with an iron fist and nothing of importance happened at Kyalami unless Alex gave it his blessing. Anyone who wanted to play a role in South African racing knew that they had to deal with Alex. If he liked you, you were in; if not, good luck.

Alex was one of the world's top race promoters. He knew the value of promotion and he would wheel and deal to help those drivers he believed would appeal to his customers, the thousands of race fans who bought tickets to Kyalami's national and international events. By 1977, he had been instrumental in forcing the change of the premier racing category in South Africa from the old Formula 1/Two and F5000 classes, to Formula Atlantic, a series that had really taken off in a big way during 1976 and 1977.

Knowing that we had no prospects for a drive in the UK, for 1978, Desiré and I decided that her best bet would be to try to find a way in which to compete

Formula Atlantic in South Africa. Desiré lines up her borrowed Chevron B34 ahead of Alex Blignaut's driver, Nols Nieman, in a Wheatcroft – one of the many cigarette company-sponsored cars in South Africa's premier race series. These macho companies didn't appreciate being challenged by a mere woman! (Courtesy Wilson Collection)

in the South Africa Formula Atlantic Championship. The first thing we did, on returning to South Africa in November 1977, was to visit Alex in his downtown Johannesburg office. He was pleased to see us and was very complimentary about Desiré's European exploits. He immediately embraced her wish to race in South Africa again and we spent several hours with him discussing opportunities, strategies, potential sponsorship sources, and possible drives. He even suggested that he might be able to offer her a ride in the second of his own team cars, alongside Nols Nieman. We left his office convinced we had something going for Des.

Alex followed up by saying his second car wasn't available, but that he would introduce us to a friend who promised to raise sponsorship. Within a week, we had two offers of sponsorship, one from the Laddiers retail clothing chain, the other from Wonder Slim, a Weight Watchers-type company. On the basis of this sponsorship, we did a deal to rent a much modified Chevron B34, from Basil van Rooyen, who had been a multiple South African Saloon Car Champion and was the owner of a large speed equipment shop. Although the car had not been raced for some time, it had been quite competitive and seemed a good car for Desiré to start her Formula Atlantic career in.

With the help of Richard Martin, a friend from our Formula Ford days, we prepared the car for the first of the summer season of Atlantic races, towing it the 1000 miles to Cape Town's Killarney circuit behind a borrowed El Camino. Without the benefit of any pre-event seat time, Des qualified the car eighth, ahead of several strong competitors, including Nieman in Alex's Blignaut's Wheatcroft. Des got a good start, passed a car or two, then stopped out on the track when a misfire terminated in an engine failure.

We hauled the car back to Johannesburg, replaced the damaged motor with Van Rooyen's spare, and took the car out to Kyalami for a test. The misfire remained and we struggled for two days to fix it. Even van Rooyen was unable to find the problem, despite spending hours working on the carburettor settings. The stuttering engine continued throughout qualifying, leaving Des mired in the midfield. It was still there when the race started. Despite this, she managed to pass several cars before the engine blew up again.

The costs of the engine rebuilds, plus the rental fee for the car, were now far greater than the sponsorship due to us – especially as this suddenly seemed to disappear: the sponsors seemed happy, but we hadn't seen their money and the fixer guy stopped taking our calls.

Now we were in real trouble, owing far more money than we could conceivably find; money that would take years of work to repay, even if we had jobs. Then we received a shot in the arm. Des was

Singing for Her Supper. Desiré tried hard to justify the sponsorship she received from Laddiers and Wonder Slim, but received nothing when the person who put the deals together vanished from the scene, forcing us to have to borrow a lot of money to pay off the loan of the car and engine rebuilds. (Courtesy Wilson Collection)

asked to drive in the next Atlantic race by Willie Kauhsen's German team. It had come to South Africa for the summer Atlantic season and its driver, Derek Bell, had returned to England. It looked as if things would be OK after all.

The next morning I received a call from a very profane Alex Blignaut. As already related, he screamed down the phone that we should get out of the country. "That's where her career is, she has no future in South Africa!"

"But, Alex," I responded, completely taken aback by his ferocity and sudden, inexplicable change in his attitude, "Willie Kauhsen has offered Des a ride at Welkom." "Her entry has been refused," Alex responded. "She will never get another entry in South Africa. She's not wanted here. Get her the f**k out of South Africa. Go back to England." He slammed the phone down, even as I tried to ask him what had gone wrong.

I couldn't believe what I'd heard. Just a day before, Alex had been happy to hear of Kauhsen's offer. Now, he was telling us that her career in South Africa was over. We were devastated. I tried to call back to get a reason, but Alex wouldn't take my call.

The South African racing scene is very small and

it immediately became obvious to us that Desiré was now persona non-grata. Alex had the message out. Basil called for his money and the engine builder wanted his. Doors closed in our faces. Des went from hero to zero in a matter of hours.

We were, obviously, extremely upset, but surprisingly, didn't see this as the end of the world. The year we had spent overseas had opened our eyes to a new way of life and one of our first reactions on returning to South Africa, six weeks before, had been the realisation that we were now uncomfortable with the political situation and the basic structure of the South African apartheid way of life. We had already held long conversations about our future and we were already considering a return to the UK, even without jobs or any racing prospects.

Alex's phone call helped us make up our minds, as did a call from Roy Thomas, who rang from England, to say that John Webb wanted Des to drive in an all ladies celebrity race at Brands Hatch. Would we be interested?

But how were we to get to England? Not only were we flat broke, we also owed a fortune to Basil van Rooyen and the engine builder. We couldn't even afford the air fare, let alone the costs of living in the UK without a job.

Roy said that he would give Des some work if we could get to England, so we called *Fairlady* magazine, which had sponsored the Merlyn during Desiré's champion year, and it came up with two one-way tickets. We settled with Basil and the engine builder, borrowed money from Des' mother and flew to the UK with less than £500 to our name.

It was funny how quickly we forgot Alex Blignaut's diatribe and how soon we were able to put our disappointment behind us. We didn't even try to find out what had made him change his attitude and why he was so desperate to chase Desiré out of South Africa. I suppose that we should have found a lawyer, gone to the media, made a big fuss, fought back, but at the time, Alex's power over South African racing was so complete, that none of these seemed to be viable options.

We just forgot and moved forward and it was only several years later we learned the reason. By then, Alex Blignaut was no longer involved in racing. His tenure as dictator had ended amid fierce criticism of a management style that had become increasingly self serving. He moved on to horse racing and played no further role in motor sports.

Some years later, Desiré and I were back in South Africa for the Kyalami 9 Hours race, where she had raced a Porsche 962 for John Fitzpatrick. We were enjoying the post-race party, at the race organiser's home in Johannesburg, when we were approached by a former president of the Sports Car Club of South Africa, who had been very supportive of Desiré during her Formula Ford years.

"Do you know why Alex wanted Des out of the country?" He asked.

We were surprised that he even knew of the conversation, but he told us that he had been with Alex when the phone call had been made. "It was the cigarette companies. They didn't want Des in the series. They told Alex that if she raced they would pull all their sponsorship."

Now, it all made sense.

The South Africa Formula Atlantic championships, in 1976 and 1977, were dominated by cars sponsored by large cigarette companies. Most of the top 12 cars in the championship carried cigarette advertising, including Alex Blignaut's own two-car team. These cigarette companies, basically, funded the premier level of South African motorsport, not only by paying for the cars to race, but also by spending huge amounts to promote the sport through advertising and promotional budgets, that were all based on the macho image of racing. They had spent hundreds of thousands of rand, invested in images of he-man drivers wrestling hard-to-drive cars around the track.

Then, along came this small, shy, slip of a girl, who climbed aboard a car that was known to be less than the best and proceeded to drive it as fast as their male stars. Petrified that their macho advertising image would now be ridiculed, several of the tobacco barons contacted Alex and demanded that he find a way to keep her out of South African racing. Alex, with the whole financial security of South Africa's premier race series at stake, had little option but to tell me to take Des back to England.

Instead of simply caving in to the tobacco companies, it might have been fairer to her, and much more beneficial for the international image of South African racing, if Alex had asked the cigarette people to put together a budget for Des to race in Europe. This could have been done, for example, under a 'Racing for South Africa' programme, which would have given the cigarette companies good mileage in the SA press. It was another lesson learned!

8

THE CHARM SCHOOL

JOHN Webb was the best race promoter there has ever been. He was the man responsible for developing Brands Hatch from an irrelevant club track into the most important Grand Prix venue of its time and had a role in helping to make British national racing the world's most significant development arena for racing drivers. His role in developing Brands and the other circuits and his creation of Formula Ford and other formula, were all backed by what became known, by others, even if he hated the name, as the Brands Hatch Charm School.

The 'Charm School' was John's most effective marketing project; the promotion of celebrity and women drivers.

John ran Brands Hatch and its associated circuits for nearly thirty years and, in all that time, hardly spent any money on regular event advertising. Very early into his stewardship of the tracks, he came to the conclusion that regular advertising wasn't a cost-effective way of promoting his events. Instead, he understood the value of editorial exposure and its ability to promote his events far more proactively than any regular form of radio, press, magazine, or TV advertising could deliver. He also realised that the best way to get Brands Hatch and racing in general into major newspapers was to present them with stories featuring celebrity race drivers – especially if these were women.

John kept a sharp lookout for stars from other sports, movies, and politics who would be able to provide him with a story and a photograph in England's national daily papers and whenever he found a willing player, he would invite them to Brands Hatch's Racing School to learn to drive a race car.

The celebrity would be trained to drive the school's Ford Escort cars until they were capable

The Slow Car That Made a Fast Career! *Desiré returned to England after the South African Formula Atlantic fiasco, to race a mere Ford Escort in a celebrity all-womens race. The best decision she ever made! (Courtesy Wilson Collection)*

of racing them against other celebrities, during a public race meeting. These simple fifteen lap contests were held at every major race event. They, typically, provided relatively uninspiring racing and occasional accidents, but they did add celebrity stature to the event and always generated free media exposure.

John's choice of drivers was as wide as the news of the day. Anyone in the headlines was likely to receive an invitation and many stars and celebrities took the plunge and made their way down to Brands for their school training. Perhaps his most visible annual celebrity race promotion was the Lords versus the House of Commons Challenge. For this event, six to eight Members of Parliament would race against the same number of Peers from the House of Lords. Over the years, many of England's leading political lights appeared at Brands. The value to John was enormous, not just for the media publicity these races would attract, but also because of the valuable contacts he made. Contacts that, for example, paved the immigration path for Des and I after we had taken unauthorised jobs at Brands and then stayed way beyond our six-month visitor allowance.

One of John's regular promotions was the all-women race, similar to the one that had launched Divina Galica's career. Now it was Desiré's turn.

With John Webb's invitation and just £500 in our pockets, Desiré and I left South Africa, talked our way through British immigration, and made our way to Brands Hatch.

Once there, Desiré dominated the fifteen-lap race, leading every lap and setting a new celebrity race record. After the race, we found our way to John's private viewing suite, above the main grandstand, introduced ourselves, and thanked him for inviting her to drive.

He asked us to come and see him in his office the following day. The meeting went extremely well for both of us.

At first, his interest was in Des. He complimented her on her drive and asked her about her plans for the season. He seemed to lose a little interest when she told him that she had nothing going and no money with which to race. He turned to me and asked about my background. We talked for a while and then, to my surprise, he offered both of us a job. He wanted me to help prepare the facility for the upcoming British Grand Prix event. Apparently, Brands had recently lost the services of its Track Manager and I presented a temporary solution to his problems. He offered Des a job in the Administration and Reception office of the Brands Hatch Racing School.

I told him that we didn't have work permits, but this didn't faze him: "We'll sort that out," he said. He turned to Des.

"I'll see what I can do to help you with your racing. In the meantime, use the School cars as much as you like. I'll see if I can find something for you to race." So, we joined the Brands Hatch family.

I was appointed as track manager of Brands Hatch and within a few months was promoted to General Manager of all four of the MCD circuits. By the end of the year, I was on the Board of Directors of

The Win That Really Mattered. *Floral wreath, chequered flag, and a future in racing – who would have guessed the consequences of a minor win? (Courtesy Wilson Collection)*

Motor Circuit Developments. During my period at the track, I had some great times, particularly helping run the British Grand Prix. These included being at the receiving end of one of Ken Tyrrell's famous froth jobs for simply following the orders of Bernie Ecclestone. Bernie had really set me up, over parking arrangements in the Formula 1 paddock. He didn't pass information on to the teams, leaving me to face the wrath of the team owners, as I tried to enforce his new arrangements! I also learned that I didn't want to get on the wrong side of John Webb; any member of staff who did would be deluged with countless memos, criticizing their work!

Brands Hatch, in 1978, was the epicenter of British national racing. More than any other circuit, including Silverstone, this was where the politics of racing were centered. The clubhouse, a charismatic old wooden barn that housed the cafeteria, a large pub, and the offices of the British Racing and Sports Car Club, was a meeting place for drivers, sponsors, officials, media, and fans. On any given race weekend, many of the most important and influential personalities in British racing could be found there. Among these were the Brands Hatch crew, a group centered around John Webb and normally found huddled together on bar stools at the far end of the counter. They included John's wife, Angela, who was the Sales and Marketing Director for Brands Hatch; Jackie Epstein, son of the famous sculptor and a former driver in his own right, who was the Operating Manager of the Brands Hatch Racing School; commentator Brian Jones; and favoured drivers such as Tony Lanfranchi. Here, together with other associates, plans were made and plots were hatched as the beer and wine flowed. This group played a huge role in making Des welcome and helping her with her career. Brian, and his wife Roz, became our very good friends, while the hard drinking Tony was always supportive and became a valued guru to Des. Lanfranchi, who was a very talented driver, had turned down an audience with Mr Ferrari because the Italians wouldn't pay for his air fare to visit the great man, and he also turned down an offer to drive for Ken Tyrrell because Ken wanted him to curb his drinking!

Des and I were welcomed into the group and, before long, we found her career falling under the hard-edged guidance of John, Jackie, Brian, and Tony. Despite, or because of the help, Desiré's first few months at Brands were very frustrating. Her day job was to handle the administration of the Brands Hatch Racing School, from 7.30 am to dusk, every day of the week. But she was far more interested in driving race cars than working behind the counter at the school. She was free to drive any of the School cars, at any time when she wasn't tied up in the office, but these offered little challenge, being far slower than anything she had driven since leaving South Africa for Holland. Yet, John would question her every day about her lap times and kept insisting that she drive them as much as she could. He even made her race the school's beat-up old Eldens in a few entry level Formula Ford races, which Des considered to be a major step backwards and almost insulting. After all, her last FF2000 race at Brands had seen her on the front row and now she was struggling to even get the old School cars onto the back of a club level Formula 1600 grid. She seethed in frustration, while John egged her on. He also made her drive hundreds of laps in a school Sports 2000, giving customers high

speed rides around the track late into the evenings, after each race event. Although she wasn't very happy, she buckled down and accepted his direction, not realising that John was deliberately testing her character, trying to ascertain how she would react under the negative conditions that, he knew, would be part and parcel of any professional racing career.

Then, early one Sunday morning, Roy Thomas came into my office in the administration building, asking for Des. She was actually at home cleaning the house. "Tell her to drop the vacuum cleaner and get here quick," he said, "I've got a drive for her."

Des arrived just as qualifying for the FF2000 race began, meeting up with Roy and a red Crosslé, in the pit lane. As she climbed in, he told me that the car belonged to a client, Nick Challis, who owned a truck trailer construction business called TDC. He had arrived at the track suffering a hangover and didn't feel fit enough to drive. Roy had persuaded Nick to allow Des to race his car.

She left the pits with less than ten minutes remaining in the qualifying session and, without making any

A Little Help From Her Friends. Throughout 1977, Roy Thomas was a friend in need and a big supporter, so when he called at the last minute to ask Des to drive a strange car, she rushed to the track and earned a season's racing. Here, Roy, Alan, and Des discuss her successful drive in Nick Challis' Crosslé. *(Courtesy Wilson Collection)*

changes to the car to suit her style, stormed to a fifth place grid position. Nick Challis was impressed, but said little until after both the races had ended, with Des finishing fifth and third and setting fastest lap in each. She also won the celebrity Escort race, with fastest lap time and a new lap record, to complete a successful, if busy Sunday. "Meet me in the Kentagon for lunch tomorrow," he said.

The next day Challis, Webb, and Desiré met in Brands Hatch's new Kentagon restaurant, which had been built to replace the old wooden clubhouse. Nick told her that he'd never managed to finish a race above 18th place and was impressed that she had been so competitive in the car. He then asked her to drive it for him for the rest of the season. He even offered to pay her £80 per race and allowed her to keep any prize money she might win.

The next weekend, we all travelled to Castle Combe, Des and I staying at a really nice hotel near the village, at Nick's expense. We arrived at the track early Sunday morning to find the Crosslé parked alongside a BMW, in which company owner, sponsor, and car owner, Nick Challis, was fast asleep. While we had slept in luxury, he had chosen to spend the night in the back seat of his car, parked in the paddock! Our surprise at the TDC team arrangements increased when, a few minutes later, Nick's father, Bill, arrived in a Rolls-Royce, wearing a business suit and tie. He promptly took off his jacket, rolled up his sleeves, and started working on the Crosslé. Over 70 years old, Bill Challis was the team's mechanic!

Nick and Bill were to become good friends who believed totally in Desiré's ability and potential and who provided her with good, fast, and reliable cars for the next two seasons. Unlike so many sponsors, they helped Des because they enjoyed racing, and, although their cars always carried the red and white TDC colours, their support remained intensely personal. It didn't take long for Nick to become a valued member of John Webb's Brands Hatch group.

For the rest of the year, Des drove the red TDC sponsored Crosslé in the BRSCC championships, in what was to prove to be a very competitive season. Although the year-old car wasn't as fast as the factory backed Lolas, Reynards, and Royales, Des was able to run amongst the front runners at every race, eventually finishing fifth in the championship, even though she missed several of the rounds. She won at Castle Combe, with a new lap record and was always a potential winner, running the rest of the

Brands Hatch Specialist. *Desiré loved the Brands Hatch short track, so when the last minute call came to drive Nick Challis' Crosslé, she grabbed her opportunity and proved her skills with two fastest laps and two great finishes. (Courtesy Chris Davies)*

season without any accidents – a great improvement over the 1977 season.

One afternoon, at the daily gathering at the far end of the Kentagon bar, John Webb casually made the announcement that he was going to enter Desiré in the upcoming British Formula 1 Grand Prix. Des and I were completely taken aback, although everyone else in the group seemed to take John's statement in stride.

Desiré didn't know how to respond. She told John that she had never driven anything bigger than a Formula Ford 2000, other than the two abortive Formula Atlantic rides in South Africa, something he knew very well. She said that she didn't have enough experience, but this didn't deter him. She said that she would need to test the car, which he agreed.

Revealingly, she never said that she wasn't ready to drive a Formula 1 car, or to go along with his wishes.

John unveiled his plans and said that he had total confidence in Desiré's ability to drive a Formula 1 car and that he had no doubts that she would be able to

The Man in the Middle. *John Webb was the most important person in Desiré's racing life. He used his promotion of lady drivers to great effect, ensuring publicity and crowds for his race tracks and creating great opportunities for the girls. This 1978 picture shows Juliette Slaughter (later Brindley), a good race driver and a brilliant press office manager, Divina Galica, who Des considers to be the best woman driver Desiré ever raced against, John, Desiré, and Annie Neal.*
(Courtesy John Webb Collection)

handle running in the Grand Prix. He then said that he had made a deal for her to drive a March, in the upcoming Tyre Test days, three weeks prior to the Grand Prix. Obviously, John's main goal in entering Desiré was to generate media exposure for the race.

The uproar in the racing press was immediate. Journalists, readers, and outraged would-be Formula 1 racers weighed in, demanding that John replace Desiré with a more deserving driver, someone English – a man. After all, why was this inexperienced South African girl to be given a Grand Prix drive when there were much more successful drivers who really needed the break? Drivers like Geoff Lees, Tony Trimmer, or Stephen South?

But John's publicity ploy worked. For the next two weeks, Desiré's Grand Prix plans were featured in national newspapers across England, while the racing world vilified John for yet another 'Charm School' promotion. Noticeably, as the specialist press and other pundits groused, her fellow competitors were more supportive.

Very few drivers have ever made the step up into a Formula 1 car with as little racing experience as Desiré had in June 1978. Today, a new driver will have competed thousands of laps in a professionally run race team, or competed in super competitive major race series, like GP2. Even then, their first laps in a Formula 1 car would, most likely, be taken under the auspices of one of the Grand Prix teams.

The Tyre Test days were a regular feature of every Grand Prix back in the 70s. A few weeks before each event, all the competing cars would gather at the track to test the different tyres that Goodyear wanted to bring to the event. The testing would last for two full days and would provide teams with the setup information they needed to compete successfully in the GP itself.

The Tyre Tests were a boon to fans, who were able to see the same stars who would compete in the GP proper under much more casual and friendly conditions. They were, also, a valuable promotional tool for the race promoters, who used them to generate large amounts of media and TV exposure for their upcoming events. John Webb made sure that Desiré was the focus of this media attention.

Consequently, when she stepped up to the white March Formula 1 car for the very first time, as the track opened for the start of the Tyre Tests, she was surrounded by photographers, radio journalists, and TV cameramen. A journalist even interviewed her for TV while the mechanics strapped her into the cockpit for the first time, and the TV cameras rolled as she started the engine. She accelerated out of the pit lane between Niki Lauda's Ferrari and Mario Andretti's Lotus!

Des had been under enormous pressure during the weeks leading up to the test days. Prior to John breaking the news to her, she had no realistic expectation of driving a Formula 1 car. While she had an interest in Grand Prix racing, she was at a stage of her career where she was looking no further than Formula Three for her next career move. Now that there was a possibility of driving in the British Grand Prix, she had to ask herself if she was ready for the huge step up to Formula 1. She was a realist and recognised her inexperience and that the Formula 1 car would require completely different driving skills. She wondered how heavy it would be to drive, for, after all, she was smaller, lighter, and less muscular than any of the current Grand Prix drivers. She thought about the immense power difference and the far higher speeds. She even wondered at her ability to learn the full Grand Prix course, for almost all her experience at Brands Hatch had been on the short 1.26 mile club track and she had very little experience of the full 2.56 mile Grand Prix layout. Finally, she also wondered how she would be accepted by the Grand Prix drivers, most of whom would never have heard of her and who would, naturally, be sceptical of an unknown girl racing amongst them.

John Webb understood these concerns and, also, knew that she would need help in making the physical transition from a FF2000 to a Formula 1 car. So, he asked Jackie Epstein to take her under his wing, to act as her driver coach, to be her guru.

Jackie may not have been a superstar race driver himself, but he had driven F5000 and top level sports cars, with some success, in events around the world. But, he was an experienced team owner and manager. He understood how to work with a driver, how to relate the driver's experience to the new car, how to be the intermediary between the new driver and the team's mechanics. He was the ideal person to help Des acclimatize herself to the Formula 1 car, to a team she didn't know, and to Formula 1. Jackie also understood how to protect her from the pressure of the media and the pressure that he knew she was putting on herself. He played an important role.

John had arranged for Desiré to drive a 1975 March, that had been partially upgraded to 1976 specifications. The factory Marches had not been the most competitive cars back then, where they could, usually, be found near the back of the field, in the Grands Prix held that year. So, Des' even older car was, by no means, competitive. Yet it was still far quicker than anything she had ever driven.

For the first day of the tests Jackie restricted Des to limited revs, as he didn't want her trying too hard. All he wanted her to do was to become comfortable with the car, to learn to accept the much faster traffic around her, to get used to the higher speeds, greater braking ability, heavier weight, and far better road holding of the Formula 1 machine.

She did her job well. To start with, she wasn't particularly fast, ending the day several seconds slower than the other cars, but slowly improved her race lines as her confidence increased. By the end of the afternoon she was tired, but sure that the following day would see some significant improvements.

They came quickly. Jackie allowed her to increase the rev limits to competitive levels and, before long,

she was lapping consistently fast, ending the day 21st fastest of the 26 cars at the test. More importantly, she never spun, never looked out of control, and never got in anyone else's way. The critics were silenced.

John then withdrew her entry for the British Grand Prix.

Des was disappointed, but not concerned. She had known all along that John's intention was to generate publicity for the GP and she knew that the chances of her actually racing had always been fairly low. More important to her was the knowledge that she was perfectly capable of handling a Formula 1 machine at a competitive level. Now, for the first time ever, she could actually aspire to, perhaps, one day, find herself racing in a Grand Prix.

In the meantime, there was always the TDC Crosslé and the rest of the season's BRSCC FF2000 championship races to contend.

The Publicity Stunt That Worked. When John Webb announced that Des would be driving in the 1979 British Grand Prix, his statement drew a storm of protest from the race world, and huge interest from the national media. After her great performance in the three-year-old March-751/761, which she used to run 21st fastest of the 26 F1 cars on hand, the race world wondered why John withdrew the entry. It was merely a publicity stunt, but it was the beginning of Des' Formula 1 career. (Courtesy CTP Photography)

9

FROM ZERO TO HERO

ESIRÉ'S performance during the pre-Grand Prix Tyre Test days had been remarkable, and was noticed by a number of important people, including Jack Kallay, owner of the High-Line Car Stripes company, which sponsored a team in the British Formula 1 Championships. We don't know whether he was influenced, or supported financially, by Brands Hatch, but regardless, he called John and asked if Des would be available to drive his Ensign for the balance of the season, starting at Oulton Park.

The British Formula 1 Championship was a race series instigated and promoted by John Webb, which he introduced at the beginning of the 1978 season to replace the ShellSport F5000 series he'd run for the previous few years. It was promoted as Britain's most important racing series, and featured one- or two-year-old Formula 1 and Formula Two cars, driven by both older, established drivers and younger drivers hoping to make their way into international Grand Prix competition. In this, it's first season, the Championship had proved very successful, both as a spectator draw and because it produced some very intense racing. The series was supported by several professional race teams, using cars that included McLaren M23s, March 771s, Lotus 78s, Ensigns, and other recent Formula 1 chassis, and by a number of quick Formula Two cars, whose nimble handling and good drivers made them very competitive with the Formula 1 cars on some of the tight British tracks. The leading drivers in the Championship were; Tony Trimmer, in the Melchester team's McLaren M23; Spaniard, Emilio De Villota, in a similar car; Geoff Lees, who drove a variety of chassis; movie stuntman, Valentino Musetti, in a March; former Grand Prix drivers Bob Evans, in a Hesketh; and Guy Edwards

First Time Out. Desiré sits in the Jack Kallay-owned Ensign MN04 at the beginning of practice for her first F1 race, at Oulton Park. Jackie Epstein crouches to her left. She qualified third on the grid, having been fastest, until de Villota and Edwards changed tyres right as the track dried, for the last two laps.
(Courtesy Wilson Collection)

and his Mopar March team-mate, Australian Bruce Allison.

Desiré's first drive in the Kallay-owned Ensign MNO4 was at the Oulton Park track, in Cheshire, where she arrived to a rainy weekend and a very wet track. Despite the conditions and her lack of Formula 1 experience, Desiré was immediately at home in the car. So much so, that, from the very beginning of the first hour-long qualifying session, she was one of the fastest drivers on the track. Fifth fastest in the first session, when the team restricted her use of revs while she accustomed herself to the car, she went even faster in the final qualifying period. She headed the times until the last few minutes of qualifying, when the team kept her on wet tyres while Emilio De Villota's McLaren M23 and Guy Edwards' March switched to dries, enabling them to push her back to third on the grid.

A second row start for her first ever Formula 1 race was a very impressive performance for the 24-year-old lady driver.

Unfortunately, the race was less so, because the clutch failed on the start line and she was forced out of the race.

An interesting situation arose between the Oulton Park and Mallory Park races, when Bernie Ecclestone and John Webb let it out that Desiré would be driving the famous Brabham 'Fan Car.' The car had been side-lined after proving too fast at the Swedish GP, although it was never actually banned. In any event, it would have been an amazing coup for Des if it had happened, but the plot went awry when Bernie said that the factory mechanics would all be at Hockenheim, so it never happened. Still, it was a great, if short lived, promotion for the Mallory event.

So, instead of with the Brabham, she arrived at the very short Mallory Park track, in Leicestershire, with a newly repainted red Ensign.

She knew the track well from her FF2000 races there, but handling a Formula 1 car proved to be a different experience. Mallory is noted for two very different challenges. The first is the very fast, sweeping, 180° Gerard's Bend, which could be taken at close to 150mph in a Formula 1 car and, at the time, was lined by railway sleepers set less than three feet from the outside edge of the track. The second is the very slow Shaw's Hairpin, which was taken at about 30mph, but which required the car to be hauled down from very high speed and wrestled through the bend and was then followed by very hard acceleration downhill, into the very fast and frightening Devil's Elbow left-hander, where, again, the guardrail was lined up against the track edge.

Desiré qualified the Ensign fifth on the grid, during a session in which she had a very scary moment: the steering wheel broke while in the middle of Gerard's Bend. One of the spokes cracked, allowing her left-hand to push the rim several inches – enough to deflect the car to the edge of the track at a crucial time. She reacted quickly, avoided hitting the sleepers, avoiding what could have been a very high speed accident, and returned to the pits to have

the wheel changed. It was a big scare and robbed her of a chance to go for pole position.

The race itself was the hardest she'd ever experienced. The high speeds around Gerards created the strongest G-forces she had ever encountered and, half way through the race, her neck muscles gave in. Without the strength to hold her head against the wind and the G-forces, her head simply flopped around, making it very difficult for her to concentrate on the task of driving the car. She also found the weight of the car to be a problem in the hairpin, requiring strong muscles to haul it through the corner.

Still, she persevered, running in fourth place until a quick spin bent her front wing against the guardrail and dropped her back into the clutches of Val Musetti. After a few laps following close to her gearbox, he made his move into the fast Esses section. Des refused to give in, matched his late braking, and drove into the first of the turns wheel-to-wheel with the March. The two cars dived to the second apex and touched. Val's front wheel ran up over Des' rear tyre, launching his March into the air, before it crashed down onto the track. Des continued, although the force of the impact caused the Ensign to slide sideways, before she could get it back under control in a move that severely wrenched her back. With neck muscles that refused to work, arm muscles

Nobody's Perfect. *Desiré nudges the Armco after a quick spin at Mallory. (Courtesy Chris Davies)*

wasted from forcing the Ensign through the hairpin, and now severe back pains, Des continued the race to finish in sixth place.

Val, whose March was wrecked in the crash, showed no animosity to Des, telling people that he had expected her to give in and that the accident had been his fault. At the following race at Brands Hatch, he joined Des in the Kallay team, driving its second Ensign. The Brands race was uneventful and saw Desiré finish fourth, from ninth place on the grid. This was after racing the TDC Crosslé to third place in the afternoon's FF2000 event.

Tony Trimmer, driving the Melchester McLaren M23, clinched the championship title by winning at Brands, and, because of a lack of funds, decided to sit out the final two races of the year. The car then became available for someone else to drive. That someone was Divina Galica.

Divi had chosen to race in the Formula 1 World Grand Prix championships in 1978, driving a Hesketh, alongside team-mate Rupert Keegan. Although she tried extremely hard, a combination of a less than competitive car and lack of testing meant that she hadn't been able to qualify for the first few events, and she decided to withdraw from the series. Back in England and without a regular ride, she was understandably wary of Desiré's sudden rise to prominence, so she jumped at the opportunity to rent Tony's championship-winning car in order to confirm her position as England's leading women driver. We didn't know how Divi had found the money to pay for the Melchester drive, but our suspicions pointed directly at John Webb, even though he never admitted to any involvement in the deal. Regardless, he jumped on the promotional opportunity and, before long, the English racing magazines were full of the up-coming 'cat-fight,' at Thruxton. For Des, this was to be round two, Divi having won their first encounter, at Snetterton, in their 1977 Sports 2000 race.

To save the long road journey to Thruxton, John offered us two seats in the light aircraft he had chartered, which seemed to be a great idea, even though Des is extremely susceptible to motion sickness and detests flying in small planes. At least, we thought it was a good idea – until we woke up to a heavily overcast sky. We took off and made our way to Thruxton, flying on instruments, until the pilot leant over and told us that although the track was right below us, he was unable to land, and we would therefore have to divert to Southampton. We

landed at about the time that the first Formula 1 practice session started, hired a taxi, and made our way to the track at speeds that never exceeded the speed limit, despite offers of a £100 bribe to get us there as quickly as possible.

Des was frantic, as she had only ever driven one race at Thruxton, her first ever English event, where she had been punted off in the opening laps, so didn't know the track very well. In addition, Thruxton was an extremely fast and very tricky layout, that was likely to be very difficult in the Formula 1 car, so Des was anxious to get as much track time as possible. Now, stuck in the back of the slowest taxi in the UK, Desiré saw her chances of beating Divi becoming more and more remote.

We eventually arrived, long after the first session was over, leaving Des just the final one-hour qualifying session in which to learn the track, set up the car, and earn a good grid position. When she returned to the pits, some fifteen minutes into the timed session, she beckoned for me to come over to the car. "Man, I'm flying," she said. "That's the fastest I've ever been. Where am I?

"You are twelve seconds off the pace."

She looked at me as if I was mad, said nothing, dropped her visor, and returned to the track. Her first flying lap was a full ten seconds faster and she eventually qualifying in seventh place, 0.4 seconds and two positions ahead of Divina's McLaren. Des finished third in the race despite losing second gear, 40 seconds ahead of Divi's McLaren. Round two to Desiré.

The final Aurora Formula 1 race of the 1978 season took place at Snetterton. Des qualified in fourth place and made a great start, moving into second along the back straight. Unfortunately, as she tuned into the right-handed Bomb Hole Corner, she felt the steering getting heavy and, two laps later, brought the car into the pits with a flat right-front tyre, losing over a lap while the team changed the wheel. She returned to the track well behind, but drove her heart out to finish the race in sixth place. During her chase back through the field, she lapped consistently faster than anyone else in the field, including race winner David Kennedy. She actually held fastest race lap, until David put in a spurt during the closing laps, just eclipsing her time.

Although she only drove in five of the season's 12 events, Desiré scored enough points to finish in tenth place in the championship. More importantly,

First F1 Podium. Desiré joins GP drivers Bob Evans and race winner Guy Edwards on the Thruxton podium, after a great drive to third. (Courtesy Wilson Collection)

Lifting Wheels. After running in second place, before pitting to change a flat tyre, Des drove the Ensign as hard as she could to make up time. Here, she lifts a wheel through Snetterton's daunting Bombhole turn. (Courtesy Wilson Collection)

she had rapidly established herself as a driver with immense promise and was now confirmed as the best lady racer in England.

Although her main focus was now on the Formula 1 car, Des continued to drive the TDC Crosslé at every opportunity, including at the events where she raced the Formula 1 car. She also drove other cars, on occasions when requested to do so by John Webb, including Ford Escorts, a Sports 2000, and a Porsche 924.

She also had her first taste of America.

The USAC Indy cars came to England in late 1978, to race at Silverstone and at Brands, in yet another major John Webb initiative, and we were able to spend time with some interesting American heroes, including Rick Mears (who introduced Des to the value of a neck collar, giving her his own to use), Danny Ongais, A J Foyt, Al Unser Snr, and Tom Bagley.

Tom, a former American SuperVee Champion, who was in his first year in Indycars, and his wife, Sally, arrived at Brands Hatch a full week before any of the other drivers, looking for an opportunity to learn the track and acclimatize, before racing his Patrick Racing-entered Wildcat. Des met them in her Race School office and immediately arranged for Tom to have free use of the School cars, a gesture which was to lead to a life-long friendship and her introduction to the United States. We immediately became very friendly with the Bagleys and arranged for Tom to be a guest commentator at the Thruxton Formula 1 event, where he was able to witness Desiré's third-place drive in the Ensign.

Several weeks after they had returned to the States, Tom called Des to tell her to get on an aeroplane and fly to Phoenix, where he had arranged for her to drive his old Zink SuperVee on the famed one mile oval.

As I was unable to travel due to work commitments, Des left by herself and, for five days, seemed to disappear. Not knowing where in Phoenix she was staying and not having a phone number for Tom, I was unable to reach her. There were no calls

from her, so I was becoming concerned when, at last, she called.

"How are you doing?" I asked, anxious to know how she was handling her first oval track experience.

"You should see the food here," she replied. "Yes, but how's the car?" I asked. "You should see the hotel I'm in," she replied.

I didn't care a damn about the food or the hotel. I wanted to know how well she was doing, if she was competitive.

"I want to live here," she said, in what was to become a prophetic statement.

Eventually, I persuaded her to tell me: she had qualified fifth, in a field of 60 cars, ahead of drivers like Geoff Brabham, the new SuperVee Champion, and just behind Kevin Cogan. She was obviously handling her transition to the banked ovals quite well.

Still, all Des wanted to talk about was the lifestyle in Phoenix, which was such a total contrast to our modular home in a trailer park in England and our pub-style food habits. She was staying at the luxurious Pointe West Resort, eating the best foods and visiting beautiful Scottsdale-type homes as the

Round and Round. *Des enters the track at Phoenix to take her qualifying run in Tom Bagley's old Zink Super-Vee. She qualified fifth of the 60 cars entered, in her first ever race on an oval. (Courtesy Wilson Collection)*

Sports Woman of the Year. *Des received the prestigious South African 'SportsWoman of the Year' award just a few months after being chased out of her home country by the local racing leadership.*
(Courtesy Wilson Collection)

Blue, Yellow, and a Coronet.
(Courtesy Wilson Collection)

guest of Tom and his sponsor, Steve Kent. She fell in love with America and, from that time onwards, we always saw the United States as our future home.

Desiré didn't finish the race, despite holding fifth place most of the way and running with the lead group. She made the typical road course drivers mistake, applying opposite lock when the car got sideways after she had turned into a corner too harshly. Instead of correcting the spin, the car turned up the banking and hit the wall. She wasn't injured and the car wasn't too badly damaged, but although she wanted to keep racing, the team retired the car. However, she had, once again, shown her ability to be competitive in yet another new type of car and on a type of race track unlike anything on which she had ever driven.

The final accolade for the year came when she was asked to return home, to receive the prestigious South African 'Sportswoman of the Year' Award, presented to her at a glittering function in Cape Town by the Minister for Sport.

Desiré's race season hadn't turned out too badly for someone who began the year by being told to get the hell out of her home country and who arrived in England with less than £500 to her name. Yet she ended as South Africa's 'Sportswoman of the Year,' as one of racing's fastest rising stars and an internationally recognised Formula 1 driver.

Soon after her first Aurora Formula 1 race, in the Ensign, Desiré adopted a new helmet design that has since become her trade mark and is now well known to race fans around the world.

She's often asked why she chose this design and whether it has any specific significance.

There are two reasons for the design.

First, we wanted to give her an easily recognised helmet that would stand out on the track, be obvious, even if she was in amongst a bunch of competitors, and which would be equally visible in colour and in black and white photos. Hence, the distinct lines and clearly differentiated colours.

Second, the design was chosen to be feminine, with what was, initially, an intricate coronet design, but which was subsequently simplified to a crown and to use the colours made famous by Swedish driver, Ronnie Peterson, a driver who Des admired for his courage, his skill, and because he just seemed to be a really nice person.

10

THE LIONESS OF AFRICA

HAT a difference a year made.

Just 12 months earlier, Desiré was in debt; had been forced out of racing in her home country; was out of a drive; out of a job, and had no prospects of continuing her career. Now, at the beginning of the 1979 season, she seemed to have the world at her feet.

Her success in the 1978 Aurora British Formula 1 championships and the support provided by John Webb and Nick Challis, had led her to becoming one of England's best known racers and to be considered one of the fastest up-and-coming drivers in the world. The new season promised to drive her career even further, perhaps to the edge of Grand Prix racing.

As the 1978 season wound down, John Webb began negotiating with Brian Morris and Alan Charles, owners of the 1978 Aurora Formula 1 Championship-winning Melchester Racing Team, for Desiré to join them for the upgraded 1979 championship season. They reached an agreement a few days before we left to return to South Africa, for the Christmas holidays.

John's plans for the following season were based around the very significantly increased interest that had arisen in the series. Substantial sponsorship and promotional support, by the Aurora AFX model slot car racing company, promised to propel the series into the limelight, as did the very strong entry list. This included two Melchester Tyrrell 008s; two Mopar sponsored Fittipaldi F5A's for Guy Edwards and Bernard De Dryver; a pair of factory run Arrows FA1s for Rupert Keegan and Ricardo Zunino; a Teddy Yip sponsored Wolf WR4 (later to be replaced by the ground effect WR5) for Irishman David Kennnedy; a new Chevron DFV to be shared by Tiff Needell, Ray Mallock, and David Leslie; two Williams FW06s,

to be driven by former multiple-World Motorcycle Champion Giacomo Agostini and variety of Italian drivers including, on occasion, Lella Lombardi; and a Lotus 78 for Spanish nobleman Emilio De Villota. There would be an LEC and a Shadow for Former GP driver David Purley, and a works run Surtees for the talented Philip Bullman. More Formula 1 cars were expected to join during the season. The field would also include several quick Formula Two cars, including the Plygrange Chevron of ex-Lotus factory driver Jim Crawford, and March 792s for Divina Galica and Derek Warwick. Fields of over twenty cars were expected at each race and competition would be much stiffer than in the previous year.

Desiré was to drive the Tyrrell 008 with which Patrick Depallier had won the previous year's Monaco Grand Prix, although a second driver was yet to be signed.

Like most of the other Formula 1 cars in the field, the Tyrrell was one-year-old and had competed in the previous year's World Championship series. The Aurora Championship rules were closely based on those of the World Championship, but specified that cars had to be at least one-year-old and had to use a single hard compound Goodyear tyre, to reduce wear and costs. These tyres would be up to two seconds a lap slower than equivalent Grand Prix rubber, but as everyone had to use the same rubber, no one minded.

The Aurora series would consist of 15 events, racing at Brands Hatch, Mallory Park, Snetterton, Oulton Park, Donington, Thruxton, and Silverstone, in the UK; Zolder, in Belgium; Zandvoort, in the Netherlands, and at Nogaro, in France. For the first time, the stature of the series was to be recognised by the FIA and by FOCA, the group that represented the teams competing in the World Championship.

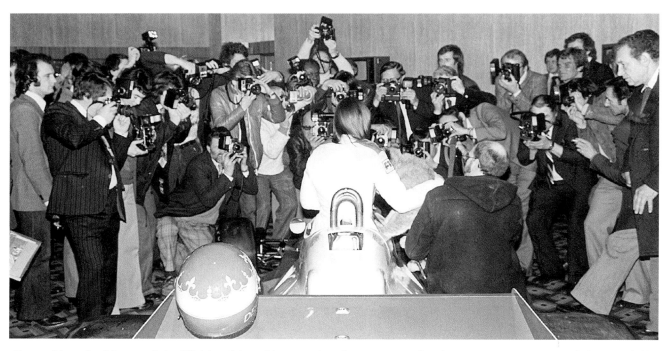

Launching the Lioness. *John Webb achieved international recognition for the Aurora F1 series, with his carefully staged launch of Desiré's programme and her 'Lioness of Africa' nickname. (Courtesy Ferret)*

Drivers in the Aurora series would be eligible to earn a coveted FIA Grand Prix Superlicence, without which they wouldn't be allowed to move up to World Championship. This elevated the Aurora series to equal status with Formula Two.

John Webb had worked his magic and Des was at the hub of his plans, driving for the Championship winning Melchester team. The season's publicity launch was held in a renovated warehouse building, in the revitalised Docklands area of London, a symbol both of the economic recovery of the city and of the new life of the Aurora series. Organised brilliantly, by Brands media wizard, Juliette Brindley, the function drew more than 50 journalists and photographers, representing media outlets all over the world and was a major success for the Brands Hatch PR machine.

As usual, John Webb was at his promotional best. On the stage, in addition to the Tyrrell, was Des' new Nick Challis run Lola T492 S2000 car, which she was to drive in the British Championships in addition to her Tyrrell commitments. Then, he hatched a name for Des that, while perfect fodder for the media, was to make Des cringe with embarrassment.

He announced Desiré as the 'Lioness of Africa,' playing on the 'Tigress of Turin' moniker he had pasted on Lella Lombardi when she raced in the earlier Shellsport F5000 series. Then, to drive the name home to the media, he added a real lioness to the show.

Without Des' knowledge and after the introductions to the media had been made, an 18-month old lion cub was released onto the stage. Bewildered by the bright lights of the hundreds of flash bulbs, the poor creature slunk onto the stage, ran straight over to the only seemingly harmless person around, and jumped onto Desiré's lap, where she sat, in the Tyrrell. Then, to drive the point home even more, it stretched up and looked up at her, as if to suggest that it had come home to mama.

The media went crazy, crowding around the car, the driver, and the lion cub, with a frenzy that resulted in front page coverage in newspapers throughout England, South Africa, and even as far a field as Brazil.

A few days later, a tall American, with a wild head of curly hair and a strong accent, walked into Des' office at the Racing School and introduced himself.

Gordon Smiley was to be her team-mate in the Melchester Tyrrell for the season.

The first race of the season was set for Zolder, in Belgium, one of Des' favourite tracks, where the team set up in a wet and dismally dreary paddock for the opening practice sessions. Despite her liking for the track and her comfort with wet conditions, she struggled throughout practice and qualifying with the setup of the car, but eventually secured fourth place on the grid, alongside Bullman's Surtees and well ahead of Smiley's sister Tyrrell in 11th place.

Des dropped to fifth at the start and began a long hard fight with Tiff Needell, which, by half distance, was for third place. Then, in three successive laps, Des got past Tiff, Bullman, and race leader David Kennedy by, each time, leaving her braking almost impossibly late at the entrance to the chicane behind the paddock. Once in the lead, she quickly opened up a thirteen second gap. But then spun and dropped back to third.

I was watching the race in the media centre and witnessed the media's excitement as history was about to be made. A woman had never won a Formula 1 race. Then she spun the car. I was devastated. I made my way back to the pits, where Des brought the Tyrrell after her third place finish. I wanted to know what had happened.

Des was blunt: "I pushed too hard and made a mistake," she said, taking full blame. That's one thing about Des. She has always been ready to accept the blame for her mistakes, even if, as in this case, there was another reason for the spin.

Desiré has always paid close attention to her pit signal board, relying on the team to give her gaps between her and the cars in front and behind. After passing Kennedy, she had seen the gap open at between one and two seconds a lap, until, with seven laps to go, she saw a plus margin of ten seconds. Then, for some reason, she didn't see the board on the next two laps and when she finally did, she saw that the sign read '+4.' She could hardly believe that someone was catching her at such a rate, but, on a track that was still wet and difficult, it wasn't impossible. So, thinking that she could still lose the race, she pushed as hard as she could, making a simple mistake and spinning the car at the Esses. After the race, she discovered that,when the mechanic held the board out over the pit rail to signal her, the number '1' in front of the four had fallen off. Instead of four, she had been a safe fourteen seconds in the lead!

Three Laps – Three passes. Des storms past David Kennedy's Wolf to become the first woman to ever lead an F1 race, having overtaken Philip Bullman and Tiff Needell in the same place on each of the previous two laps. (Courtesy Wilson Collection)

Such is the effect of small things on fate and history!

After Zolder, the Aurora field moved to Oulton Park, where Des crashed in practice, damaging three corners on the car. She qualified in tenth place, but drove through the field to finish third – a position she duplicated later in the afternoon, in the Sports 2000 race.

Next was the Race of Champions, at Brands. Aurora cars were combined with a field of invited regular Grand Prix cars, in a race that replaced the Formula 1 event, cancelled due to snow a few weeks before. Des qualified second and finished third in the Aurora class. This came in the aftermath of an accident in the earlier Sports 2000 race.

Wanting to concentrate on the Formula 1 race, she tried to qualify the Lola in a minimum of track time but, again, pushing hard for pole position, she dropped a rear wheel off the track at Brand's very fast Westfield corner, causing the car to spin wildly into the infield guardrail. The impact was extremely hard, significantly damaging the car, and flung Des backward so far that her seatbelts stretched, allowing her helmet to hit the roll bar above the passenger seat.

In the Medical Centre she was examined by the doctors, but she pretended that she was OK, even though she didn't feel too good, with a severe headache and concussion. But she knew that if she was to admit this to the medics, they would forbid her from driving in the Formula 1 race later in the afternoon. She eventually persuaded the doctors that she was alright and they released her to drive just a few minutes before the start of final qualifying for the Formula 1 race, where her second place time showed her tenacity and her ability to put aside real pain in her determination to succeed.

Later, still suffering from a headache and starting to stiffen up from the bruises and strains she had suffered in the Lola crash, she drove a steady, if not spectacular, race to the finish, having to deal with a badly misfiring engine. Very near the end of the race, the underpowered engine caused her to lose second position to Bernard De Dryver's Fittipaldi, giving her yet another third place finish.

At Mallory Park Des qualified back in eighth and entered the race a lap down from pit lane thanks to a flat battery. She then lost first gear, but still managed to finish tenth, ahead of, amongst others, Lella Lombardi, who she had out-qualified by 1.6 seconds. Qualifying was problematical again at Snetterton, where the Tyrrell suffered yet another misfiring engine, leaving her seventh on the grid, after which she retired from the race with terminal engine problems.

Des starred in a wet qualifying at Thruxton, holding a front row grid position until an optimistic move to slick tyres backfired, dropping her to third. She drove carefully, nursing an overheating engine, to her fourth third place in six starts. Once again, Des had to jump from the Tyrrell directly into the Lola, for the S2000 race that followed immediately after the Aurora race. Despite being exhausted from a gruelling hour in the Formula 1 car, she fought a race-long battle with Ian Taylor and Jeremy Rossiter, to finish in yet another third position.

Despite Desiré's consistent performance, near the front of a very competitive field, all wasn't well within the Melchester camp. Gordon Smiley wasn't a happy camper, being in constant and very open conflict with Brian Kreisky, the video producer, who was the owner of Des' Tyrrell. Gordon and Brian had taken an immediate dislike to each other from their first meeting and the feelings only worsened when the confrontational Kreisky went to extremes to upset the already very fragile and increasingly worsening psyche of the American. From the first time he had sat in the Tyrrell, Gordon had shown

Race of Champions. *Driving in pain and with a concussion after crashing her Sports 2000 Lola earlier in the day, Des spent most of the Race of Champions lying second in the Aurora category, but dropped to third when the engine started to misfire a few laps from the end. (Courtesy Chris Davies)*

Pressure to Perform. *The 1979 Race of Champions, at Brands Hatch, saw the Aurora race integrated into an invitational Formula 1 field that included some of the world's best drivers. Here, Desiré shares a media interview with the late, great Gilles Villeneuve, World Champion-to-be Mario Andretti, McLaren driver John Watson, and World Champion Niki Lauda. (Courtesy Wilson Collection)*

himself to be a very nervous and highly strung driver and his histrionics in the pits did little to endear him to his team.

Brian quickly took advantage of this and did everything he could to unsettle him with taunts, teasing, and some despicable actions – such as arranging for the theft of Gordon's passport, when we were in Holland. Add to this Gordon's inability to match Des' speed in the similar cars and the atmosphere in the Melchester pits could be cut with a knife.

With tensions already high, the team then lost three engines in as many races and Gordon crashed badly at Mallory Park, resulting in a switch to the previous year's championship winning McLaren M23, which actually suited his driving style far better than the finicky Tyrrell. The team now found itself faced with major budget issues, which resulted in Des having to race the engine that overheated at Thruxton in the next race, at Zandvoort. Des was able to qualify only tenth, although she hung on to finish fourth, after holding off a hard-charging Rupert Keegan with some demon-late braking. The tensions in the team reached breaking point when Kreisky's in-your-face taunting of Gordon, in the pit lane at Zandvoort, not only ended in a fist fight, but led Gordon to split from the team. He didn't race at Donington; instead, his newly rebuilt Tyrrell was taken over by a surprisingly fast Neil Betteridge, against whom Des had raced many times in FF2000. Des lost most of her qualifying session when she was taken off the track by a back marker F2 car, resulting in a broken gearbox casing and she qualified ninth, three places behind Neil. Struggling with gearbox trouble, which would lead to her retirement, she had the humiliation of being overtaken by a very on-form Divina Galica, in an F2 car. Divi was the undoubted star of this race, suggesting that, had she been able to compete against Des in equal machinery throughout the season, the on-track fighting between the two ladies would have been both very close and very exciting to watch.

At Oulton Park, Des continued to struggle with a car that the team couldn't get to handle properly, changing springs, ride height, and even wheel widths in an effort to overcome power oversteer. Add the two hours of seat time in the Tyrrell to her Lola S2000 commitments and it was a very exhausted and frustrated Des who ended up behind both Betteridge and Gordon Smiley, tenth on the grid. Gordon had reappeared in the series, driving the factory

Surprise! Desiré drives her Tyrrell around the outside of a surprised Gordon Smiley, in his factory Surtees, around the 'impossible-to-pass' Druids Corner at Oulton Park. Des qualified halfway down the field after suffering handling problems, but then raced up to third – before the dreaded misfire returned, dropping her to a fifth place finish. (Courtesy Wilson Collection)

run Surtees, a car he found to be much more stable and significantly faster than the Tyrrell 008. In the race, Des moved up to third, before fluctuating fuel pressure caused the car to lurch violently as the engine power kicked in and out, making her feel very ill in the car. Her fifth place finish was another testament to her unwillingness to quit. Des then climbed into the Lola and decimated the field to win the S2000 championship race, leading every lap and setting a new lap record for the class.

The field then travelled down to the bottom end of France for a race at Nogaro, in the Armagnac brandy region, a rustic track noted for its disgusting toilets. In sweltering temperatures, Des and the team struggled with a Tyrrell that was becoming increasingly difficult to set up, the car switching between drastic understeer and near terminal oversteer, seemingly without rationale. After another round of spring changes, including one after qualifying and before the race, she hung on in the race, still fighting vicious understeer, to finish fourth.

The frustrating season continued at Mallory and featured an incident which could have been devastating, or even fatal to her. Late on the Thursday afternoon before the event, after some TV promotional work, the team took advantage of an open track to try to do some development work for that weekend's race. The mechanics and I were standing in the pit lane, listening to the car as she accelerated away from Gerards Bend, when we froze as the scream of the engine suddenly cut dead. Holding our breaths, we waited for the sound of a big impact and were relieved to see the Tyrrell freewheel into sight, through the link road that bypassed Shaws Hairpin. As the car approached the pits we saw that it was leaving a huge trail of oil behind; as it came closer, we could see that sundry pieces of cabling, pipes, and even the starter motor were dragging on the ground.

Team boss, Alan Charles, immediately lost his temper at this expensive engine blow-up. When Des brought the car to a stop, he leant over the cockpit and started to give Des hell. Meanwhile, Mark Freeman, her lead mechanic, lifted off the nose cone of the car, looked down, and immediately leant over and touched Alan on the shoulder, pointing down to the accelerator assembly. Alan stopped in mid shout and went white as he saw the stretched cable wrapped around the throttle stop: this had caused the throttle to stay wide open as the car entered the Esses.

Fortunately, she had reacted immediately by pushing in the clutch in to stop the engine from driving the car off the track and into the barriers, even though this resulted in the engine blowing to pieces. But she'd averted a life threatening 175mph shunt. Later, Charles apologised and agreed it was her only course of action.

Three days later Des put the car in seventh on the grid, ahead of Neil, but with a time that was half-a-second slower than her previous Mallory best and she then dropped out of the race, after 15 laps, with a broken drive shaft.

The season which had started so strongly had, by mid-season, degenerated into a series of troubled races and an increasingly disenchanted race team. Her car was becoming more and more unstable with every race, in direct contrast to Neil Betteridge's recently rebuilt ex-Smiley chassis and she had suffered a series of engine, fuel system, and gearbox problems that had compromised much of the season. This lack of success soured the relationship with team manager, Charles, who, frustrated at his inability to overcome the handling issues and reliability problems, was now openly questioning Des' driving skill and commitment. He arranged for rival Philip Bullman to test the car at Thruxton and although he was slower than Des and reported similar handling problems, the relationship between Charles and Des was damaged. This was a real pity, as although Des was herself

Banger Racing. Des raced her S2000 Lola at many of the same events as the F1 car, finishing third in the British S200 Championships even though she missed several rounds. Here, she leads a really aggressive Ian Taylor at Silverstone, in a race that left both cars with scars down each side from the side-by-side racing they enjoyed. (Courtesy Wilson Collection)

growing more despondent as the season progressed, she was still driving the car as hard as she could. Neither she nor the team seemed able to identify the cause of the handling problems with her chassis.

Hard evidence that something was seriously wrong with the car came at the second Brands Hatch round of the series, where Des couldn't get within two seconds of the times she had done, even with the headache and misfire, at the Race of Champions. She constantly complained that the car was twitching violently under transition to full acceleration out of the turns, especially at the bottom of Paddock Bend, yet the crew could find nothing wrong and Alan simply assumed that she was driving badly.

The team never did find the cause of the problem, which persisted to the end of the season. It was several years later, when Des was approached at a race event by a mechanic, that she found out the answer. The mechanic had been hired by the car's subsequent owner to completely rebuild it. He told Des that the rivets which bound the chassis panels together had become badly stretched, causing the chassis to lose much of its rigidity, causing the twitchiness that she had experienced.

Things improved a bit for the next Thruxton race, where Des was able to get the still oversteering car handling a little better and qualified clearly the fastest of the non-ground effect cars. However, an early pit stop to replace a blistered front tyre dropped her a lap back to a seventh place finish. She repeated the feat of being the first non-ground effect car at Snetterton with a demon lap, and told the team afterwards that she had "gone berserk." Despite a misfire she qualified ninth, with a time that was below the old lap record, even though she was forced to do so using an older set of tyres. She ran the race without incident to finish sixth, once again leading the non-wing cars home.

The final round of the 1979 Aurora series turned out to be a tremendously exciting event, with the Championship ultimately resolved in Rupert Keegan's favour, after he and David Kennedy tangled with each other. At the Woodcote chicane, they slammed into the already crashed car of the only other driver with a chance to win the title, Emilio De Villota. All three cars ended in the catch fences, from which only Keegan was able to escape. Rupert went on to finish second and win the title. A rejuvenated Gordon Smiley, who, since moving over to the works Surtees team and their new TS20+ ground effect chassis, had become more and more competitive, won the race.

1979 was her first full year in Formula 1 and Des was able to finish the Aurora series seventh in the Championship. Clearly the most successful of those drivers who never had the huge advantages of ground effect machinery, by the end of the season Des had established herself as a serious Formula 1 driver.

But the season had been spoilt by issues within the team. Escalating car handling problems; the limited amount of time Des was able to spend with team manager, Alan Charles, to try to solve the problems, thanks to her need to race her Lola S2000 at most of the same events; and her time-consuming commitments to her media responsibilities all contributed. As a result, the season that started so well at Zolder turned sour, as the spirit within the team ebbed away.

This was unfortunate, as the whole rationale for John Webb placing Des in the Aurora series was to use her to promote the championship to the public. This meant that she was always the leading personality in the series, constantly the centre of media attention. Despite her natural shyness, she rose to the task and did an excellent job for the series, earning it and herself countless pages of press coverage and many hours of airtime on TV and radio. This focus, however, had its price; the time spent with

the media often cut into essential face-to-face time with Melchester team management, and this was to become a significant contributor to the breakdown in relations between her and Alan Charles. To add to the pressure, she wasn't only working as a race driver: she also held down a 7.30am to 6.00pm job every day that she wasn't racing, working in the Brands Hatch Racing office during the week and in the promotional caravan set up in the spectator area.

There were times during the season when these problems did get to Des, but she carried out her commitments to the full, drove brilliantly, and, ultimately, ended the season a more experienced, wiser, and stronger person.

Her S2000 season had been a pleasant counterbalance to her Aurora problems. Nick Challis built a great transporter, with its own hospitality lounge for the team (a unique facility at the time), which gave Des a haven in which to relax at the track and supported her with a well prepared and competitive car. With this car, she finished a close third in the Sports 2000 series, even though she missed several rounds, due to conflicts caused by racing the Formula 1 car on the Continent and at other events, where the sports cars were competing at alternate venues.

The 1979 season closed on a high note for Desiré when the FIA and FOCA listed her as one of only forty drivers in the world who would be granted a Formula 1 Superlicence, making her eligible to compete in the 1980 World Championships.

"If the Aurora Formula 1 Championship has proved one thing, it has proved that Desiré is a racing driver. All the old clichés about lady drivers have been discarded. Her car control is nothing short of magnificent, her consistency is amazing, her actual racing a revelation.

If you've not seen Desiré, you might be excused for thinking she's some kind of an Amazon, such is the talent she displays on the track. She's not. She is a petite, gentle woman with a shy manner and a quiet sense of humour. You could imagine her as a secretary, or doing the shopping – the Lioness of Africa popular press image seems a little silly.

Why not promote her as the finest lady driver ever to sit in a Formula 1 car?

Because that's what she is."

Russell Bulgin – Car & Car Conversions magazine.

11

A LITTLE BIT OF HISTORY

For 1980, Des expected to be driving for Team Surtees in Aurora Formula 1, but, as Christmas approached, John Surtees withdrew from the series. However, it seemed that as one door shut, another opened: Desiré was contacted by representatives of Chrysler's MOPAR parts group, who had sponsored Guy Edwards the previous season.

With their contract with Edwards at an end, it wanted to put together a two car team for Des, using the very successful 1979 Ligier JS11 DFVs driven to victories in the Argentine and Brazil by Jacques Laffite. As the cars were, at least, the equal of the very successful Williams FW07s, it looked to Des that she would be in for a great third season of Aurora Formula 1 racing. But she didn't get any time to get excited about the opportunity; a few days later Guy himself called and told her that there could be no deal. He invited her to visit him in London, so that he could explain and, when she arrived, handed her his one inch thick contract with the parts company.

She'd never seen anything like it. In fact, Des had never seen a driver contract of any kind until then, her arrangement with John Webb being one of simple trust and friendship. When she saw Edwards' contract she understood the difference between enthusiastic support and professional sponsorship.

The contract was specific to an extent that amazed her. Where Des had considered herself lucky to get a new set of tyres for a race weekend with Melchester, she read that Guy was guaranteed eight new sets every event! While Des had to suffer a misfiring engine for four races in a row, she saw that Guy received a newly rebuilt motor for every race. Testing, for her, was a rare experience; for Guy it was a contractual requirement before each race. And Guy got paid!

Then Guy showed her the clause that killed her hopes for the year. His contract very specifically noted that MOPAR were not to be allowed to undertake any form of motor sports sponsorship for a year after its contract with him expired and he was holding them to it – to the extent that it even had to remove its name from Chrysler's own factory rally team!

Guy Edwards was known in English racing as the best sponsor finder in the business. He was famous for bringing companies like Barclay's International into the sport. He had ridden his sponsorship finding skills all the way to a full-time Formula 1 Grand Prix drive with Graham Hill's Embassy sponsored team, before turning to the Aurora series after Hill's death in a plane crash. While never a top line GP racer, Guy was, nevertheless, a more than competent journeyman driver. His main recognition had come from his bravery, helping pull critically injured Niki Lauda from his burning Ferrari, at the Nürburgring, in 1976 – a feat for which he was awarded the George Medal.

Des talked to Guy about him looking after her sponsorship needs, taking whatever cut he wanted, but Edwards was still too involved in his own racing and he knew that John Webb still controlled her racing programme, so declined. Des left Guy's flat with no drive for 1980 and, because Britain had started to slip into one of its deepest recessions in years, not much hope of finding the sponsorship to buy one.

With the 1979 season at an end, John and Angela Webb left for their annual vacation in Barbados, leaving me to run Brands and Des to look forward to a bleak new season.

Then, two days before Christmas, she received a call from Ron Frost, promoter of the New Zealand

Tasman race series and operator of Auckland's Pukekohe race track. He wanted her to fly out for their four race series, starting on January 1, offering her a 1977 March Atlantic car and a drive in a Ford Escort in a support series.

It took us about thirty seconds to accept the offer, even though we knew that John would likely be upset that she was racing without his clearance. Little did we know that he had turned down Ron's request the previous year, without telling Des that an invitation had been extended!

It took two days to get visas and work permits arranged and to rush around London collecting a load of parts that the team needed for the car. On Boxing Day, we were on the plane, to Los Angeles for a stop-over and then on to Auckland, where we arrived the Monday before the first race. We had an interesting arrival in New Zealand.

The parts we'd been asked to pack in our suitcases could almost have built a new car and mine was so heavy that, even with two hands, it was almost impossible to lift it onto the customs inspections table. The customs official interrogated Des and when he saw that her work permit applied to her racing, he immediately started on about how racers were always trying to smuggle parts past him. Looking me straight in the eyes, he warned me about the consequences of trying to avoid the 100 per cent duty and then proceeded to open every other passenger's suitcase – while he studiously avoided watching me drag my bloated case across the floor! I decided there and then that I liked New Zealand!

The Tasman series had been a major race series during the 1960s, when drivers like Jim Clark, Graham Hill, Jack Brabham, Derek Bell, and Bruce McLaren gave it world-wide status. Even though the big names no longer competed, in 1980 it was still a serious and fiercely competitive series, now running to Formula Atlantic rules.

Des' car was a three-year-old March. The car was looked after by Graham Cooke, who had experience in the UK and was helped a by a friend who just happened to work for New Zealand customs, at the airport, and helped on a part-time basis. Although the car carried Nashua sponsorship and was owned by long time race team owner Colin Giltrap, it was being run on a tiny budget and right from the outset, Des realised that the package was never going to be competitive against a very strong field.

This included two factory supported Marchs, to

New Zealand Adventure. The opportunity to race an old March 77b in the New Zealand Tasman Series, allowed Des to start the British Aurora Championship driving at her very best. (Courtesy Wilson Collection)

be driven by Andrea De Cesaris and 18-year-old rising star Mike Thackwell; new Ralt RT1s for Steve Millen and Dave McMillan; a Chevron for Dutchman Huub Rottengatter; Ian Flux in Dr Elrlichs F3 car, transformed to FAtlantic spec; and strong Australian and New Zealand contingents that included ex-Formula 1 driver Larry Perkins and F3 star Brett Riley.

The series started at Pukekoe and raced at Manfield and Wigram. Despite trying her hardest and putting in every penny of the money that Ron Frost had pulled together for her (as well as contributing all her prize money to buy tyres), the unreliable March just couldn't compete with the newer cars and she found herself, typically, fighting for fifth or sixth at each race.

She also had some experiences on the track that added to her reputation for not putting up with any bullying, especially from teenager Mike Thackwell, who seemed to find it especially unacceptable to be beaten by a girl. After several close races, he eventually put his rear wheel between her front and rear wheels while racing along the straight at Wigram; he then tapped his brakes, causing her March to leap, almost onto its nose, when their wheels touched. Fortunately, the car didn't tip over completely and Des was able to regain control after a big moment. She made up the gap and, subsequently, proceeded to give him a lesson in track management, taking him to the edge of the very wide airfield track and forcing him to run onto the grass and into a wide ditch. He never bothered her again.

Although the Tasman series wasn't successful for Des on the track, it played a major role in the successes she achieved when she returned to the UK; it enabled her to start the British season already on top form.

Once John Webb had made it clear that he wasn't amused by Des' show of independence, he set his anger aside. He put together a deal for her; to drive for Teddy Yip in the Sid Taylor managed Theodore Racing Wolf WR4. The WR4 was the same car that David Kennedy had abandoned, half way through the previous season, in favour of the newer, ground effect WR5 version. Geoff Lees would be her team-mate.

Although the Wolf was now in its fourth season of racing and had no ground effect technology, it was small, nimble, and well balanced and could well have been designed to suit her driving style. At the opening Oulton Park race she was immediately at home in the car, despite no pre-event testing. She qualified in third place, ahead of Geoff and behind Edwards and de Villota. At the start, Geoff slipped past Des, but she held on to his tail for several laps, before a broken CV joint put her out of the race.

Understanding. Julian Randalls was an excellent team manager who immediately bonded with his new driver and put every effort into helping her go quicker. (Courtesy Chris Davies)

The team packed up and drove through the evening to Brands Hatch, for Sunday's practice for the Easter Monday Aurora Championship race. Des will tell that, from the moment she arrived at Brands, she knew she was going to win. Drivers are like that. There are times when they believe they are invincible, when they have absolute confidence that the stars are aligned. Des began practice knowing she was going to deliver – and deliver she did.

Right from the start she was quicker than her much more experienced team-mate, Geoff Lees. She and team engineer Julian Randalls found themselves working well together and the whole team sensed something special was happening.

Then came qualifying and Des flew, getting the Wolf around in 1:22:02 in the first session, despite heavy understeer. The crew dialed this out between sessions and she improved to the low 21s from the start of the final qualifying period, a fraction behind the de Villota Williams ground effect car.

With only a few minutes left in the session, she pulled into the pits to discuss things with Julian, who asked what she needed done to find that final tenth of a second.

"The problem is the gearing," Des told him. "With the ratios in the box I have to change up after Dingle Dell and then drop down again into Stirling's, which costs time. If I hold it in gear I will over rev the engine. But if I could just hold the lower gear I know I would be faster." Julian listened, leaned over into the cockpit, and flicked off the switch that controlled the rev limiter.

Des left the pits in a blur of wheel spin, built up speed, and put everything she had into one flying lap.

De Villota's team, which was garaged at the entrance to the pit lane, put their stop watches on her and as she came out of Clearways they recorded a time of 1:20:20, split seconds faster than Emilio's best of 1:20:49. She had taken pole at the last minute.

Except that the car rushed past them in silence. The engine had blown as she turned into Clearways and she was forced to free wheel that last three hundred yards to the finish line, where the official time keepers recorded her at 1:21:40 – second fastest. The Teddy Yip team was thrilled at her speed, knowing that the blown engine had cost her the pole position. John Webb was much less amused, as the £10,000 engine bill was coming straight to him! Despite the lecture in the Kentagon that evening and the realisation that the next blown engine would mean the end of her race season, Des maintained her confidence. She went to the grid the next day absolutely certain that, as long as she could be in the lead at Paddock Bend on the first lap, she was going to win the race.

Brands Hatch is a peculiar circuit and drivers who know its intricacies will always have an advantage. Des was a Brands specialist and she knew that pole position wasn't the advantage it might have seemed. The track is heavily cambered along the straight and cars which line up on the right-hand side of the front row have to climb a steeper hill to Paddock Bend, as well as fight a tendency for the rear of the car to slide to the right, down the slope, under fierce acceleration.

Consequently, when she lined up on the staggered grid next to Emilio, she deliberately placed her car so that he had to park further down the slope than normal. When the lights turned green, she took advantage and shot into the lead, drew ahead through Paddock Bend and Druids, and had opened a gap of several car lengths by the time she turned onto the long track at Surtees. Then there was an accident at Bottom bend and the red flags began to wave. She had to do it all over again.

Favourite Car. Although the Wolf was already four years old, well used, and didn't have any ground effect technology, Des loved it and drove it to the very limit. Here, she leads the much newer and more advanced Wiliams FW07 of Emilio de Villota.
(Courtesy Chris Davies)

Her second start was even better than her first and she immediately took the lead, opening up a gap of over second per lap on the field, until she was a full 22 seconds ahead. Then she slackened her pace, holding her position to run the rest of the 40 laps in total command of the race.

From her position at the head of the field, she could judge her lead by watching the second place Lotus 78, of Scotsman Norman Dickson, emerge from Paddock Bend while she turned onto Bottom Straight: every time he closed the gap she simply went faster. Eventually, she maintained a fifteen second advantage all the way to the finish line. To rub things in, after cruising comfortably for the whole race, she set her goals on achieving the fastest lap, which she did on her final tour around the course. There may not have been any racing for the lead, but the large Easter crowd at Brands Hatch didn't mind.

Des was their home driver. They'd become strong supporters through the 1978 and 1979 seasons and she was their star. Many knew her well, as she had always been accessible and friendly to them. They had talked to her in the paddock, in her office at Brands Hatch Racing, and, many times over the past two years, when she manned the Race School sales caravan behind the grandstands. Not only were they watching a favourite driver win, they also knew the importance of what they were witnessing. When Desiré received the chequered flag to become the first woman ever to win a championship race in a Formula 1 car, the crowd erupted into a wave of cheers that she heard above the scream of the engine as she crossed the line.

It was an unbelievable and very emotional moment, made more so by the absolute ease with which she had won the race.

Des' win was obviously a huge moment – for her, for John Webb, for Brands Hatch, and for me – and it resulted in a wave of publicity that reached across England, into Europe, and back to South Africa.

Some drivers were impressed, including the current World Champion, Jody Scheckter, who was quick to salute her achievement in his column in the Johannesburg's *The Star*. Less so was his brother, Ian, whose derogatory comments came across as sour grapes and was, perhaps, back-handed recognition of how fast she had been when racing the old Chevron Atlantic against him at Kyalami, at the beginning of 1978.

In reality, Des' performance in being the first and (so far) only woman to win a championship race in a

Winner! *The first three set out on their parade lap in front of the supportive Brands Hatch crowd. Des is understandably happy, Eliseo Salazar and Norman Dickson less so. (Courtesy Ferret)*

Formula 1 car, doesn't rate that highly in the annals of motorsport. Des has always seen herself not as a woman race driver, but a race driver.

So, winning the race wasn't a score for the feminine gender, but a score for Des the racer. Obviously, the win was to be the defining moment of her career and she does believe that it was one of the best races she ever drove, but it was, perhaps, no better than her two World Championship sports car wins in the de Cadenet, or her drive at Fuji in the Porsche 962.

There are those who say that the Aurora win means nothing because it wasn't a full-blooded Formula 1 Grand Prix. But, at that time, in the world of racing, her achievement was very meaningful. A little bit of history was made at Brands on Easter Monday, 1980.

Two weeks later Des qualified the Wolf fifth at Silverstone, but jumped into second place at the start. She then held third for the next 28 laps, harrying De Villota's much quicker car. All the way, in fact, until her gear lever broke-off in her hand, leading to a pit stop and an eventual eighth place finish. Despite this

bad luck, she was still hailed by the *Daily Express* as the star of the race.

At Mallory she qualified third, but broke a CV joint after only three laps. The series then moved to the very fast Thruxton track, in Hampshire.

Des qualified fourth, dropping back over the first few laps, but then she began a charge that became a highlight of the Aurora series final season. First, she passed Villota and then closed behind Salazar's similar Williams. For lap after lap she fought to find a way past, then, with just nine laps to go, she left the track and went onto the dirt when Eliseo closed the door on her, in the chicane. The gap immediately opened to over ten seconds as she found her way back onto the track and shrugged-off the gravel that was sticking to her tyres, slowing the car down. But she wouldn't give up. Each lap she made up time until, at the start of the final lap, she was three seconds behind the Williams. With a superhuman effort, she raced up to his gearbox and pushed her way alongside, as the two cars raced through the final chicane. But, the

Winners Both! *Both Desiré and John Webb were winners at Brands Hatch. (Courtesy Ferret)*

Williams had the better line and crossed the finish just two one-hundredths of a second ahead.

Despite her success and the value she brought to the Aurora series, Des' position in the series was becoming less and less secure. John Webb's budget to support her position, in the Teddy Yip-owned team, was virtually non-existent, decimated by the engine blow-up at Brands. Now, Teddy's focus switched to American Kevin Cogan, who had joined the team at Mallory Park.

Kevin had a strong competition record in Formula Atlantic racing in America. He was immediately quick in the Wolf, qualifying on the front row at the first Mallory event, before crashing out of the race. At the second, he and Des fought a hard battle for position, until Des used a lapped Formula Two car to force him to make an engine destroying mistake. At the second Brands event, she was almost two-and-half seconds a lap quicker than him and when the series arrived at Snetterton she had him totally out-psyched. After the first practice session, when she

was, again, significantly quicker, the team swapped the two cars' engines – but she went faster still. Then, they switched chassis and, finally, switched engines again: yet Des remained quicker, through all the changes.

In the meantime, Sid Taylor, Teddy's race representative, had been very vocal to the media about Kevin's Grand Prix potential, disparaging Des' ability to compete at that level despite the fact that she was consistently and significantly quicker than Kevin. So, it was no surprise when Teddy Yip, who seldom attended any races and relied completely on Taylor for input, finally pulled the plug on Desiré, leaving her without a drive.

Her Aurora career ended with a final drive in Colin Bennett's Aurora AFX sponsored Lotus 78, the ex-Villota/Norman Dickson car, at Brands Hatch. After qualifying on the second row, the rear suspension broke, at Bottom Bend on the first lap. Des was unhurt, but both her and the car's Aurora Formula 1 careers were at an end.

12

"YOU DRIVE THIS CAR ... IT'S GOING TO KILL ME"

FOR over 50 years, there have been two major championships in the world of racing: Formula 1 Grand Prix and the World Sports Car Championship. Formula 1 has, generally, evolved with few major changes to its formulating regulations. The sports cars have competed in many guises, often driven by the power of the Le Mans 24 Hours race, sometimes by competing manufacturer influences, and sometimes by the nationalistic goals of the FIA.

In 1980, the World Sports Car Championship was promoted as the World Endurance Championship, and was undergoing a transition from its previous open cockpit Group 6 form to a closed, more production-based Group 5 series. Brands Hatch was the host for the opening round and the race attracted several Group 6-type cars, including two very quick Joest 908 Porsches and a host of Group 5 Porsche 935s. More significantly, the two car factory Lancia team, with its Grand Prix drivers, Ricardo Patrese and Eddie Cheever, Michele Alboreto, and World Rally Champion Walter Rohrl, were there.

Once again, John Webb saw in Desiré an opportunity to get free editorial coverage for the event, so arranged for her to drive with Alain de Cadenet, in his Le Mans car. As Alain remembers, he received a call from Angela Webb, who asked him if he had a second driver committed to his car. He was a little surprised when Angela said his co-driver would be a woman.

After a slight pause and Angela's assurance that Des was completely capable of driving his car, Alain agreed. He immediately found that they complemented each other perfectly and, after some initial handling problems which Alain quickly sorted out, Des was soon at home in the dark green

de Cadenet DFV, qualifying fifth overall. Alain chose to drive the first three hours of the six hour race, stopping once to refuel, before handing over to Des at the halfway mark.

Des ran consistently in third and then moved up to second, chasing race leader Patrese hard, before briefly taking the lead when he stopped for fuel. However, the race was then halted: there had been an horrific accident in which British driver Martin Raymond was killed. The race resumed after an hour-long stoppage and Des went on to bring the car home in third place, behind the two Lancias, taking Group 6 honours.

Des had driven extremely well in an unfamiliar car, and showed that she was fully capable of racing head-to-head against some of the world's best drivers. John Webb was also pleased; the race had attracted a good crowd, again fuelled to a large extent by the pre-race publicity Desiré had helped to generate.

Desiré's drive with Alain de Cadenet at Brands Hatch was meant to be a one-off event and, despite the success, it was never intended to be a harbinger of anything more substantial. Des and Alain, however, found that they worked extremely well together and quickly became friends, so, it wasn't a total surprise when, a few weeks later, Des received a phone call from Alain, telling her to find her way to Italy for the following weekend's Monza 1000 World Endurance Championship event.

I stayed behind, working at Brands, and Des travelled to Italy for the first time. She found the de Cadenet much the same as it had been at Brands Hatch, even fitted with the same engine, which was facing its third major race without a rebuild. Ranged against the de Cadenet were several Group 6 cars and a strong Group 5 class. These included; the two factory turbo-charged Lancias, to be driven by Eddie Cheever and Piercarlo Ghinzani, and Ricardo Patrese and Walter Rohrl; and a number of Porsche 935s – the strongest being a factory supported car for Le Mans-winning drivers Henri Pescarolo and Jurgen Barth. But, there had been some changes to the de Cadenet line up.

First, there were only two mechanics; Don Halliday and John Anderson. Second, the air jacks and compressed air-powered wheel nut tool systems needed to make quick tyre changes were missing: Alain had sold them to raise cash! So, Don and John would have to change tyres using a hand-held quick-lift lever-type jack, an old copper headed mallet, and a crossbar wrench borrowed from Alain's prewar Alfa Romeo Monza. If this wasn't a slow enough method of changing tyres in the heat of battle, the two man crew soon found that the front splitter was so low they would have to physically lift the whole front end of the car off the ground to get the jack underneath. To compliment the crew, Alain found two young Italians hanging around in the pit lane and roped them in to help.

Alain practiced first and almost immediately had brake problems, causing the front left wheel to seize up at high speed. He saved the ensuing moment and brought the car into the pits with the tyre in shreds and the bottom half of the wheel completely ground away.

"You drive the damn thing ... it's going to kill me!" He shouted to Des, visibly shaken by the incident.

The crew repaired the car and Des quickly learned the historic track. Alain decided that they shouldn't push for pole position and the team spent the rest of the pre-race sessions getting the car set up for the race.

There was another incident to come when Desiré was at the wheel during the final qualifying period. Approaching the Parabolica Curve at very high speed behind a smaller, 2-litre class Osella, the Osella suddenly shed its bodywork. Right behind it, Des had no time to react other than to duck her head as the fibreglass mass flew over the de Cadenet. By the time she looked up, she was way past her braking point and, despite hitting the brakes as hard as she could, went off the track at the end of the straight in a cloud of dust and stones, coming to a standstill in the middle of a large gravel trap.

She immediately tried to drive through the trap but to no avail, the spinning wheels simply digging the car deeper into the stones. She switched off the car and undid her seat belts, wanting to get out of the car and behind the barriers as soon as possible, conscious that the car was stuck in a very dangerous position. But the marshals seemed more interested in leaving their posts and having their photos taken with her than with extracting the car.

Only in Italy!

The car was eventually freed from the trap and towed back to the pits, where Alain looked it over for damage. He called Des over to where he was peering down the throttle slides into the piston chambers. His penlight torch illuminated the crowns of the pistons, which were covered in small stones and gravel, ingested when she tried to drive her way out the trap.

"That's stuffed it," he said. "It will never last. We'll just start the race to collect our start money and then pack it in. Sorry old girl."

That night, with the pressure off, Alain and Des had a relaxing and interesting dinner as guests of Count Johnny Lurani, the fabled driver, historian, and Italian racing legend, in his castle outside Monza. After an excellent meal, the Count showed them around his private car museum, ending up in a basement room that had featured in a scene with Eva Marie Saint and Yves Montand in the 1960s classic race film, Grand Prix.

The wall was covered with hundreds of autographs, all of famous race drivers. The Count turned to Desiré and Alain, saying that he would be honored if they would add their signatures to the amazing collection.

The two drivers looked at the wall, realised that the majority of signatures were those of dead drivers, and both responded immediately: "Thank you very much, but no way." Neither was prepared to push their luck that far!

Alain chose to start the following afternoon's race, intending to nurse the damaged engine for a few laps before retiring the car, but soon found to his amazement that the tired engine was running like a train. He drove the first three hours of the race, running consistently in the top four or five positions, then handed over to Des for her three hour stint with the car in third place.

She quickly moved past Pescarolo, in the Porsche and then took over the race lead when Patrese stopped for fuel. For the rest of the race Desiré and the Frenchman raced for the lead. With two hours to go,

Winning. *Des drove the de Cadenet to a World Championship Endurance victory at the Monza 1000, after a race filled with incidents. (Courtesy Wilson Collection)*

Pescarolo led, but, ten laps later and after the Porsche pitted for fuel, Desiré held a 25 second advantage. Then Des pitted for her refuel stop and the Porsche moved ahead. With 55 minutes remaining, the Porsche started to splutter with a minor turbocharger problem. Des closed the gap, making up as much as seven seconds a lap on the French driver, before sweeping past into the lead, which she immediately opened to around twelve seconds.

Now in the lead, she concentrated on saving the car, watching the large scoreboard near the start line that showed her distance ahead of the Porsche. She maintained a steady pace and a safe lead until, with less than an hour to go, it started to rain!

Under normal circumstances she would have driven into the pits to change to wet tyres, but,

without the efficient equipment that Alain had sold, she knew the pit stop would take several minutes. She decided to stay on the track and prayed that the rain would not last too long. Pescarolo, however, dived into pit lane, emerging some 30 or so seconds later on a fresh set of wet tyres. He immediately started lapping at speeds significantly faster than Des could manage, despite her every effort to push the de Cadenet as fast as she could on the slippery track.

Driving right on the limit, she approached the very fast and treacherous Lesmo turn, to see corner workers standing at the entrance to the corner, gesticulating wildly for her to stay on the outside of the turn. After a couple of laps, when she could see no obvious reason for the cautionary signals, she realized they were actually giving her advice to use a wider but drier line. She tried it and they gave her the thumbs up. Amazingly, they were trying to help her win the race.

Every lap after that they enthusiastically waved her on; but Henri Pescarolo had the advantage of rain tyres and, slowly but surely, closed the gap, eventually passing the green de Cadenet with just 30 minutes left in the six hour race. Des hung on as best she could, disappointed to lose her lead but satisfied that she had done everything she could to keep the car on the track in the treacherously wet conditions, happy, at least, to finish second in a World Championship race.

She drove through the Parabolica at ten minutes before the six hour mark, 20 seconds behind the Porsche, and accelerated past the pits – only to see, to her total surprise, Pescarolo pulling into the pit lane. The Frenchman's team had made a mistake, miscalculating the fuel strategy. He drove furiously through the pits and tried to catch her in the last few laps of the race, but she refused to give in, holding him off to sweep past the finish line and win the Monza 1000 by just 9.9 seconds.

On the slowing down lap and for the first time in the race, Des noticed the spectators cheering her as she drove past, their shouts clearly audible above the sound of the Cosworth engine. They were going crazy, climbing the fences, waving flags, banners, shirts, and anything they could hold. Monza's famous tifiosi had recognised her performance and were showing their respect ... one of the greatest moments of her life.

This was before the advent of mobile phones, so I hadn't spoke to Des for five days. There was no internet, either and no instant results on a computer, so I called Monza. All they could tell me was that some woman from South Africa had won. The Brands Hatch family celebrated hard and long in the Kentagon that night.

Fourteen days later, Des and Alain repeated their feat to win the World Championship 6 Hours race at Silverstone, this time vanquishing a much stronger field of cars, many of which were using the Silverstone race to prepare for Le Mans.

Being his 'home' race, Alain dug deep into his pockets and sent the engine to John Nicholson to be refurbished and the car turned up for practice as a crowd favorite to win the race. Once again following his mantra to save the car for the race, neither Alain nor Des pushed hard in qualifying, taking sixth place some four seconds behind John Fitzpatrick's Kremer

Porsche 935. Alain started the race and immediately jumped into second place. For his three hours behind the wheel he fought for position behind Fitzpatrick with a pair of 935s, driven by John Cooper and American John Paul Junior. When Fitzpatrick stopped for fuel, Alain moved into the lead, but then had to fight off a challenge from Jurgen Barth, who was driving Siggi Brunn's Porsche 908. When the time came to hand over to Des, near the half way stage of the race, Alain pulled into the pits, losing a narrow lead to the Fitzpatrick-owned Porsche, now being driven by Axel Plankenhorn. Des raced out of the pits and snatched the lead back on her first lap. Fifteen minutes later the Porsche blew its engine, handing second place to the Siggi Brunn/Jurgen Barth Porsche. The race then settled into a straight fight between Siggi and Desiré.

Alain had noticed a small misfire, caused by a dodgy fuel pump, during his last few minutes in the car; now Desiré found it getting worse and worse. The car also began to suffer brake problems; not only were they overheating and fading, but the pedal travel was getting longer and longer, making Des, who was secured firmly in her seat by her safety belts, stretch her legs to their limit to slow the car. Soon, the stretching turned into pain, then painful leg cramps.

This combination of problems allowed Brunn, in the 908, to close-up and an hour later he was just 25 seconds behind. Des pushed as hard as she could, pushing to the limit, but she could do nothing to get away from the hard-chasing Porsche. With just an eight second lead and an hour-and-a-half to go, she tried to overtake a back marker into the Woodcote chicane, missed her braking point, and shot across the infield, passing over the white line that meant she would immediatelybe given a one lap penalty. Although she slowed down to a virtual standstill to see if the officials would accept this as her penalty, her pit board soon told her that she was now a lap down, so the damage was done. She pitted for her final fuel stop, allowing Brunn to move into what was now to become a one-and-a-half lap lead.

Desiré now began the race of her life, driving the stammering – and almost brakeless – DeCadenet to the absolute limit. She began closing on the 908 at some four to five seconds a lap, eventually passing him with 73 minutes left in the race, but still a whole lap behind. Now she was stuck behind a Porsche 935 which was blocking her in the corners – and time was

Celebration. *Alain hoists the trophy while Des gets the toys! The pair had just won their second in a row World Championship race. (Courtesy Sutton-Images.com)*

running out. In the end, she passed with a demon-late braking move into the chicane, followed by a light touch of her brakes, causing the Porsche driver to get off his accelerator and lose his turbo boost. This prevented the faster-accelerating 935 from re-passing her.

It was all the advantage Des needed and she was able to maintain her lead to the next corner, where she immediately opened a wide gap on both the 935 and Siggi Brunn, who hadn't been able to take advantage of the 935s hesitation and was still trapped behind it.

She now drove even harder to take advantage of the situation, pulling away at several seconds a lap to open a gap. The gap became even greater when Siggi dived into the pits for a quick stop to fix a problem with his car's throttle slides. When he returned to the track, the Porsche was running much better, but Des was just 36 seconds behind and closing fast.

With 26 minutes to go she was right on his tail. At Copse Corner she moved to pass inside him, but he closed the gap. At Club and Abbey they were side-by-side, but, at Woodcote, the de Cadenet was in the lead. Des drove away to win her second World Championship race by eighteen seconds.

The Silverstone win immediately raised Desiré's profile in the racing world. In the space of just two-and-a-half months she had won a British Championship Formula 1 race, finished a great third behind the turbocharged Lancias, at Brands Hatch, and then won two back-to-back World Championship Endurance races. There was now absolutely no doubt that she could race at the top levels of the sport and win.

The British media were now suggesting that the de Cadenet crew were one of the favourites for a Le Mans victory. Desiré was at the top of her world.

13

BRITISH RACING GREEN AND FRENCH RACING BLUES

THE three most important race events in the world are, in no particular order, the Monaco Formula 1 Grand Prix, the Indianapolis 500, and the 24 Hours of Le Mans. Each has its own majesty, its own traditions, and its own unique character.

All have run for many years; Indianapolis since 1911, Le Mans since 1923, and Monaco since 1929. Only one driver, Graham Hill, has won all three and no other driver seems likely to emulate this feat.

Desiré never had the opportunity to race at Monaco and her Indianapolis exploits are told elsewhere in this book. Her Le Mans experiences are some of the most memorable of her career, if not for outright success, but because some of the stories are almost too bizarre to believe!

Alain brought with him both an intense desire to win Le Mans and extensive experience in a variety of cars over the past several years of Le Mans events. He'd previously raced there in a Ferrari 512, then, in several, first Brabham, then Lola-based cars. Alain raced the first de Cadenet Le Mans car, initially painted in yellow Duckhams oil colours, with Chris Craft as his co-driver, at Le Mans in 1975. He had commissioned his close friend, the famed Brabham, and, later, McLaren Formula 1 designer Gordon Murray, to devise an aerodynamic shaped racer that would maximize its performance along Le Mans' 3.5 mile-long main straight. Working late at night so as not to compromise his Brabham Formula 1 duties, Murray drew up a design based on a Brabham BT33 Formula 1 car. The later version used more Lola parts, but still the Murray-designed bodywork. Gordon had been one of the guys in our group during my first days racing in South Africa, when he raced his homemade IGM sports car while I raced my Yamaha, at Roy Hesketh.

Knee-high to the proverbial grasshopper, the car Des raced was low, narrow and sleek. Fitted with a de-tuned Formula 1 Ford Cosworth DFV engine putting out around 400bhp, the car proved to be capable of nearly 230mph down the long Mulsanne straight, achieving excellent fuel economy, too. That it worked so well in a straight line was the result of a compromise in design that meant that the cornering ability wasn't exactly the greatest, although it was certainly stable and capable of handling the needs of the Le Mans track. Brakes, too, were built for endurance, with big thick pads that offered average braking ability but exceptional life. The de-tuned Formula 1-based engine offered longevity, if driven with care, but still had enough power to make the de Cadenet a very competitive race car for the 24 Hours.

As a self-funded and privately built car, the de Cad, as we called it, had none of the high tech materials, advanced equipment, wind tunnel developed aerodynamics, or unlimited budget that was available to the 1980 race's top favourites. The French Rondeaus, or the factory Porsches, whose support numbers included large teams of highly practised and experienced factory mechanics with endless spares, top quality tools and equipment, and the support of dozens of helpers, cooks, masseurs, timekeepers, and other staff. The de Cad team was closer to the other end of the spectrum, with just three experienced mechanics and three guys drawn from Nick Challis' trailer construction company. The car was, however, painted in traditional British Racing Green, which made up for the lack of technology and funding!

Based out of a London mews flat, Alain de Cadenet was and still is one of the real characters of racing. Always fighting with the establishment and always doing things his own way; seemingly impecunious, he always raced on minimal funding or with someone else's money, yet still had the ability to own fabulous (and very valuable) old sports cars, fly his own Spitfire, and hob-nob with the rich and famous. A true individualist, Alain would have been a picture-perfect World War 2 fighter ace, dashing, irreverent, always up for a party, devil-may-care in life – but deadly serious, skilful, and ambitious in his aim to win Le Mans.

Thanks to his image and his lifestyle, few people took Alain seriously as a driver, yet he was an outstanding endurance racer who was capable of setting very fast laps that were always within his and the car's limits and he always drove with a sensitive feel for the machinery. Alain would have made a great factory endurance driver, if his public persona had not so clearly defined him as the loner and outsider he chose to be. To us, Alain's greatest attribute was that he knew how to work with and get the best from Desiré.

One of the biggest problems Desiré has faced throughout her driving career is that she has almost always been faster than her team-mates, many of whom haven't been able to handle the thought of being slower than a woman. This has led to instances of frustration and anger and has even resulted in team owners deliberately trying to slow Des down to satisfy the sensitivities of the slower team-mate. None of this applied with Alain.

Des and Alain had never met before John Webb arranged for him to give her a drive in the Brands Hatch round of the World Championship early in 1980. Yet when Desiré immediately showed that she was the faster driver, Alain, instead of getting upset, simply put every effort into making her even faster. Alain supported Des and taught her as much as he could about endurance racing during their race winning charges at Monza and Silverstone, so that, by the time they arrived at Le Mans, the two were as good-a-pairing as could be imagined. The team added a third driver for the race.

The officials at Le Mans have long had the reputation of not only being difficult (particularly with the British), but also favouring local teams and drivers. Consequently, Alain knew that he would need to add a French driver to the team, to give the car a local interest and to enable them to benefit from any 'French' decisions that might be made during the weekend. He chose Francois Migault – a driver with both Formula 1 and Le Mans experience – who

3D. Des, Alain, and the de Cad. Privateers who took on the Le Mans establishment and lost a political battle! (Courtesy Wilson Collection)

offered the benefit of owning a magnificent old château close to the track, complete with haunted tower and erratic electricity!

Another very important member of the team was an expatriate Brit living the high life as a senior advertising executive, in New York, named Murray Smith. Murray is, now, well known in historic racing circles, in both the UK and America, has his own collection of historic race cars, and is, in his own right, an excellent and very fast race driver. As a long standing friend of Alain and, perhaps just as validly, as someone with valuable connections within the Ford Motor Company, Murray was appointed as team manager. Murray Smith is another character of note, with a sense of the ridiculous that, when interacting with de Cadenet's over-the-top and overtly ribald anti-French taunting, caused a shy and well mannered Desiré total embarrassment whenever they drove through the streets of Le Mans!

The crew was unusual, too. Unable to afford large salaries, Alain used his powers of persuasion to bring in Don Halliday and John Anderson, two young Antipodean ex-McLaren Formula 1 wrenches, both of whom were to later move to America to make their names as race engineers. The third member of the mechanical team was the genial, bearded, historic car specialist, Tony Dutton, who was also later to move across the Atlantic, to start his own restoration business on Long Island.

While this trio was the lead crew, additional help was provided by Nick Challis, who not only brought three mechanics from his semi-trailer manufacturing business, but also contributed the team's magnificent transporter. This was to be a major asset in the then very basic and rough paddock. (Unfortunately, we still had to use the paddock toilet facilities, which were simply disgusting and, seemingly, unmaintained throughout race week!

Le Mans has a long tradition as a charismatic and exciting endurance race, and also as an event compromised by politics, extreme over-officiousness, and French nationalism. The 1980 event was to prove no different. First, the rules for this race were to be significantly different to previous events.

Innovations included the decision to establish qualifying positions on the average lap time of each of its drivers, based on their best single lap. This immediately meant that any team with one slow driver would be severely handicapped, but ensured that a well balanced team of quick drivers would have a clear advantage in qualifying. Then, they ruled that each car had to use the same engine for qualifying and the race. This meant that many teams, de Cadenet included, would need to limit their qualifying to a minimum of laps to ensure reliability for the race. Finally, the rule-makers decided that only the fastest 80 per cent of cars in each class would qualify, with a maximum of 50 cars allowed to start the race. This rule would have the effect of potentially eliminating some of the fastest cars in the field: a car that qualified seventh in the eight-car Group 6 class (potentially the race's fastest cars) would be eliminated while, for example, the fifteenth-fastest car in a well supported slower class might still make the field, even though its race speed would be as much as half-a-minute or more per lap slower than the disqualified faster car!

Add to these rules the decision to have just one qualifying session, during which all three drivers would have to qualify under both daylight and night conditions and the scene was set for drama.

The first practice was scheduled for 4.00pm on Wednesday and was set to run until midnight. It started in a haze of drizzle, light mist, and cold winds. Alain set the policy for the night. Each driver would go out and do a couple of laps and then the car would be parked. There was no need to chase pole position and there was certainly no need to risk damaging the car, as it wasn't official qualifying. He drove first, did a few laps, and handed over to Francois who did the

Team de Cadenet in the Le Mans Paddock. *From left to right: Francois Migault, Des, Don Halliday, Alain de Cadenet, John Anderson, Tony Dutton, a TDC helper, Nick Challis, two more TDC guys, and Murray Smith. Race cars don't get much lower than this. (Courtesy Wilson Collection)*

same. Then Des climbed aboard for her first laps of the famous Le Mans course.

Desiré's first ever lap was in steady rain, deepening dusk, and hard on the throttle. There had often been times since I quit my own racing when I had looked at Des in some race car or other and wondered whether I could be doing as well as her, or maybe nearly as well, if I had continued racing. Her first lap of Le Mans quickly dispelled those fantasies.

First time out on a strange track, in the wet and dark, and never having been in a car at any speed approaching 200mph, she simply put her foot down and flew, hitting 219mph on her first run down the Mulsanne. Returning to the pits four laps later, her lap time was faster than either Alain or Francois and among the ten fastest drivers of the night.

A perfect practice session, three outstanding drivers, a car built to win Le Mans: what could be better? Add the sheer fun and excitement of being at one of the world's greatest race events, with its incredible atmosphere and history. Magic! The car was eighth fastest. The drivers relaxed and, overnight, the mechanics changed to the race motor.

Qualifying the next day was, again, wet and slippery, and Alain decided that there would be no need to run early, hoping for drying conditions later in the evening when each driver could do their three laps in the dark (a provision of qualifying). No need to stress the car and no need to push hard for qualifying position. After all, the car and the drivers were certainties to make the field. Speed in qualifying wasn't that important: speed, endurance, and reliability over 24 hours was.

As soon as it became dark enough and when it seemed that the rain was going to last for the duration, Alain, then Migualt, and finally Desiré, each did their three laps, comfortably qualifying the car in the top ten.

Don, John, and the mechanics, pushed the de Cad back to the paddock and the drivers retired to Challis' transporter to discuss strategy for the race, while waiting for the midnight end of qualifying. Then it stopped raining and lap speeds started to increase. Soon it became obvious that the drivers' lap times were, now, no longer fast enough to guarantee that they would qualify for the race. The mechanics rushed to get the car back onto the pit lane and fitted it with slick, dry weather tyres.

Alain went out first, did one flying lap fast enough to qualify, and handed over to Migault who did the same. Finally it was Des' turn, but now there was only eight minutes remaining before the midnight end to qualifying.

Her out lap was quick and she came past the pits to start her first flying lap, running as quickly as she could in the treacherous conditions. 3 minutes and 53 seconds later, the green de Cadenet again blasted past the pits, completing its timed lap just seconds before the clock turned to midnight and the flag signalling the end of qualifying came out.

Murray looked down at his stop watch and smiled. She was the fastest of the three. But, in the car, Desiré had no way of knowing how fast she had gone, or that she had qualified the car, so she set out on her last lap with fierce determination to make her final lap as fast as she could.

There were no effective pit-to-car radios in 1980 and, even if there had been, the de Cadenet team would not have been able to afford them, so they had to rely on the traditional method of driver communication; hanging out the pit board. In those days, the signal area wasn't at the pits, but just after the Mulsanne Corner, half way round the course. However, by the time Des reached the corner, Tony Dutton had left, thinking the session was over.

Driving fast on a drying track is a challenge all of its own. The racing line, carved out by the cars ahead, is a narrow grey lane set in a wide expanse of shining, treacherously wet asphalt. Keep the car on the dry line and you can run almost as fast as on a perfectly dry track. Step an inch or so off – and all hell can break loose.

The headlights of the de Cadenet cut a swath through the dark and the spray hanging over the track, highlighting the 8ft wide dry line that twisted through the fourth gear, 140mph Porsche curves. Passing Pete Clark's Lola on the entry, Desiré found herself slightly off the dry line as she turned into the corner. The car lurched sideways as the outer wheels touched the wet surface on the edge of the dry line and scrabbled for grip, snapped sideways, and nosed into the Armco at 120mph.

It's amazing how, in the midst of a tumultuous accident, a race driver will feel as if the whole world has suddenly slowed down. It's a sensation that every race driver knows but that non-race drivers will seldom experience. Like the cogs inside a slow motion movie camera, the senses and reflexes are moving so fast that real life seems to slow right down. The accident, over in split seconds, seems to take minutes to unfold.

Immediately upon losing control, Desiré understood what was about to happen. She had seen the guardrail in her headlights and knew that the car would strike it at an angle which should not cause too much damage – maybe some torn bodywork and a few broken but replaceable suspension parts. No big deal. She braced herself and waited for the impact. The de Cad hurled itself at the barrier, impacting with a loud thud, followed by silence. Instead of spinning around, the de Cad had launched itself off the guardrail and was flying through the air. It pirouetted along its length, then slammed, upside down, onto the tarmac, in the middle of the track.

Momentarily stunned, it took Desiré a few seconds to get her wits together and when she did, she went ice cold with fear.

She smelt – and then felt – the cold flow of the pure racing fuel that came pouring down onto her legs and chest, released from it's aluminium-encased safety bladder through a broken filler tube, and she heard, in the silence, the steady ticking of the electric fuel pump, greedily sucking air.

The potential for a major fire was all too real. She was trapped under the weight of the open cockpit car, her helmet wedged against the asphalt, her body still strapped into the seat by her safety harness. Disoriented she searched for the master on-off switch, fumbled, found it, switched it off, and breathed a sigh of relief when the fuel pump stopped ticking. Then she saw the nozzle of a fire extinguisher that squirmed into the cockpit and blasted a cloud of ice-cold fluid over her body and knew that someone was outside trying to get her out of the car.

Back in the pits we were oblivious to the accident and were starting to pack up the equipment safe in the knowledge we had qualified. We waited patiently for the car to return, but it soon became apparent that something had gone terribly wrong as a long line of cars slowly began to enter pit lane. One stopped next to us. Its driver, Martin Birrane, now the owner of Lola race cars, climbed out and walked over to Alain.

He described the wreck, lying in the middle of the track, upside down, its bodywork strewn around, twisted and broken; officials on their knees peering into the cockpit; ambulance lights flashing; people running around; torches flashing.

"It's bad," he said.

It is difficult to describe the feeling in the pit when the crew learns that their car has crashed and that the driver may be hurt. People stand around with stunned expressions and then they quietly begin to talk to each other, trying to surmise what might have happened.

I stood there, suddenly alone, because no one wanted to talk to me, not knowing how I would react if Des was badly hurt, or worse. I waited a few minutes then left pit lane, walked along the passage behind the pits, and out to the paddock. I made my way to the track hospital where the doors were already open and doctors and nurses stood by, waiting for the ambulance to arrive.

After what seemed like hours (but was, probably, just a few minutes), the blue Citroën van with flashing light and siren slowly approached, turned around, and backed-up to the hospital doors. The attendants opened its doors, lifted the stretcher, and carried it into the hospital. I could see Desiré lying flat on her back, covered in dirt, fire extinguisher foam, and smelly gasoline. She saw me and smiled; she was OK. Which is more than could be said for the car.

Desiré remained in the medical centre while the doctors checked her out and gave the green light for her to race on Saturday, while I returned to

the transporter where a crowd of onlookers had gathered around the wrecked de Cadenet. It looked pretty bad, but Don and John soon declared that it was repairable. With help from the rest of the crew, they began a night and day of frantic work, intent on getting the car ready for Saturday's morning warm-up, the only opportunity that Alain would have to test the car before the start of the race.

When we arrived back at the track, early on Friday morning, we were amazed at the amount of work that had been accomplished. Confident that the car would be in great race shape, the three drivers settled down in the transporter, talking with friends, and generally getting into the spirit of the 24 Hours experience. In the meantime, Murray went off to the race administration offices to handle the formal nomination process that would confirm the team's entry into the race.

A few minutes later, a blast of profanity preceded his angry return to the trailer.

"They say we haven't qualified, that we're out," he said. "They say that we didn't go fast enough to make the 80 per cent class cut-off point!"

Murray grabbed the lap scoring and timing sheets that he had used to record our times during qualifying and he and I went back to the race office, where Race Secretary Alain Bertaud was holding court.

According to Bertaud, the three drivers' average speeds were too slow, but when Murray pulled out our records it was easy to see the problem. The officials had a record of Francois' dry lap time, but only the wet times put in by Alain and Desiré. With all three dry times averaged we were not just in the fasted 80 per cent of the class, we were comfortably in the top ten overall.

Murray, who speaks fluent Fench, presented our case, but Bertaud was adamant that the time keepers couldn't be wrong and a loud and heated argument followed. He could not, or would not, explain, for example, how they had a dry time for Migault but not one for Alain, who had run his dry lap before the Frenchman. After almost an hour and with the official cut-off time for driver nominations fast approaching, the timekeepers finally admitted that they did have a dry time for Alain and Bertaud was forced to concede that the car could now qualify if the average of Alain and Migault's times were to be used.

"What about Desiré?" Murray asked.

"She didn't do a dry lap," was Bertaud's response.

Again the argument flared, but now a new factor cropped up.

"We do not have time to look through the time sheets for a faster lap for Madame Wilson," said Bertaud. "You have to nominate your drivers by ten o'clock, and that is five minutes from now." Catch 22.

"You can submit a formal protest," Bertaud said. "Then we can look for the time, but you cannot nominate her with the time we have because the car will fall below the 80 per cent mark."

Murray asked him what the protest fee would be and how he should write the protest, and noted the words that Bertaud dictated. He handed over 5000 francs, completing the procedure just as the ten o'clock deadline arrived.

Murray looked up at Bertaud and said, "Now, let's look for Desiré's time."

"Why?" said Bertaud, "It does not matter if we find a faster time as you have not nominated her as a driver, so even if she has a faster time, we cannot allow her to race." We had been stitched up. Desiré wasn't going to be allowed to race.

When the news reached the paddock the reaction was immediate. Alain and Desiré were swamped by journalists, other drivers, and team manager; all, including influential French drivers and industry figures, came out in support of the team. French Formula Two driver Patrick Gaillard who was driving a Group 6 car (which happened to be sponsored by Longines, the official timekeeping company of the 24 Hours race) in the same class as the de Cadenet, went into the media tent and demanded that his car be disqualified to allow Desiré to get into the race. He claimed that, as he was much faster than his two co-drivers, he had worn their crash helmets to fool the officials into believing that they were driving and ensure that the car would qualify!

We were approached by Ian Bracey, owner and driver of the Ibec Group 6 car, another all-British entry. His car had also been disqualified from the race and his driver's dry times also ignored. Convinced that Bertaud's actions were deliberate and were intended to lessen the English challenge for victory, Bracey had already sent someone into town, seeking a lawyer to try to get an injunction against the organisers.

The injunction failed, but the sheriff was instructed to take possession of the official time-keeping records.

Bracey's team opened the file, a bound pad of green and white bar computer paper about three inches thick, and read the very first page. There it was, as clear as daylight: car number eight, the de Cadenet; Desiré's dry lap time; one of the fastest ten lap times of the night! She had qualified. No doubt about it.

Yet, even with this evidence, Bertaud refused to change his mind, and Desiré was forced to sit out the biggest race of her life, one in which she could have been a major star and which she had a very realistic chance of winning.

Bertaud and his officials went on to allow several cars which didn't qualify on speed to race, because they were deemed "Cars of particular technical interest." Drivers who didn't even qualify were allowed to compete. These included French film star Jean Louis Trintingant, who was way off the pace. One Ferrari was allowed to change an engine, another wasn't. All seven GTP class cars were allowed to start, yet the 80 per cent rule was rigidly applied to the Group 6 class. The organisers even increased the starting field to fifty five, in contravention of their own pre-event rules limiting the field to 50 cars.

Yet Desiré, winner of the past two World Championship races, a potential race winner, holder of a Formula 1 Superlicence, one of the most promotable figures in road racing, and a sure fan favourite, was refused the chance to drive. It was unbelievable!

Alain and Francois raced the car to seventh place, losing valuable places when fighting for third after a chassis member cracked, most probably as a result of the accident.

We never did find out the reason behind Bertaud's actions, There was, however, an incident several years later that reflected on these events. I was a race steward at the Daytona 24 and, during a pre-race cocktail party, IMSA President John Bishop and I were talking, when the door opened and Alain Bertuad walked in.

John immediately made the introductions, not knowing that I already knew who Bertaud was. He introduced me as Alan Wilson, the Columbus street race promoter, which left Bertaud totally unfazed, but, when he said that Bertaud probably knew my wife, Desiré, Bertaud's face flushed bright red and he turned and immediately left the room.

14

From Hero to Zero

Unlike some kids, Desiré wasn't born wanting to be a Formula 1 driver. Some children study every available racing magazine, watch every race on TV, and all the drivers and statistics. She didn't.

Des went through her teenage years without any particular interest in Grand Prix racing. Even while racing micro midgets to win-after-win, she never had a fantasy of becoming a World Champion or driving a Formula 1 car. With no TV (South Africa didn't get TV until 1975!), there was only the annual South African Grand Prix to generate interest. When she started racing her Formula Vee and attended the annual GP event at Kyalami, she took no special interest in the World Championship, as a whole. Even when she led the Formula Ford supporting race in front of 100,000 fans at the 1976 South African Grand Prix, she never envisioned moving from her Formula Ford to a Formula 1 car.

By 1980, however, she didn't just want to get into Formula 1, she felt she was ready to succeed in it. She had won the famous Brands Hatch Aurora race, earned her Superlicence, and won two World Championship sports car races. She was widely regarded as the best woman driver in the world and, regardless of gender, one of the best of the up-and-coming drivers looking for Grand Prix opportunities.

So, it was with a high level of confidence in her ability to qualify that John Webb arranged for Des to be entered in the 1980 British Grand Prix, at Brands Hatch. The cars were now considerably different from the old March Des had tested two years earlier, in John Webb's publicity stunt. Ground effect technology had evolved quickly and had changed the way the cars needed to be driven. Apart from the astonishing new speeds, the cars handled completely

differently. They stopped much better, but overtaking was more difficult, corner speeds were much higher, and even the racing lines were different.

The driver had to get used to these new characteristics, as well as some strong side effects. G-forces were more severe and braking forces much more dramatic. The cars were very uncomfortable to drive, lacking almost any suspension travel and drivers needed to be stronger and fitter.

Ground effect cars work better the faster they go; the greater the amount of air flowing under the car, the greater the pressure forcing it onto the ground. But, at the other extreme, the cars give little or no warning to the driver when reaching the limits of handling. Consequently, the number of high speed accidents in Formula 1 had increased significantly.

Formula 1 teams and their mechanics, too, were on a fast-track learning curve. In the past, car setup and interaction with the driver was carried out by highly experienced mechanics with years of hands-on experience. Now, engineers and highly qualified aerodynamicists were required to assess and understand the foibles of ground effect technology and the best of these were snapped up by the leading teams. This resulted in a growing gap in on-track performance between the top teams and those at the back of the grid and made it almost impossible for smaller teams, running one-off or occasional Grands Prix, to be even remotely competitive.

As a consequence, Formula 1 racing in 1980 was significantly different from the Aurora series in which Des had gained her Formula 1 experience and a 1980 specification Formula 1 car was a whole new animal when compared to the Ensign, Tyrrell, and Wolf Des had raced before.

As was the case for the 1978 British GP, the tyre

companies hosted pre-event test days at the track some six weeks before the event. These were split into two segments for the Brands Hatch race, one for Goodyear runners, the other for Michelin.

John Webb, working with race sponsors Marlboro to promote his event, arranged for Desiré to drive a one-year-old Williams FW07 in both the test days and the Grand Prix event itself and contracted with the RAM team's John MacDonald to run the car. This promised to be a good combination because John had run the March for Des during the 1978 test days and currently ran two, one-year-old Williams FW07 chassis in the Aurora Formula 1 series, for Eliseo Salazar and Emilio De Villota. He had also run a newer car for Emilio in the Spanish Grand Prix earlier in the year, so could be expected to be familiar with current GP standards. John was also providing a similar car for Rupert Keegan, so the potential for an effective race seemed good.

Although Marlboro were instrumental in putting Desiré into the race, it wouldn't allow its logo to appear anywhere on the car, thanks to its policy of not sponsoring women, so, it, in turn, gave the sponsorship space on the car to American clothing manufacturer, Murjani Jeans. The car that turned up for the test days was beautifully turned out in its green and white corporate colours. It also sported TDC decals, indicating an unknown level of support from Nick Challis that he refused to discuss with us.

The car wasn't the only part of the team to attract attention. By the end of the tests, Desiré was just outside of the top ten of the 21 cars that tested. New to the car, to the team, to ground effect, and to Grand Prix level Formula 1, she immediately set out to establish her credentials in the field. She lapped a full five seconds quicker than her near-lap record pace in the old Aurora series Wolf. To put her times in perspective, she was over 1½ seconds per lap quicker than, the then current World Champion, Jody Scheckter and his team-mate Gilles Villenueve had been, in their factory Ferrari's, just a week earlier. She was also faster than Mario Andretti in the Lotus.

The differences between the Williams and her old Wolf were dramatic. In the Wolf, she had braked hard for the right-handed Hawthorn turn, at the end of the long back straight, changing down a gear to take the corner. In the Williams, Hawthorn was now flat out in fifth gear! The Wolf had 760lb springs, the Williams 3600lbs. The Wolf had light steering, the Williams required all her strength to turn. The

Getting on with the Job. Des and John MacDonald in the pits during the pre-GP Tyre Test days. The relationship couldn't have been better, and they worked together to achieve a great result. What a difference to race weekend! (Courtesy Chris Davies)

Wolf provided plenty of feedback to the driver, who had time to sense when the car was on the verge of control. With the Williams, the car was either completely stable or completely out of control, with no warning as to when the edge would be reached.

Des also enjoyed working with John MacDonald's team. The car was well prepared and fast out of the box. It required almost no changes during the entire test period, so she was able to concentrate on her driving and didn't have to waste time chasing a setup. Macdonald seemed supportive and the team worked well together. She was consistently faster than Rupert, a former F3 Champion, who already had Formula 1 experience.

Despite her unfamiliarity with the car and her intentional caution not to get in the way of, or upset, the established Grand Prix drivers, she pushed as hard as she could, learning all the time and getting quicker and quicker as the tests drew on. Although on limit, she made no mistakes and by the end of the test days she was both comfortable with the car and her ability to drive it very fast. She was certain there was at least a second-or-more to come, especially if she could have the use of the softer compound tyres used by some of the major teams (as a privateer, she wasn't eligible to try the softer qualifying specification tyres).

Recognition. Even Barry Foley's Catchpole recognised Des' Tyre Test achievement. (Courtesy Autosport/Barry Foley)

Ultimately, her fastest lap of 1min 15.6 seconds, driven on hard rubber, saw her in the middle of the time sheet and faster than the two factory Ferraris that had practised the week before.

Desiré's performance was one of the highlights of the test days and garnered extensive media coverage, both in the general press and the specialist racing media. Drivers like Jochen Mass, who was slower, were quick to praise her, saying he'd long waited for a woman driver with the talent to race competitively in Formula 1 and that Desiré was that woman.

Even Ken Tyrrell, who, when interviewed before the tests, had stated that he didn't believe any woman would ever be in Formula 1 on a serious basis, tempered his views as a result of Desiré's performance. He now suggested that she would easily qualify somewhere in the top 16 or so amongst the 30 expected entries. Jody Scheckter, again, praised her, and John Webb placed a £500 bet with Lotus sponsor David Thieme, of Essex Petroleum, that Desiré would out-qualify Mario Andretti. Everyone was impressed and everyone, including Des, believed that she would qualify for the British Grand Prix.

Quietly confident in her ability and buoyed by the car, the team, and the knowledge that she still had plenty in hand, Desiré went about preparing for the biggest race of her life. We fitted out our garage as a home gym and she spent hours each day working with weights and on the treadmill, trying to build up her strength and endurance – although the efforts also resulted in her slimming down to a mere 125lb. She stayed remarkably calm and focused, although, as race week closed in, this became more and more difficult, thanks to the immense media pressure she faced.

Fuelled by the efforts of the Brands Hatch press office, Des became the single most visible news story

Great Car – Great Performance. Des impressed everyone with her performance in the Williams FW07 during the Tyre Test days, a few weeks before the 1980 British Grand Prix, running faster than many established GP stars. (Courtesy Wilson collection)

Bad Car – Bad Result. *The team changed cars for the race, presenting Des with an upgraded Aurora spec car that had been hastily repaired after a major accident. This car ran several seconds per lap slower than the car the team had 'borrowed' from Emilio de Villota for the test days. (Courtesy Chris Davies)*

of the Grand Prix. The fact that she was a woman – and one with a real chance of making an impact on the race – brought out the national media in droves.

The pressure was immense. Hardly a day went by when she wasn't being interviewed, photographed, posed on cars wearing, against her will, as little clothing as the media could get her to, and asked the same questions over and over again by writers who had little or no knowledge of her, racing, or what she was trying to achieve.

Through all this she tried to remain as calm as she could, and did a great job of not allowing her sudden fame to get to her as she concentrated on her race preparations. But the 1980 British Grand Prix turned out to be the biggest disappointment of her life.

The first thing she noticed when she arrived at Brands for the opening practice session was that the car was painted in different colours than at the test days. In addition, the seat was different and the pedals totally altered; even the steering wheel and mirror positions were different. The car no longer fitted her. She called John Macdonald over and asked what was up, but he denied anything was different from the test and said she was imagining things. Des is no fool: she immediately knew that something was wrong.

The feeling was reinforced when she ran her first laps. The car was terrible – it wouldn't handle, it was inconsistent, it seemed to flex when it should have been solid. It had major oversteer leaving the corners, and the tyres immediately started to show very unusual wear patterns. During the test days, the car had been very susceptible to minor changes, but, with this chassis, even drastic changes made little difference. At one stage Des shifted both stabiliser bar controls to opposite extremes and, even then, the handling didn't change: a sure sign of a major chassis problem.

Des looked at the chassis plate and saw that the car didn't have the same chassis number as her test car. She said nothing, but John kept on telling her it was the same car and suggested, to others, that she was feeling the pressure of the occasion.

A race driver is a funny animal and little things can mean a lot to their psyche. Des was no different. As a perennial underdog, always up against better funded teams and better equipment, she had come to depend on people having a positive attitude around her. She also wanted and expected absolute honesty. Now, at the most important race of her life, she found neither.

The situation deteriorated even further when Des began to overdrive the car, trying as hard as she could to extract speed that just wasn't there. It got worse again when she asked for changes to be made and her requests were met with sullen faces and a complete lack of enthusiasm.

Even worse, she could see a complete difference in attitude between the team and her and the team and Rupert, who was getting constant attention and, as a result, was going really well, almost reaching the times Des had achieved during the test days. Not that Rupert was being unfriendly; he just wasn't being helpful. He was also using this race to try to make an impact and to reinstate himself as a full time Grand Prix driver and knew full well that any hope of doing this required him to outperform Des. So, he used his experience and subtle actions to try to unsettle her, such as ensuring that his car was always parked at the door to the pit lane, so Des always had to wait for him to leave the garage before she got onto the track. And he always took his time getting into the car and onto the track, which unsettled her and lost her valuable track time. When she eventually did get out on course, she found herself running relatively slowly on cold tyres, while all the other cars on track were up to speed. Being a rookie, she was intensely aware of not getting in their way. Simple things like this suddenly began to become an issue.

On the track, too, she found a difference in the attitude of the other drivers. Gone was the relaxed atmosphere of the test days. Now, when she tried to pass someone, they fought back with a vengeance. When she let someone past her, they gave no thanks, demonstrating their superiority. Then Jacques Laffite pushed her off the track.

Des had just emerged from the pits and was getting up to speed along the straight below the pits, when Laffite came up to pass her, going much faster. Seeing him in her mirrors, she moved to the right to give him plenty of room to turn into Surtees Bend. She let him past, expecting to follow him as he turned inside her, but, instead, found him taking her right off the edge of the track, causing her to spin and damaging the sliding skirts. She returned to the pits but the repairs were too significant to complete before the end of the session. This ruined the first qualifying session before she had a chance to run on qualifying tyres and, so, put in a faster lap.

Macdonald immediately blamed her for going off the track, ignoring Laffite's role. But Jean Sage, team manager for Renault, made a point of finding me in the pit lane.

"Laffite is telling everyone that he drove Desiré right off the track," he said to me. "He's saying than no f*****g woman belongs in Formula 1 and he's going to do whatever he has to, to keep her out. Tell Desiré that the next time she sees him on the track she must drive him off, even if it means he has a big crash." She never had the opportunity.

In the final free practice, she continued to struggle to get the car up to speed, without avail. The same pattern followed in the last qualifying session, where her best time, 15 minutes or so before the end of the session, was 0.8 seconds per lap slower than Keke Rosberg at the bottom end of the grid. She was failing to qualify and time was running out.

But she still had her qualifying 'C' compound tyres, softer rubber that was at least a second-or-more per lap faster than the race rubber that she had been using. She came into the pits to have the qualifying rubber fitted. The team raised the car on stands, took off the wheels, mounted the rears, and then tried to fit the fronts. The wheels wouldn't fit. For the rest of the session the car sat on its stand, while her last opportunity to qualify for the race slipped away.

Desiré was devastated. I was devastated. John Webb was devastated. John Macdonald didn't care a damn.

It was her fault, he told the press, she was too intimidated, she just wasn't fast enough. She wasn't even as fast as she had been in testing, six weeks before!

The next morning I received a phone call from Emilio De Villota.

"I am very sorry that Desiré didn't qualify but I could not let her use my car." He explained.

The car that John Macdonald had provided for the test days was Emilio's 1980 specification Grand Prix car, his personal property. John had used it without telling Emilio and without his permission. Quite rightly, Emilio had refused to let the car be used for the British Grand Prix, so John had taken the car that Eliseo Salazar was using for the British Aurora series. This was a one-year-old car setup to run without skirts, which were banned in the Aurora series. Worse, Eliseo had comprehensively crashed the car at Monza, the Sunday before the British Grand Prix. The car had been rushed back to the UK and hastily rebuilt in time to be taken down to Brands on the Thursday. The repairs were rushed, resulting in a chassis that flexed so significantly that it reduced the effectiveness of its ground effect, making

Friends. Kevin Cogan, Desiré's team-mate during part of the 1980 Aurora series, and journalist Russell Bulgin, were good friends to have during the traumas and dramas of the British Grand Prix weekend. Russell followed her progress throughout the weekend, and wrote a well balanced and very fair report in Cars and Car Conversions magazine that told what really happened behind the scenes. (Courtesy Wilson collection)

it unpredictable and unstable, ensuring that it would be a pig to drive.

Then, throughout the first day of practice and qualifying, Macdonald had refused to acknowledge that the car might have a problem. After all, he still continued to insist that it was the same car Des had driven in the test days. Thus he wasted valuable time by refusing to try to sort out the problem, telling Des she was to blame. Worse, the team didn't have the experience or knowledge to sort out the problems. Their performance was a disaster made worse by the car substitution that wrecked Desire's career.

Desiré's dominant need, throughout her life in motorsport, has been to have the respect of her peers, her fans, and, above all, the teams for whom she has driven.

This need for respect has always required that the team believe in her ability to drive the car as fast as anyone, that they believe that she will always try her hardest, which was what Julian Randalls and Alain de Cadenet had done.

John MacDonald didn't believe in Desiré. He was running her car for money. His interests lay only in the pay cheque. Throughout the weekend he had refused to acknowledge that this was a different car, and wanted Desiré and the media to believe that Des was the issue, not the car.

Had John simply called Des before the event, told her that he had to run another car, told her that it may have some problems as a result of its accident, and then simply got on with the task of making it work, the whole weekend would almost certainly have worked better. Des would have accepted the bad news and made the best of it. If she then didn't qualify, the fall-out would have been manageable, even if she would have been very disappointed.

Yes, the history books say that Desiré failed to qualify for the 1980 British Grand Prix. Yes, ultimately, the driver must always accept the blame. But in this case, John Macdonald must carry a large part of the responsibility. Although Desiré's failure to make the show was a big disappointment for her and, really, signalled the end of her upward progress in racing, it should also be put in context.

Most telling, perhaps, is that John MacDonald ran his FW07s at the remaining races of the season for Rupert, who failed to qualify in Germany, Zandvoort, Canada, or at Watkins Glen, while Kevin Cogan (Canada) and Geoff Lees (USA) both failed to qualify the chassis that Des had found to be so evil at Brands.

The failure to qualify for the British Grand Prix remains Desiré's greatest disappointment in racing, but what was even worse, was that it signified a sudden and dramatic end to the wave of success that she had enjoyed, so far, in 1980.

Almost immediately, the funds behind her Wolf campaign in the Aurora series dried up and, despite being third in the Championship, she was suddenly out of a drive. There were no more endurance races, as de Cadenet had already run out of money for the season. There were no Sports 2000, FF2000 or any other cars to drive. Suddenly, Des was on the sidelines.

For the rest of the year she sat in her office, wondering what had happened to a stellar career that had promised so much.

After racing almost every weekend, now, other than two Formula Atlantic races at Mallory and Macau, she was almost completely idle.

15

JUST A HUNDRED THOUSAND POUNDS

ONE hundred thousand pounds is nothing in the world of Formula 1 racing, but it's a fortune to someone who doesn't have it. The whole world of Grand Prix racing was in turmoil during the 1980 and 1981 seasons, thanks to Bernie Ecclestone's fight for control of the sport with FISA (Fédération Internationale du Sport Automobile), racing's international authority. This resulted in a short period when the FOCA (Formula 1 Constructors Association) teams, who supported Ecclestone, set up their own independent World Championship series, although this didn't have the support of Ferrari, Renault, or Ligier.

Consequently, the world of racing entered the 1981 season in a state of chaos, waiting to see what would happen at the year's opening event, the South African Grand Prix. A few weeks before the race, Bernie Ecclestone called Des and said that he was planning to run her in a works Brabham, alongside Nelson Piquet and Argentinean Ricardo Zunino.

The deal for Des to drive the Brabham didn't materialise, but instead resulted in a phone call from Ken Tyrrell, two weeks before the South African Grand Prix.

"You'll be driving for me," Ken said. "Get down to South Africa and I'll see you there."

In recent years, new Grand Prix drivers would typically run many hundreds, perhaps thousands of miles, in highly structured tests before ever driving a Formula 1 car in a Grand Prix event, or will have enjoyed many hours at the wheel of a highly advanced simulator, learning the car and the tracks they would be racing on. But this wasn't to be the case for Desiré.

She arrived in South Africa on Sunday morning, spent a few hours with her parents, and then joined the team at the Kyalami Ranch hotel, just outside the circuit gates, on Sunday evening. Monday and Tuesday were almost exclusively spent undertaking media and PR activities for the car sponsor, Deutz tractors. On Wednesday, she spent most of the day with the team having a seat fitting and meeting team number one driver, Eddie Cheever. She drove the car for the first time during the opening practice session on Thursday morning, her first time at the wheel since early November, three months earlier and fully seven months since her last drive in a Formula 1 car. Once again, the pressure was enormous.

As the only South African in the race, she was, again, the centre of major media interest and was followed everywhere by a phalanx of reporters and photographers. She was also acutely aware that she was getting a second chance at Grand Prix racing and was determined to make up for the Brands Hatch disaster. Equally, she was worried that her time away from driving had left her rusty and, finally, she desperately wanted to impress Ken Tyrrell, perhaps the most respected team manager in Grand Prix racing.

Ken and the team worked hard to make her feel at home. There was none of the mistrust that she had found with Macdonald. Instead, the mechanics acted as if they were pleased to have her in the car, although the look on one individual's face, when he had to put his hands down between her legs to fasten the crotch strap of the safety harness, was pitiful as he looked up at me, as if to ask permission! Similarly when, securely strapped in the car, she needed to get hold of some paperwork from her purse and had to ask a team member to fetch it for her; he carried it across pit lane, accompanied by laughs from the rest of the crew, using the tips of his fingers and with a look of acute embarrassment on his face.

Des didn't find Eddie to be very friendly, but wasn't concerned. She was simply a one-off team-mate, who was only in the car because she was a local driver in the local Grand Prix. Although they had raced against each other in World Sports Car races, it would certainly never have occurred to him that she might, in any way, be competition to him, either on the track, or within the inevitable team pecking order. He wasn't unfriendly, just distant. Des could not and didn't expect anything else. Ken was exceptional.

He sat her down and told her that he didn't have great expectations; that his car wasn't going to be very competitive, and that he had no doubt that she would drive it as fast as it could go. He asked her to take things slowly, to get used to the car, not to overdrive it, not to try too hard until she was totally ready. He wanted her to enjoy the experience of driving for him. What a contrast to John Macdonald!

Des didn't cover herself in glory during the first day of practice and qualifying. She did try to follow Ken's instructions, but was soon pushing hard. Unfortunately, this resulted in two spins, one of which cut short her qualifying period, late in the afternoon. There was no doubt that she was still rusty from her long time out of the cockpit and she found the Tyrrell to be less effective than the Williams in its ground effect abilities. Moreover, its steering was incredibly light at slow speeds, which took some getting used to, but loaded up so much at speed, that she could barely turn the wheel through the fast Barbecue and Jukskei sweeps. Still, at the end of day one she was just over one second slower than Cheever.

When she returned to the pits, Ken sat her down and talked over her performance. He didn't mince his words, telling her just what he thought, which was

The Boss. *Ken Tyrrell was the best possible team manager for a new driver entering Formula 1. He was firm, patient, and had the great ability to instil confidence, even while he was being critical. Ken tried very hard to keep Des in his team for the entire 1981 Grand Prix season.*
(Courtesy Wilson Collection)

that she was trying too hard too soon and making unacceptable mistakes. Then, Ken showed the skills that made him such a great developer of racing talent. After giving Des a talking to, he sat back and listened to her side and settled the discussion by saying;
"You're driving faster than my car can go."

This was how to talk to a new driver. Ken knew exactly how to make his point, how to criticise, and yet at the same time, how to bolster a driver's confidence. No wonder he had been so successful over the years in getting new drivers up to speed.

Des listened to him, acknowledging some of the criticism, but defended herself on one count. She told him that she wasn't happy with the tyres on the car. Although all the tyres in the race were to be same specification Goodyears, she knew this set wasn't working well, causing her to spin the car a couple of times. Ken listened to her and, even though he remained sceptical, said that he would give her a new set for the next morning's practice.

The car was immediately better on the new rubber and she quickly cut her lap times, stayed on the track, and moved up the grid, finally qualifying in 16th place, just 0.6 of a second slower than her far more experienced team-mate. Ken was very impressed and let her know how he felt.

Grand Prix racing is, perhaps, the world's most glamorous sport, surrounded by parties, beautiful people, never ending social activities, the media, and thousands of fans. Drivers are an essential part of a Grand Prix weekend's menagerie of pre-event activities and Desiré, as the only South African driver in her home Grand Prix, could have been expected to be at the centre of the social whirl.

Far from it.

Desiré and I spent the evening before the most important race of her life driving around

Johannesburg looking for a coin-op laundry. The one we eventually found, in downtown Hillbrow, was dark, dirty, and empty. Des only had one good set of driving overalls and wanted to at least have them clean for her maiden Grand Prix, so, she insisted on washing them instead of joining the pre-race parties that were a feature of the Kyalami Ranch pre-event night life. Some glamour!

Thursday and Friday had seen typical hot and dry South African summer weather, but Saturday's race day dawned cooler, overcast, and drizzly. Ken was concerned that Desiré's lack of experience would work against her in the rain and wasn't mollified when she was immediately among the top ten drivers during the very wet morning warm-up session, calling her back into the pits after only a few laps. As race time drew near, Des looked at the weather and, more familiar with Kyalami's weather patterns than Ken, asked to start the race on dry weather tyres, even though the track was still damp and there was still a light drizzle falling on the 100,000 race fans, but Ken disagreed.

For the one and only time in her entire racing career, Desiré stalled at the start of a race.

Sitting on the grid directly behind Eddie Cheever and alongside factory McLaren driver, John Watson, she noticed water seeping through the gap between her visor and helmet, spreading down the inside of the perspex, so she began wiping it clear with her glove just as the flag dropped to start the race. Caught unawares, she hurriedly dropped the clutch but, anxious not to get too much wheel spin on the wet track, gave too little throttle and stalled the engine.

The field raced away, leaving her stationary on the grid. The track marshals reacted quickly and soon arrived to push-start the car, but, by the time she got under way, the rest of the field was disappearing around Crowthorne Corner, at the end of the straight.

I watched the start from the Ford building in the pit lane and groaned when I saw what had happened, timing her at 15 seconds behind the next last car as she passed the pits on her first flying lap.

For the first few laps she followed the field at a distance, but I soon saw that she was catching the tail-enders very quickly and, sure enough, within a handful of laps she was starting to work her way through them as she moved up the field.

Although easier than with current Formula 1 cars, passing in Formula 1 has never been simple, but Des was making short work of overtaking as she worked

Des and Eddie Cheever sit in their Tyrrells in the very narrow Kyalami pit lane. This was state of the art in 1981! (Courtesy CAR magazine).

her way up the field. Grand Prix drivers never give way if they can help it and Nigel Mansell was no exception. Still in his early years in Formula 1, Mansell was driving a Lotus as team-mate to Elio de Angelis. Of all the drivers she passed, he was the only one to crowd her, taking her to the edge of the track as she drove past. But she forced her way ahead and then left him behind at over a second per lap.

She came up on the Arrows of Sigfried Stohr, who had won the previous year's F2 championship. By now, I had moved down to the signalling area and was standing next to Ken Tyrrell when Des and Siggi raced past the pits, absolutely side by side, heading for Crowthorne. We watched as the two cars entered the braking zone side-by-side and saw one of the cars plunge off the track in a cloud of dust. Not knowing if Des had gone off, we waited to see which of the two would come past on the next lap – Desiré, thank God. Siggi came up to us with the wry comment "I no break, she no brake. I no brake, she no brake, I no break, I crash. She turn!"

Important Pass. *Des leads team-mate Eddie Cheever,*
after passing him early in the race.
(Courtesy Malcolm Sampson)

Her most important overtaking manoeuvre followed a few laps later, when she saw that the next car in front of her was that of her team-mate Eddie Cheever. At Grand Prix level, a driver's greatest competitor is his team-mate, because a driver who cannot beat his team-mate, in cars that everyone assumes have the same performance, is marked as the slower. So, Des knew that she could expect a tough fight from her vastly more experienced team leader. As she closed the gap on him she planned how to get past, deciding that she would, really, only have one chance, which was to take him by surprise.

She reckoned that he would expect her to close slowly and sit behind him for several laps while she worked out where she could pass, which would also give him the chance to develop his own strategy to keep her behind. So, instead of waiting for the opportunity to pass, she created her own by making an extra effort to close the gap as rapidly as she could. She judged her approach so that she arrived at his gearbox in the braking area for the tight, left-handed Clubhouse Corner. Seeing her coming, Eddie braked as late as he could, but Des held back, entered the corner much faster, and pulled alongside him as they accelerated out of the corner, taking the inside line for the following left-hander, where she out-braked him and slipped past. She immediately drew away from him.

By now, the rain had stopped and the track started to dry out. Cars began to enter the pits to switch to the faster dry tyres. Ken called Eddie in, but kept Des out for several more laps. I asked him when she would be coming in, as I could see her making hand signals from the cockpit and knew that she wanted to come in to change rubber. But Ken chose to keep her out, saying that he wanted her on wet tyres until the track was completely dry.

Eventually she came in, but not before a large cloud passed over the Kyalami Ranch Hotel just a half mile south of the track, pouring rain. How I prayed for that cloud to move up to the track, because, with Des driving the only car in the race still on wets, she would have had a great chance to move to the front of the field. But she had no such luck.

Des went back into the race on dry tyres and continued to make up positions until, around the $\frac{2}{3}$-mark, she was 30 seconds ahead of Cheever in 12th place and was fast closing-in on the top ten.

Even though she was doing very well, she wasn't running as fast as the race leaders and first Carlos Reutemann, then Nelson Piquet came up to lap her. Being very aware of her rookie status, Des had no intention of getting in their way. She allowed Reutemann to pass and moved out of Piquet's way as she accelerated out of Leeukop Corner, the tight hairpin leading onto the straight. Unfortunately she went a little too wide, ran onto the marbles and spun the car. Then, seeing that she was in Piquet's way, she allowed her car to roll back to give him room to pass safely and struck the outside wall, damaging the wing enough to force her into the pits – and retirement.

It was one of two mistakes she made, one at the beginning and one at the end of her race. In between, she had driven extremely well, most notably compared to her team leader Eddie Cheever, who she chased down from a 15 second deficit, overtook, and then driven away from to a 30 second advantage before her accident. Her drive from last place to the fringe of the top ten proved that she was fully capable of racing amongst and against established Grand Prix drivers. Des had done enough to show that she deserved a place in Grand Prix racing even if she was never to graduate to that level.

Despite the accident, Ken was impressed and invited her to his office the week after the race. He told her that he wanted her in his team for the rest of the season, but needed to find £100,000. While this was a vast amount for Des and I to find, it was really

Finish. Des crashes the Tyrrell out of the race while trying to give Nelson Piquet room. A simple error that ended her last race in a Formula 1 car.
(Courtesy Malcolm Sampson)

a small price to pay for a full time Grand Prix drive. Ken himself tried hard to source the money, as did Des, but no one wanted to sponsor a South African at a time when anti-apartheid fervor was at its height.

Ken called Chris Pook, in America. Pook had arranged for Michelob to sponsor Kevin Cogan in the second Tyrrell for the Long Beach Grand Prix and Ken tried to persuade him to switch the beer company's funding to Des – but to no avail. Then he told Des to meet the team in Long Beach with her kit, as he would do what he could when he got there to get her into the race. In the event, her race gear was stolen from the trunk of her rental car and Kevin failed to qualify.

Then Ken told Des to get her visas so that she could race the car in Brazil and Argentina. Both Brazil and Argentina had 'No-Sports with South Africa' policies, so Des had to ask Mark Thatcher, son of British Prime Minister Margaret Thatcher, to 'arrange' visas (which would have cost us £5000 each, at a time when Des' total annual salary working at Brands Hatch was around £7500). We didn't have to spend the money because, a few days later, Ken told her that Ricardo Zunino had come up with a bundle of money for the drive. However, he told her that she would be driving for him in the European races.

Finally, Ken called Des and told her that, as much as he wanted to give her the ride, he had been offered a large amount of sponsorship money by an Italian ceramics company to give the drive to a young Italian

named Michele Alboreto. Her Grand Prix dreams ended right there.

Desiré was, quite naturally, upset that things didn't work out for her, but was also very realistic. She had two chances to make the grade. The British GP failure was the result of a combination of problems, the South African largely her own mistakes. Had she not stalled, had she not spun and damaged the wing, she might have finished in the top six or seven, in which case, maybe – just maybe – her career could have moved on.

In the 60 years of the Formula 1 World Championship, all the drivers have been male except for Des, Lella Lombardi, Maria Theresa De Filippis, Divina Galica, and Giovanna Amati. Only these five women and Des reached the level of Grand Prix fame. Lella, sadly no longer with us, was the only one to race regularly and the only one to earn points, albeit just half-a-point from a race stopped early. But for £100,000, things could have been different for the girl from Brakpan.

Desiré believes that, had she been able to secure a regular drive in halfway decent equipment, she would have been a regular midfield runner, with the potential for earning a few points each year and maybe finishing the occasional race in the top five or six. Certainly, she felt totally comfortable running with drivers as highly respected as Derek Daly, John Watson, Geoff Lees, Eddie Cheever, and even the Nigel Mansell early in his career. She was happy to run with Elio De Angelis in the wet, outbrake Siggi Stohr in the damp, and pass Eddie in the dry.

She was certainly not out of place amongst the Grand Prix drivers of the day.

Although Desiré qualified for and drove in the 1981 South African Grand Prix, her name does not appear in the official Formula 1 history books as ever having driven in a Formula 1 Grand Prix. The reason for this is that, after the Kyalami race had been run, settlement was reached between Bernie Ecclestone and Jean-Marie Balestre whereby FOCA and the FIA agreed to work together. Part of that settlement included dropping the South African Grand Prix from the events that were to count for 1981 World Championship points, because Ferrari, Renault, and Alfa Romeo had not competed. So, while Des competed at both the British and South African events when both were genuine World Championship qualifying races, luck and politics conspired to keep her from the history books.

16

TRAGEDY AND TRAUMA
AT THE BRICKYARD

BY 1982 Desiré, the girl from Brakpan, South Africa, had climbed two of the three biggest peaks of motor racing – Le Mans and Formula 1. The third remained to be challenged. In 1982 she discovered the rock face that was the Indianapolis 500.

Just as neither Formula 1 nor Le Mans had ever been targets of any youthful ambition, so the Indy 500 wasn't something she had ever seen as a goal for her racing. Not while she raced in South Africa and not even while she pursued her Aurora Formula 1 and British Grand Prix hopes in Europe. It's not that she didn't want to race there, just that she had very little knowledge of the event, its stature, or its position in the world of racing.

While this may seem surprising to American-born race enthusiasts, to a South African whose interest – even in the European world of racing, before she won her Driver to Europe award – was minimal. The Indy 500 was just another race and, even then, it featured an alien type of racing.

Even her 1978 drive in a SuperVee, on the Phoenix oval, did little to stimulate any serious interest in Indycar racing. And that year's appearances at Brands Hatch and Silverstone of the USAC Indycar field simply showcased the relatively unsophisticated, but dramatic and very powerful, oval cars running, like fish out of water, on road courses.

So, when Teddy Yip, owner of her Brands Hatch-winning Wolf, told her that he planned to enter her at Indy she accepted the offer, not for any burning desire to compete in the 'Worlds Greatest Auto Race', but as just an opportunity to compete in another major event.

Teddy's offer came early in 1980, soon after she won the Brands Aurora Formula 1 race. However, the offer wasn't for the 1980 race, nor for 1981. Instead, Teddy, who was enthusiastically in awe of the pageantry and traditions of the 500, wanted Des to attend the 1981 race as a spectator so that she would learn to respect the famous race and so that she would not be overawed when she arrived to compete in 1982.

Des travelled to Indy in May, 1981 and was suitably impressed with the grandeur and patriotic fervour of the famous race, but not overawed by the actual racing. It was, to her, just another major event in which she was going to race and another type of car which she was going to drive.

True to his word, Teddy made arrangements for her to compete in 1982. The plan was for her to drive a brand-new March 82C with a similarly new Cosworth DFX engine.

The car was to be run by Bob Fletcher's Phoenix-based race team with Englishman Derek Mower, an acknowledged Indianapolis expert, as crew chief. Teddy's trump card was to arrange for Des to be coached by Bobby Unser. Teddy's plan also called for her to run a preliminary race at the Phoenix mile, a month or so before the Indy event, before she would have to go through the traditional Rookie Test programme at the Indianapolis Speedway, in late April. It sounded fantastic.

Step one in Teddy's programme was for Des to spend time away from the track with the great and famous Bobby Unser, three times winner of the 500 and a legend in American racing. During this time he would imbue her with his skills and experience. She flew from London to Albuquerque, New Mexico, to meet the great man. It took her about 30 seconds to see that this wasn't going to work.

Bobby Unser may have been a great driver and a

Super Fan. Teddy Yip was a huge fan of the Indy 500 and wanted to make Des a star of the show, but his decision to involve Bobby Unser was unfortunate. Here, Teddy talks with Des as she gets ready to make her only qualifying run. (Courtesy David Hutson)

legend, to himself and his fans, but his chauvinism did not impress Desiré. Obviously 'helping' Des simply to keep Teddy, a long-term sponsor and patron, she saw that Bobby had no real interest in helping her and that he certainly didn't believe that she, or any other woman, would ever be able to run competitively at Indy. When she returned to the UK, she summed up his education process thus; "He made me sit down and read all his scrapbooks."

Unfortunately, Unser's 'help' didn't end there.

The first thing he did was persuade Teddy that Desiré didn't need to race at Phoenix, claiming that the Phoenix oval was so different to Indy that she would get no benefit from driving there. Forget that she would get experience in the heavy, turbocharged cars, with far greater horsepower than she had ever handled. Forget, most importantly, the oval racing requirements of rolling starts and re-starts, multiple pit stops, banking, the need to drive on a knife-

edge of precision, and even familiarity with other competitors. At Bobby's recommendation, Phoenix was scratched from the programme. This was bad enough, but there was worse to come.

Bobby persuaded Teddy that the March was the wrong car for her. Rather, he insisted that she should, instead, drive an Eagle. In particular a one-year-old Eagle that had been designed for a Chevy V8 stock block, but which Des should race with a Cosworth engine. Strange; Bobby just happened to have such a car! A car that was a far cry from a brand new March 82C and was instead a collection of bits and pieces lying in Bobby's garage that still had to assembled and tested before it could be driven in a race.

Teddy listened to Bobby and agreed that Des should drive the Eagle and the order for the March was cancelled.

Interestingly, Bobby then signed-on to manage a team for young Mexican driver Josele Garza, for the 1982 Indy – and guess what car he bought? A brand-new March 82C.

The Indy Rookie driver's programme is a Brickyard tradition that was generally viewed with disdain by Indy's new European drivers. Most of theses drivers, whom had achieved considerable success in major road race events across the Atlantic and who couldn't understand why, with all their experience and skill, they would have to go through an initiation programme before they would be permitted to race in the Indianapolis 500.

The Rookie Tests were a long standing programme that required every driver new to the Speedway to post a series of ten-lap runs at fixed, relatively low speeds. The runs would be observed by experienced Indy drivers and officials. Only when satisfied with a driver's performance at one speed would the officials allow the rookie to increase speed by another few miles-per hour for another ten laps, with the procedure repeated until competitive speeds were attained. A new driver would only be granted the opportunity to qualify for the Indy 500 after proving their competence in this way.

Even Jimmy Clark had to go through the Rookie Tests, as did Jackie Stewart, Graham Hill, Jack Brabham, and Denny Hulme – all Formula 1 World Champions. While European fans considered it an insult to their heroes, the tests were considered to be an important necessity by Americans and the American's were right. Oval racing and the Indianapolis Speedway in particular offer an incredibly dangerous package and the race is very different to European style road racing. The whole purpose of the Rookie Tests is to familiarise drivers with the value of precision driving at the very edge of car control; the need for total smoothness at the controls; the importance of establishing and maintaining a consistent flow around the unbelievably fast track – and the reality that there is absolutely no room for error. For Des they promised even more; the opportunity to get familiar with a strange car.

Unfortunately, the Rookie Tests didn't serve their purpose for Des. The problem was simple: the damn Eagle never lasted long enough to allow her to run the required number of laps, at any speed!

The car broke down every time she went out on the track during the five day Rookie Test. It had gearbox problems, engine problems, turbocharger problems, and suspension problems. The car was a joke. Hastily assembled from boxes of miscellaneous parts, nothing fitted. Changing springs took as long as an engine swap – eight hours of overnight labour. The mechanics worked their butts off and Desiré sat in the pit lane getting more and more frustrated while the other rookies went through the programme. Eventually, even the hard-nosed Indy officials saw that there was no point in her continuing. However, they had watched her handle the frustrations, observed her during her few laps on the track and realized the experience that she brought with her, so, in a very unusual move, they gave her the OK to quit the tests and to enter the race. A few weeks later she returned to Indianapolis for the month of May.

I need to set the scene and describe the Indy 500, because it was, then, so completely different to any other car race in the world. First, it started in 1911 and is the world's oldest surviving car race. Consequently, it has an enormous base of tradition – and tradition is everything to the fans, officials, and participants in the event.

Second, until recently, the testing, practice qualifying, and race was spread over the whole of May and the race itself had, for years, been the world's largest one-day spectator event, attracting around 400,000 fans.

The grid was always limited to 33 cars, not drivers, a point not often understood outside America, where enthusiasts would sometimes learn with amazement that a car had been qualified by someone who would not necessarily drive it on race day. Qualifying was spread over two weekends, with open practice during the week. Cars that qualified on the first weekend 'locked-in' their grid positions, even if other cars went faster on the second weekend, until the grid was full. Cars could attempt to go faster than already qualified cars and, if they did, they would 'bump' the slowest car off the grid. Thus, cars that were considered to have qualified could easily be removed at the last minute, contributing to the interest and excitement of the event.

The was no track activity during the week before the race, except on Thursday, which was known as 'Carburetion Day,' and was the last opportunity to ensure the car was ready for Sunday's race. This was always held in conjunction with Memorial Day, even if the May 31 date didn't coincide exactly.

For more than 60 years this format had contributed to the excitement of the event, made more dramatic by large entries and huge crowds.

In 1982, for instance, there were 108 cars entered for some sixty or so drivers, all trying to qualify for the 33 car grid. The first weekend of qualifying drew between 150,000 and 200,000 spectators each day, the second over 100,000, both qualifying events attracting more spectators than any Formula 1 Grand Prix of the time!

When Des arrived at the track for opening day, she made her way into the famous old Gasoline Alley which was, in 1982, a far cry, architecturally, from today's featureless concrete garage blocks. Back then, the garages were housed in long, single-story, green-roofed wooden sheds with green and white farm barn-type doors, each unit just a little bigger than the race car within. Garages were assigned on a long-time use basis and many teams retained the same garage year after year.

Desiré made her way to the Fletcher garage, situated close by the gate controlling pedestrian access to the paddock and just across a narrow roadway from the security fence. Throughout the month, thousands of fans would stand against the fencing for hours on-end, waiting for the drivers to walk by, hopefully scoring autographs and photos, and maybe even a quick chat with their heroes. There was a surprise waiting for Des when she entered the Fletcher garage.

The two-bay shop held two cars; her white, freshly rebuilt Eagle and a red and white March 81C, covered in Intermedics sponsorship and with Gordon Smiley's name written on the side of the cockpit. Her team-mate for the month of May was

Talking it Through. *Former Wolf team-mate Kevin Cogan was a great help to Des during the Rookie Test. Here, he and Crew Chief Derek Mower discuss the track with Des. Kevin, who was seldom as quick as Des in comparable F1 cars, put his Penske on the front row of the 1982 race. (Courtesy David Hutson)*

to be her old Melchester Tyrrell friend from the 1979 Aurora Formula 1 series.

Des had a lot to learn. Apart from the sheer lack of miles in the Rookie Tests, during which she completed just 47 laps in a whole week, and in addition to the many mechanical and other woes suffered by the car, there was also the peculiar nature of the Indy track.

The 2½ mile, four turn Indy circuit demands extraordinary levels of commitment and extreme precision, in both driving style and car setup. All of these can be affected by any number of small problems, from wind to track temperatures, that would change every time a cloud crossed the sun. Consequently, arriving at a definitive balance that would result in the fastest lap speeds could take hours of work by driver and crew, and then be totally negated by a change in temperature, a new set of tyres, or even the amount of rubber laid down on the track by a large number of cars running on-track simultaneously.

Worse, however, was the never-ending frustration created by the yellow lights which would cause all cars on the track to immediately slow down and

return to the pits when they came on. While a few instances of this were caused by accidents or spins, the majority, by far, were accompanied by the public address announcement of "a track inspection." At such an announcement, a fleet of red service trucks and similarly clad workers would move onto the track and drive, slowly, around the course looking for oil, spilt gas, a part that may have fallen off a car, or, as became the standing joke amongst the European-based drivers, the ant that was crossing the track.

Without intending to criticise the officials, whose only objective was to locate any possible debris or fluid spill which could cause a car to crash, it seemed to Desiré that the number of times the track action was brought to a halt by these inspections was over the top, to the point that it was very difficult for any driver to run more than a few laps at a time without interruption. This, together with the ongoing car problems and the length of time it was taking to make any changes, meant that during the first week, even though she spent almost every minute of every day in the pit lane, she actually ran only a mere handful of meaningful laps.

She noted in frustration: "I got more time on the track in a single qualifying period in the Aurora series than I got in a whole week at Indy."

Racing is a sport whose fans are legend and, like Le Mans, Indy spectators are a race apart. With the event lasting a full month, the race draws enthusiasts from all 50 states of the USA and from countries around the world, many of whom spend every day of the entire month at the track. Many will have attended every Indy 500 since their infancy, first attending in the arms of their parents, later carrying their own children, and then coming as full families with grandparents, children and grand children together. Many would sit in the same seats every year, seats that were reserved, by Indy, for its most faithful fans and handed down from generation to generation. Thus, for many, the month of Indy was more than a race, it was a reunion of friends, an outpouring of enthusiasm, a chance to let inhibitions go, a chance, perhaps, to drink way too much beer.

The enthusiasm spread from the most sophisticated to the most base, as could be witnessed amongst the recreational vehicles parked side-by-side along 16th Street, the main thoroughfare that passed by the entrance to the Speedway infield. Here, drunken fans could be heard late into the night, playing loud music, singing along, cheering and jeering at passing fans, and ogling girls, almost always accompanied by the theme phrase of the Indy 500,

"Show us your tits!"

When Des started practice on the first Monday of race month, she found a group of these enthusiasts ensconced in the stands immediately behind her pit box. Obviously not fans of Janet Guthrie, this group was very evidently not in favour of another woman driver shredding the traditions of male macho Indy. The group attended every day's practice and spent much of their time catcalling, jeering, and asking Des to remove her top.

Instead of an angry response, or even ignoring the unfriendly calls, Des responded with smiles and laughs, making a point to stand at the fence to shake hands, talk, and laugh with members of this group. Within a few days, their attitude changed from taunts to full support. It wasn't long before the grandstand, full of orange T-shirted fans, rose to cheer and clap every time she left the pits or returned from the track, quickly becoming as loud and vociferous in her support as they had been in her opposition, just a few days before.

Tight Fit. *The '81 Eagle wasn't the world's safest car. I was constantly aware of how dangerous it was if Des had hit the wall.*
(Courtesy David Hutson)

So, it was with no surprise that, when Des walked down pit lane towards her car for the start of the morning open practice session before Saturday's qualifying, the grandstand section behind her pit, now completely filled with orange T-shirts, stood, whistled, and clapped as she approached. What was a surprise, however, was the 30 foot-long banner they unfolded: "Superboobs 82."

Des was very much a centre of attention and, thanks to extensive media cover, under immense pressure. This pressure was made more intense by her bad luck (or was this scripted?) in drawing the number one qualifying position, so, when she left pit lane to make her first qualifying run, the pressure on her was enormous. She wasn't just a rookie and not simply the only woman in the field. She was the centre of attention for 150,000 rabid race fans, every team in the field, and every other driver. Yet she amazed everyone with her ability to put this pressure aside and focus on her job. Despite the bad luck that kept her from the race, Desiré was able to prove, through the month of May, that she, a woman in a male world, could stand up to pressures that would fold many a male at the knees.

Then there was the Gordon Smiley situation. Gordon, remember, was Des' team-mate in the Melchester Tyrrell Formula 1 team in the 1979 season, during which time they became good friends. Because Gordon's wife, Barbara, was only able to come over from America to be with him for a few short trips during the year, Gordon was often lonely and turned to us for company and for support in what was, for him, a very traumatic year. A year made much worse by the difficult relationship he endured with Brian Kreisky, who owned Des' Tyrrell and who took great pleasure in taunting the American at every opportunity. At one point during the year Gordon suffered a psychological breakdown and was admitted to Dartford Hospital, whose old-style buildings and English social medical system he quickly came to hate and which did nothing to aid his recovery. Seeing how miserably unhappy he was, Des and I checked him out and brought him home, where Des nursed him back to health.

I arrived in Indianapolis, from England, an hour or so before Des' qualifying attempt, and stood with Barbara Smiley as Gordon prepared for his run, fifth in the line of the 60-odd drivers attempting to qualify for the race.

Des ran first, but came into the pits when the team waved her off after three laps. She moved her car to the back of the line so as to make her second qualifying run, not happy with the tyres fitted for her first attempt.

Gordon was fifth in line – and in a state. His friend, Gilles Villeneuve, had been killed at Zolder, in Belgium, the previous day.

He was overwhelmed by the pressure of the qualifying for the 500. Indy qualifying consisted of a single car on track at a time, doing two warm-up laps followed by four flying (timed) laps and one slowing down lap. The average speed of the four flying laps sets the 'mark.' In 1981 drivers were under great pressure to reach the 'magic' speed of 200mph and all morning Gordon had been hyper, hardly standing still, totally wound-up in his intent to break the 200 mark.

While Des, Derek and others tried to calm him down, she and I were not overly surprised at his state of mind, having seen him display similar, if less extreme, anxiety back in the UK. Gordon left the pits

If Only the Bird Would Fly. *The '81 Eagle was a dramatic-looking car with a very unusual approach to ground effect technology. Although it went well with the Chevy V8 for which it was designed, it was much less effective when fitted with the Cosworth DFX that Des ran at Indy. (Courtesy IMS Photo)*

with wheels spinning, raced up to speed, completed his first warm-up lap, and then started on his second. We watched the lone car turn into Turn One and listened as the announcer described his passage through Turn Two and down the long back straight.

"He's crashed, Smiley has crashed in Turn Three."

The announcer said nothing more and the public address system went silent.

Derek Mower turned to the crew and swore in frustration, "The fool. The stupid fool." A sentiment repeated by many along the pit lane and acceptable because most accidents at Indy, while violent and car-destroying, usually result in little more than damage to the driver's ego and hard work for the mechanics.

Very quickly, however, it became apparent that something very bad had happened.

Even though I was standing right next to Barbara, I didn't see the officials who quickly came and took her away, but we all saw the instant response from the rescue crews. Trucks and wreckers immediately started and raced back up the pit lane into Turn Four and out of sight as they hastened to the accident scene. These were followed by a number of official cars – a very unusual sight, as these seldom went to accident scenes.

This was bad. The pit lane soon reflected the severity of the crash. People stood around in small groups, some just staring at the ground, some talking quietly, others looking up at the PA speakers, waiting to hear word of Gordon's condition.

Smiley's crew quietly, but quickly, packed their tools and tyres onto their pit wagon and towed it back down the pit lane, into Gasoline Alley and to their garage. Des' crew followed behind, towing the Eagle with Des sitting in the cockpit, to avoid her having to interact with the crowds that were becoming denser and denser as they approached the garage. Moving people aside, the crew opened the garage, parked the car, and closed the door against the crush of silent fans who, by now, had completely blocked the roadway.

We stood around in silence in the small garage, some 12 or so of us, not knowing what to say. No one wanted to be the first to suggest that Gordon might be dead. A few minutes, that seemed like hours later, Derek Mower walked in and quietly gave us the terrible news. Gordon had been killed instantly.

It's very difficult to describe the feelings that saturated the small garage. There were a few muffled sobs but very little conversation. No one wanted to leave the room, no one wanted to face the mob outside who suspected, but didn't know, the truth. Gordon's crew went to one side, while Des' mechanics began to work halfheartedly on her car, trying to give their minds something else to think about, but with any thoughts of getting it ready for a second qualifying run that afternoon well and truly set aside. A few people from other teams came in to offer their commiserations, for although Gordon's death hadn't been officially announced, the word was out and everyone seemed to know.

We waited for some time before a truck backed-up to the garage, allowing the crew to unload the shattered remains of the March.

The severity of the accident was immediately apparent. Apart from the engine which had broken away from the car under impact, nothing left of the car was bigger than the remains of the foot box, a distorted piece of aluminium no bigger than 2ft x 2ft 6in in size. Every other piece could be carried in one hand. Even the gearbox was in two separate pieces, its internals twisted and broken by the impact. This wasn't the debris from a car crash; it was more like the residue of an explosion. The remains were simply thrown away. Gordon had no chance of surviving such a wreck.

Des and I left the track and returned to the hotel, where we stayed in a room, not wanting to talk to anyone. Des had very little to say and I could see that she was bottling up her emotions. Gordon had been a friend, as well as team-mate, and his death wasn't easy to take.

When I turned on the TV it was full of graphic images of the crash, images which Des didn't want to watch, so, while she turned away I, drawn, I suppose, by morbid curiosity, watched as the crash was repeated over and over again, both in real time and in excruciating slow motion.

Drivers handle the death of their compatriots in many ways, but a common thread, always, is the need to know and understand the cause of the accident. Somehow, if they know that the accident was caused by driver error, the fatality is easier to deal with. If it's caused by car failure or by other factors out of the driver's control, they feel vulnerable and, perhaps, scared for themselves.

I insisted that Des watch to see what happened and finally she did. She sat up and silently viewed yet another replay of the crash, thought for a while and said,

"OK, it was his fault."

While this didn't lessen the sadness that she felt, I could see that, by recognising the basic driving error Gordon had made, she could now live with the situation, confident that she would not make a similar mistake.

The error that killed Gordon was as simple as it was tragic. Brought up in the world of road racing, where the natural instinct when a car starts to spin is to turn the steering wheel into the slide, so correcting the breakaway, Gordon had immediately reacted this way when the car, entering Turn Three far too quickly, had broken away at the rear. By applying opposite lock he instinctively tried to stop the car from spinning, but on a banked oval and with ground effect technology designed into the car, it overreacted, turned sharply to the right, and plunged head-on into the outer wall, where the impact came at nearly 200mph. Death was instant.

The shocked crew wasn't willing to run the car on the second day of qualifying, so Des and I stayed away from the track, returning on Monday morning to try to get the car up to speed.

Dan Gurney was a big help to Des during the week after Gordon's crash, giving her confidence in herself by telling everyone who would listen that she was lapping at 192mph, although running only 198mph on the straights. He refused to let his driver, Mike Mosley, drive Des' car, saying that she was already driving it faster than it could go and that she needed a faster engine. Yet Dan underestimated her when he claimed that she had been affected badly by Gordon's death.

He didn't know, for example, that Des tried to persuade the team to let her run on Sunday. Not knowing her, he failed to recognise her refusal to show emotion, or the resolve and determination that she hid behind her quiet demeanour.

Late on Monday afternoon, when attempts to get the car to speed were not being successful, Des told me she was going to take all four Indianapolis corners flat out – it was the only way she could get a competitive time.

She climbed into the car and was strapped in by the crew, before setting out for her make-or-break attempt. I was left to ponder, with concern, the stories circulating the Speedway that only Rick Mears and Tom Sneva were ever said to have run all four corners without lifting.

For three laps she allowed the car to build up to racing speed and then, as she flashed past the pits, she called into the radio, saying,

"I'm going for it."

The car turned into the first banked corner at unabated speed and then the yellow lights flashed on and the Speedway suddenly became silent. Derek Mower went completely white and the whole team held their breaths. I heard nothing for a few long seconds, until a calm voice came over the headphones.

"It's OK, I didn't hit anything."

When she returned to the pits, along with an Eagle whose front tyres sported fist-sized holes in the flat spots, she described the near accident.

"The car turned in well," she said, "but as I hit the apex of 1 it just broke away. I started to correct it but then had a vision of Gordon's accident and hauled the wheel in to the left, making the car spin completely around. Then I was able to guide it as it ran backwards down the middle of the track until I got it stopped at the entrance to Turn Two."

Thank goodness Des had watched Gordon's accident on TV, because her natural road racing reactions were tempered by what she had seen and she had responded to the spin in precisely the right way. Derek Mower, completely shaken by such a near miss so soon after Gordon's accident, immediately told the team to put the car away for the night, but Des argued with him, demanding to be allowed to get back on track. While they argued, the crew towed the car to the garage, replaced the wheels, and returned it to the pit lane. Des climbed aboard and immediately ran two laps in excess of 192mph – her fastest laps of the day – then parked the car for the night.

To say that the team was impressed is putting it mildly. They were amazed, both at her speed and the fact that the very nearly disastrous spin hadn't fazed her in the least.

Then there is the story of the missing engine. After the spin, the team decided to switch to their final motor, the brand-new Cosworth designated as the race engine. Des was thrilled. Now she would have the latest specification motor with much more horsepower. The car was sure to fly. Qualifying would be easy.

Bad news. There was no new motor. All she had was the old, rebuilt, Rookie Test engine. The new engine was sitting in one of the Bobby Unser-managed, Josele Garza driven, brand-new March 82Cs. The Fletcher team wasn't amused!

The week went from bad to worse: the rebuilt engine blew within four laps of being fitted. The team rented an engine from Al Unser's team – it also blew before she could get up to speed. Finally, they rented an engine from Mario Andretti's team, which Des immediate realized was way more powerful than any of the others she had used ... but it, too, blew within four laps! Later inspection showed that there was a blockage in the fuel-injection system which caused the engines to run too lean.

So, Des and the Eagle didn't get another chance to qualify.

When Desiré failed to qualify for the Indianapolis 500, she joined many famous and brilliant drivers who also went home early, in other months of May. Drivers that have included future four-time winner Rick Mears and Indycar champions such as Emerson Fittipaldi and Al Unser Jnr.

Indy is a unique event, where otherwise undistinguished drivers have starred, champions have failed, legends have been created, and some of the world's greatest drivers have simply walked away, uncomfortable with the speeds, the walls, and the peculiar traditions of the event. Not making the field may have been one of Desiré's greatest disappointments, but it did little to lessen the respect she gained amongst the other drivers, the fans, and the media who attended the Speedway during May 1982. They all knew that, with a just a little bit of luck and with equipment the equal of other cars in the field, she would have been a certain qualifier in the world's greatest race.

17

CART RACING

Des returned to Indy in May 1983, at the invitation of Herb and Rose Wysard. Their brand-new March 83C was being driven by former Ensign, Tyrrell, and Williams Formula 1 star Derek Daly. Their 1982 model March, run at Indy the previous year by Johnny Parsons Junior, was on standby as a back-up car for the Irishman.

Herb and Rose were property developers from California whose enthusiasm for racing brought them to Indy, as one of the many small teams with bags of enthusiasm, limited resources, and the hope they might get to race in the top-half of the field. For 1983, however, they had a brand-new car that was capable of winning races – at least when it came out of the factory. In Derek Daly they had a rookie with a major reputation in Formula 1 racing, who had driven extremely well in the pre-Indy 500 rounds of the CART Championship on the Phoenix and Atlanta ovals.

Flushed with enthusiasm and, perhaps, with a sense that Derek might not stay with the team for long, they invited Des to join them, offering her the older car to run during the opening days of May, but with no promises of allowing her to qualify. They just wanted to give her a chance to show her skills, but couldn't afford to run the car for the whole month of the race, especially as their team only had two engines.

Des sat in the car on just two days and quickly got up to speed, but her short opportunity ended early when Derek's engine blew and hers was handed over to Derek. Although she didn't get a chance to qualify for the race, it wasn't a wasted opportunity; she had met and worked with Rose and Herb and to impress them with her ability, determination, and personality. It also put her at the top of Rose's shopping list when Derek announced, after finishing 19th in the 1983 race, that he was leaving the team. Having spent the past few seasons driving for top Formula 1 organisations like Williams and Tyrrell, the small and under-financed Wysard team had come as quite a shock to his system.

Des received the call from Rose while competing at the Oulton Park Gold Cup race, where she was driving a Porsche 908, with a view to possibly joining the team for the rest of the season.

We flew back to New York and Des immediately went on to Indianapolis. There she ran her CART Rookie Test at Indianapolis Raceway Park, a small road course near the Speedway, before travelling in the team transporter up to Cleveland for the 500 kilometre race.

This event, a round of the prestigious CART PPG IndyCar World Championship, attracted 38 cars to the Burke Lakefront Airport, where a temporary circuit had been set up on the airport runways. Fast, wide, and very bumpy, the track offered the potential for almost unlimited overtaking, ensuring that the event would attract a large crowd.

Sure enough, race weekend opened in hot, humid weather in front of thousands of enthusiastic fans. For Des, the experience of competing in the CART series was very new and very exciting. Here, at last, was an opportunity to run with the very best American drivers, Mario Andretti, Al Unser Snr and Jnr, Tom Sneva, Rick Mears, Danny Ongais, Johnny Rutherford, and a host of Indianapolis heroes. Forget that the under-financed Wysard team was hardly noticeable amongst such big name teams as Penske, Truesports, Newman-Haas, and Patrick Racing – this was a chance to drive a powerful race car on a road course at the top level of American road racing.

Des was eighth-fastest in the first practice session, something of an eye-opener to many in the pit lane. So, when the time came to get ready for the first official qualifying session, Des was quietly confident that she could easily do better as she became more familiar with car and track.

She left the pits, ran two laps, and came back in complaining that there was something wrong with the turbo pressure-limiting pop-off valve. The crew removed the engine cover, couldn't see a problem, and then talked Des through the system for setting pop-off levels from within the cockpit. She went back on the track and immediately returned.

"It's still not working." She said, "It's popping off way too soon. There's just no power."

The pop-off valve was intended to limit the power and extend engine life, the pressure being regulated by CART. The system used a heavy spring which compressed when turbo pressure reached the mandated limit, reducing turbo pressure, which it did with a distinct 'popping' sound – hence the name – not unlike a kitchen pressure cooker.

To ensure that all pop-off valves worked at exactly the same pressure, CART owned and controlled every unit and issued them to teams on a random basis for every session. CART also recognised that some pop-off valves would, inevitably, not work correctly, so they had agreed that any team suffering pop-off problems could call for a replacement which would be installed on the car in pit lane, under the watchful eye of a CART technical inspector.

The Wysard team called for a replacement, but, instead, were approached by CART's technical chief, who ruled that no replacement would be made as he believed the valve was fine. He got quite agitated when Des and the team insisted there was a problem and he blamed the problem on Des' lack of experience with turbocharged engines.

The more the team argued, the more the official dug in, wasting the remaining qualifying time while Des sat, frustrated, in the car in pit lane. The session ended with Des' only recorded lap time a full 2.5 seconds slower than her first, track learning, practice laps just an hour or so earlier. 23rd of 36 cars, with only 25 cars allowed to start the race.

The pop-off valve was removed from the car and taken back to the CART trailer for inspection, where it was immediately found to be faulty. Des was right,

CART was wrong. But there was still a session to go. She completed her first two laps relatively slowly but, then, as she began to get up to speed along the back straight, her left front wheel detached itself from the car and rolled across the safety zone to the edge of the airfield.

One of the best attributes of CART-type racing, especially when compared to European traditions, is that the organizers usually do everything they can to keep cars in the race, often dispatching tow vehicles into the heat of competition to bring a wounded car back to the pit lane, where it can be repaired and returned to the race. Typically at CART events, stranded cars were towed quickly back to the pits. But Des' March was left on the side of the track, so, without an opportunity to run at speed, she would start a disappointing 23rd.

The whole team was angry and frustrated at the two situations that had prevented her from qualifying well. Rose and Herb tried to get an explanation from race control, returning convinced that, for some reason, their team and Desiré were the subject of discrimination and unfair rulings; a judgment which was hard to avoid in the light of CART's own rules and regulations.

Race day temperatures soared to 100°F and humidity was around 99.9 per cent. The drivers – clad in long-john underwear, three layers of Nomex fireproofing, and their heads encased in a balaclava and tight fitting helmet – faced more than 3½ hours of intense competition, roasting in the close confines of the cockpit, where the temperature would rise well above 130°F.

The first lap at Cleveland is always a mess, as the 25 car field enters the tight first turn five or more cars abreast and there are always incidents. Sure enough, two cars in the middle of the pack ahead hit each other, causing those following to scramble in avoidance. Someone got sideways in front of Des so she deliberately spun her March to avoid him, having to get a tow start from a rescue truck before lining up at the back of the field for the rolling restart of the race. From this inauspicious beginning to her Indycar career, she quickly settled down and soon carved her way through the back of the field until she was comfortably circulating just out of the top ten. She maintained this position for lap-after-lap, running close behind former Champion Tom Sneva, making no mistakes and conserving her energy.

It was one of the hottest races on record and

several drivers had to quit with exhaustion, some even needing oxygen to revive them. Des carried on, circulating steadily, although I could see that she, too, was beginning to feel the effects of the heat. Every time she came into the pits to refuel, Rose would ask her if she wanted to quit, saying that they had a standby driver available. But Des refused, simply asking that water be thrown over her. After that, at each pit stop, a full bucket was dumped on her shoulders and she soon found herself driving around with several inches of water surging around her legs and seat.

Eventually the race dragged to an end, 3¾ hours after it started, with Desiré finishing in tenth position. Her final lap, after receiving the chequered flag, was very slow and I thought that she might be on the verge of passing out, so I asked for a medical team to be on hand when she came into the pits.

To everyone's surprise, she stopped the car in the pit lane and sprang out, sweaty and bedraggled, but looking remarkably fit. The waiting TV interviewer, the photographers, and the mob of people crowding around her car were amazed at her condition, impressed no-end by her performance in the race and the stamina that enabled her to last through the hours of heat. It was a great start to her CART career and a great result for her first ever Indycar race, for which she was presented with the Hilton Hotel 'Hang Tough' Award.

The season's next Indycar event was the Michigan 500, but instead of driving, Desiré found herself in the radio announcers box assisting with the nationwide broadcast of the event, thanks to a pair of injured legs that prevented her from racing. Driving in the Momo March Porsche IMSA GTP car the week after Cleveland, she had suffered an enormous accident: a suspension failure caused the car to launch into a series of barrel rolls, destroying the car, breaking her right leg, and badly bruising and spraining her left foot. As a result, the Wysards brought Geoff Brabham in to drive their car, which he took to an 18th place finish. But she was determined to drive two weeks later, at Road America.

Despite undergoing therapy, neither her foot nor her leg were, by any means, healed in time for the race, but, as she was insistent on driving, she had me cut off the plaster cast and – not wanting anyone to know the extent of her injuries, which could have resulted in the CART doctors forbidding her to drive – she also abandoned her crutches.

She hobbled into the paddock on the Thursday afternoon to find a team that was almost completely different from the crew that had supported her at Cleveland. Herb and Rose had brought Donnie Barsala as their new crew chief and he had, in turn, replaced most of the mechanics, keeping just two of the previous crew. More significantly, Barsala had made major changes to the car. All the cockpit-adjustable driver aids, such as brake balance and front and rear sway bar adjustment levers, had been removed. Worse, he had replaced the limited-slip differential system with a locked system – common to sprint cars and used on the ovals, but certainly not compatible with road racing.

When Des asked what had happened to the brake and sway bar adjustments, Barsala said that he would be responsible for the car setup and that she should just drive the car: he didn't want her interfering with the setup that he wanted! Hardly a good start to the relationship.

Barsala's motives for this soon became evident. He had very little working experience with Indy cars, having spent his career in short-track dirt-oval racing, where the traditional role of the crew chief was to exercise complete control over the car setup and where the driver would, in fact, just drive. That this was absolutely not the case in road racing was completely alien to him. He had no concept of the driver's need to balance braking forces between front and rear axles as fuel loads changed, or the importance of being able to adjust front or rear sway bars, changing the handling characteristics of the car as tyre wear increased or track conditions changed.

The decision to switch to a locked differential was even worse and, with this sprint car setup, the car's predominant handling characteristic would be extreme understeer when powering into a corner and when accelerating along the exit trajectory, making the car extremely difficult to drive smooth or fast.

This was certainly the case with the Wysard March and the problem was made worse by Desiré's injuries. With feet and legs still painful from the IMSA crash, she also found that her leg muscles had weakened considerably while in their plaster casts, making it impossible to use the brakes properly; she just couldn't push down hard enough.

During qualifying, she struggled to get the car handling correctly, so, she asked Barsala to manually adjust the sway bars in an effort to balance the car. Each time she asked, he would go the front and rear of the car, look down at the suspension, and then come back to her and tell her that they weren't adjustable. Frustrated, she simply got on with the task of driving the car as it was. But, immediately after the session ended, she took a look for herself: both bars were normal and easy to adjust. Barsala just couldn't figure out what to do. A few minutes later, he took her to the back of the transporter, where no one could overhear their conversation and asked her to explain to him how sway bars worked!

Despite all these problems, Des qualified the car 12th out of 35 cars and, in the race, found herself fighting for tenth position amongst a tight group of cars that included Pete Halsmer, Howdy Holmes, and Tom Sneva.

Then, second gear started playing-up; sometimes it would go in, sometimes not. As a consequence, she began to drop back from the group. Then the yellow flags came out, signifying a full course caution. She saw them for the first time just as she started to accelerate out of the tight Canada Corner and immediately slowed down. She tried to get second gear, but the 'box jammed and, instead, locked-up the rear wheels. The car spun to the infield – right into the path of an approaching rescue vehicle. The two cars struck each other, the smaller March sliding its nose under the chassis of the wrecker. For a few minutes there was chaos, as workers jumped out of the truck to see if she was OK and to get her out of the car. Then a second wrecker had to be called to free the March. There was surprisingly little damage to the car and she was able to get back in, accept a tow start, and drive back to the pits.

When the race resumed, she was back on course, a lap or so down, but in the same racing group as before, with Holmes and Halsmer in front and Tom Sneva behind. They resumed their battle.

With no cockpit adjustments available and her inability to brake hard, she was struggling; but the lurid power-slides she induced to overcome the limitations of the locked diff made for great spectator viewing. Despite the handicap, she was still able to hold her place in the battle around her, but was eventually put out of the race when a yellow flag came out, the front three cars slowed, and Sneva, engrossed in the battle, slammed into the rear of Des' March, launching his car over her head and smashing it's gearbox onto her right-front suspension. She drove slowly back to the pits and climbed out.

A few minutes after the end of the race, she was

Des Leads Danny Ongais at Road America. Driving with a recently broken leg and with a car that she wasn't allowed to adjust during the race, Des fought hard to get to the top ten, until gearbox problems led to a series of dramas. Her performance upset some of the old-school oval drivers. (Courtesy RMA-Torres)

approached by an official, telling her that she was needed for a meeting with Wally Dallenbach, CART's highly respected Chief Steward.

He showed her an official protest note, signed by several drivers, including oval expert Pancho Carter. The protest claimed that, due to her inexperience and inability to drive an Indy car, she should be banned from competing at subsequent events!

She was astounded and so were several SCCA officials standing nearby in the control tower, who immediately collected a petition of their own from workers around the circuit. This told Wally that Des wasn't only one of the best drivers in the field, but that she was also the most polite – and respectful of faster cars.

Wally dismissed Pancho's protest out of hand, but the incident left a sour taste in Des' mouth. Was the discrimination she had faced in qualifying at Cleveland now spreading to some of the older, oval-based drivers?

The next race was to be at Pocono, a very fast and tricky Superspeedway and was to be her first experience of actually racing in such an event. Just before the start of the race, she asked me to take a look at one of her crewmen. I did and I saw the crewman's pupils were very dilated and he had a

Super Speedway. *Pocono was Desiré's first super speedway race. She raced through the field, passing Al Unser Snr, among others, in the first few laps, but then had a major accident when a universal joint broke, throwing the March into the wall at Turn One. (Courtesy RMA-Torres)*

dreamy, far away look on his face. As we had already heard rumours of drug use by some of the crew and their associates, this seemed to confirm our fears. For a while, Des was on the verge of refusing to drive the car, not knowing whether the mechanic had done his job of preparing the car or not, but she eventually decided that she had to take the chance.

Starting 18th of the 35 or so cars, after running out of fuel after just one lap in qualifying, she lost a lot of ground at the start, but then quickly worked her way back up the field to 13th, passing, among others, Al Unser Snr on the way. Al was later to comment that he was so concerned with the bad handling of her car that he left her plenty of room. The handling was due to the car's setup. Barsala had set the car up for minimum downforce and minimum

drag, a good policy for an experienced driver like Tom Sneva (whose setup he had copied), but hardly the setup to impose on a rookie driver in their first Superspeedway race. It would have been far better to have started with more downforce and, then, over the period of the weekend, progressively flatten the wings as the driver became more confident in the car. Still, Des had coped and the accident, when it came, had nothing to do with the setup.

Des happened to be the car nearest pit-in when the first yellow caution period of the race began and she was able to duck into the pits for fuel a full lap sooner than the race leaders, which put her right behind the pace car when she came out of the pits. Recognising that she was slower than the real leaders, Rick Mears, Mario Andretti, and John Paul Jnr, she planned to

Women in Racing. *Des and Rose Wysard wait for the car to come into the pit lane from the paddock. Rose, Herb, and Jeff Wysard put everything they could into their small team, providing Des with some of the most memorable racing of her career.*
(Courtesy Wilson Collection)

There was immediate chaos. Mears managed to find a way by, but John Paul and Mario slammed into her car, followed by several others. Des immediately called back to the pits on her radio and apologised to the team for crashing, believing that the car had just got away from her.

While the track was cleared and the race restarted, Des was taken to the medical centre and then to the local hospital, where her legs were X-rayed to see if she had suffered any further injuries. Fortunately, she had only sustained more bruises, so she was able to return to the track – where she found that she was the subject of a typical Mario rant against rookie drivers. In contrast, John Paul simply asked if Des was OK.

As the mechanics had already packed the wrecked March in the transporter and left the track, Des was unable to look over the car. The ride in the ambulance had given her a chance to try to work out why she had crashed and, after a lot of thought, she came to the conclusion that she had done nothing wrong and that there had to be some other reason for the spin. When she talked with the Wysards, on her return to the paddock, she found that Herb had similar doubts. The way the car spun was, he said, totally abnormal.

It wasn't until the very end of the season that Lew Parks, a close friend of the Wysards and the one team mechanic who seemed to believe in Des, told her that the cause had been a broken universal joint, a common failing among 1983 series March Indycars.

The 83C March was badly damaged in the incident, so for the next few races the team brought out their one-year-old 82C version, the same car Des had driven briefly at Indianapolis. But this car was both uncompetitive and very unreliable, breaking in every subsequent race. Nevertheless, she was able to perform well while the car lasted. However, there was one bright spot.

A bolt fell out of the right rear suspension during the race at Mid-Ohio, forcing Des to drive slowly for almost the entire length of the track to get back into the pits. Des did her best to stay off the racing line and out of the way of faster cars. Then, as she approached the famous Mid-Ohio Hill, she saw Pancho Carter approaching. Her car – ever so accidentally – moved a foot or so away from the kerb. After all, with broken suspension, who could have kept the car from straying a little? Pancho, intent on getting past Des' stricken car as quickly as possible, moved to his left and put his outside wheels on the slippery rubber debris along the edge of the narrow racing line, flying

get a really good jump on the restart to allow her to get through Turn One without holding them up, after which it would be easy and safe to let them by. Her plan worked perfectly, and she was already over a hundred yards ahead as the field crossed the restart line, so, she was almost on her own when she turned the car down into to the apex of the first corner. All went well until, when the car was at the lowest point of the banking, it suddenly swapped ends, spun once, and plunged headfirst into the outer wall.

What Can We Do? Des and, Aussie Ron Baddeley, who had previously been Mario Andretti's crew chief, ponder the problems he inherited with the car when he took over as team manager at the Las Vegas race. (Courtesy Wilson Collection)

off onto the grass in a long, slow slide. Des smiled as she watched him struggle to get the car under control. No damage, just payback.

She went on to race the '82 March at Riverside, where gearbox problems in qualifying relegated her to the back of the grid and an overheating engine dropped her from the race after she had worked her way into the top ten. She was happy to have the '83 car returned for her to use at Las Vegas.

This was to be run on a 'roval;' a temporary track laid out in the parking lot of Caesars Palace casino, that, while not a pure oval was, also, not a proper road course. She was, also, happy to find yet another new team of mechanics, this time run by Ron Baddeley, who had been Mario Andretti's crew chief, but who was now working for the Wysards, through the balance of the season, prior to returning to his home in Australia.

What a difference. Unfortunately, Ron's first view of the car was in the garage at Vegas, as he had played no role in the rebuilding of the car or its preparation for this event. So, for the first few practice and qualifying sessions, he and his crew struggled to get it to work properly. For final qualifying it was much improved and Des put in a flyer – a full two seconds faster than she had managed before – to give her a

top ten start. The race was less satisfactory, as the car quickly ate its front tyres and she soon dropped back through the field, before coming into the pits for fuel, a wing adjustment, and new tyres. Then, as she accelerated back into the race, she felt herself struggling for breath and getting really hot. The car was on fire.

She drove through Turn One and steered the car to an opening in the crash barrier, where she knew there would be some corner workers with fire extinguishers.

An Indycar fire is not a typical car fire. Indy cars used methanol instead of gasoline for fuel and methanol burns with a clear flame; the only indications of fire are the extreme heat and shimmering, colourless heat waves. Seeing these, a worker ran past Des to extinguish the fire on the car, without noticing that she, too, was burning. Reports in the following day's Las Vegas paper showed a sequence of pictures of the worker running past her, then her tapping him on the shoulder, pointing to her own flames, then a blast of fire extinguisher fluid over her head and shoulders that put out her fire.

Grateful for his intervention, she raised her visor to say thanks – at which point he put the nozzle of the extinguisher into the opening and blasted her with a face- and lung-full of extinguishing agent. Des promptly dropped to the ground, gasping for breath!

The next race, at Laguna Seca, wasn't particularly successful either (even though Ron had fitted the car with a limited-slip differential), as the engine blew up soon into the race.

The final race of the season was the 200-miler, on the one mile Phoenix oval and Des even managed to get a day's testing in advance. This helped her to qualify 13th and, after 200 miles without a single full course yellow, she finished 11th, being lapped for the first and only time at the beginning of the last lap. With lap times of around 22 seconds, this showed that, despite everything, she was more than competitive in Indy cars and could hold her own against any competition.

Her first year in Indy cars had been fraught with problems and many changes to the team. The team had a very limited budget, which meant that other team's secondhand parts were often used. Yet she had done well enough to prove that she belonged in America's top road racing series.

1984 was much less successful and after failing to make the grid at Long Beach in the '83 March (mainly due to problems which limited her practice and qualifying time), she arrived at Indy hoping to make her way into the field.

Unfortunately this wasn't to be. With yet another new team manager – this time a German who had never been to Indy before – and a year-old car, she was already at a disadvantage. But the car was distinctly worse than it had been the previous year, when Derek Daly had qualified it at 197.74mph: the Pocono accident had significantly damaged the car. The team, instead of replacing the carbon fibre monocoque tub, repaired the chassis by cutting the tub in two and riveting on an aluminium nose section. While the workmanship was exquisite, the repair failed to meet one very important requirement which, at Indy in particular, was a major problem. The very high cornering speeds and severe G-forces caused the car to flex, loose stability, and handle inconsistently, with the result that it was both difficult to drive safely on the limit and it wasn't as fast as it had been the previous year.

Des struggled with the car through the first week of practice, while she tried to get it up to speed. Despite asking for key changes to be made to the setup to resolve some of the handling issues, she was simply told that the problem was her driving, not the car, so no changes were made. This led to Des making the decision to get out of the car and leave the team.

This, of course, led to a flurry of media releases as the team tried to justify their preparation of the car and they eventually hired Indy veteran Johnny Parsons Jnr to drive the car. In order to justify their contention that the slow speeds were a driver, not a car problem, they made a point of telling the media that Johnny would drive the car exactly as Des had left it.

Des had run laps in the region of 196mph before she quit. Johnny's first few days in the car saw speeds no greater than 188mph. Only when the team finally began to respond to his requests to make changes similar to those that Des had requested did he get over the 190 mark. He failed to qualify for the race.

Desiré was very disappointed to have to leave the team, but she had become very uncomfortable with the contention that lack of speed was a driver issue and the team's failure to work with her to get the handling sorted. While she really liked Herb and Rose Wysard and respected the effort that they put into their small team, she now realised that her career would never prosper if she continued to run

at the back of the field in a year-old, underpowered, unreliable, and bad handling car. She didn't drive an Indycar again until 1986.

In the interim, Des did very little racing. Three World Endurance races, in Porsche 962s, a British Formula 3000 race at Brands Hatch, driving for Derek Mower, in which she finished a close fourth to Damon Hill, and a few drives in Saleen Mustang production cars did little to keep her busy. The rest of the time she worked as a Pace Car driver for PPG, the series sponsor for the CART championship. This enabled her to travel to all the Indycar races and it was at one of these, Pocono, in mid 1986, that she had a chance conversation with Andy Kenopensky, the irascible and unconventional team manager of the Machinists Union Indycar team.

The Machinists Union had run a team in the Indy series for many years, but, thanks to lack of funds, was never a consistent front runner. Nevertheless, the team was well presented, appeared at all the races, and was a key part of the CART family. Des and Andy happened to be standing at the fence watching a practice session, when she asked him who was going to replace the injured Mike Nish in the car for Mid-Ohio. She suggested he give her a chance.

Andy called a week later, offering her the drive. He had needed to go to the Machinists Union Board to get permission for a woman (and a South African at that) to drive the car.

She raced the Machinists Union March three times. At Mid-Ohio she qualified in 18th place, a typical starting position for the Machinist's cars. She made up a few positions in the early laps and was following team leader Josele Garza, when he had a major accident at the end of the short straight in front of the pit lane. Des passed under the ensuing flying debris without damage and continued to the end of the race, finishing 13th.

Andy was extremely happy with her performance, as she had brought the team its first race finish in many races and he confirmed that she would drive the car for the final two races of the year. There would be no second car, as Garza was too badly injured and the team was now down to their last car.

At Road America, driving in torrential rain, she was positioned around 12th, after a restart, when she found herself joining several cars that plunged off the end of the straight. She had moved across to allow race leader Michael Andretti to move up on her inside on the approach to the corner and, because of

Fast Work. *The Machinist Union team makes short work of a pit stop at Mid-Ohio, during Des' first drive with the team. (Courtesy RMA-Torres)*

the spray from the cars in front of her, was caught by standing water on the much wetter outside line.

Her final race in an Indycar was at Laguna Seca and it summed up the hassles and problems that were so much a part her Indycar career.

The engine misfired from the minute she drove out of the pit lane for the first practice session and, despite the efforts of the team and their engine builder, the problem was never resolved. It soon became evident that the problem lay deep inside the motor. She asked for the engine to be replaced, but was told that the team had no money for two rebuilds. She would have to persevere with the one she had. Unsurprisingly, it blew up during the race. And there ended her Indy car career.

Des was the third woman ever to race an Indy car and she opened the door for a new wave of lady drivers with her competitive driving and friendly attitude, which earned her the respect of her competitors. Subsequently, a number of other women have successfully raced Indy cars, including Lyn St James, who was the first Indy 500 female Rookie of the Year; Sarah Fisher, the first woman to earn an Indycar pole position and who now runs her own race team; Danica Patrick, who has become a highly paid sports star in America and who became the first woman to win an Indycar race (Motegi in Japan); Katherine Legge, and Simona De Silvestro, perhaps the lady racer with the greatest potential of them all.

Wet Work. *Conditions were so bad at Road America that the race was called off and restarted the following weekend. (Courtesy RMA-Torres)*

18

F*****G FAST HAUSFRAU

ESPITE – or because of – their 1980 experiences, both Alain and Desiré wanted to return to Le Mans. Alain, realising that the now three-year-old DeCadenet wouldn't be eligible when the new Group C class began, commissioned the design of an all new Ford-powered car. That car wouldn't be finished until 1982, so, for the 1981 Le Mans, he rented the DeCadenet to a Belgian team, leaving Des without a drive.

However, things looked good the following year, with the new car being close to completion a few weeks prior to the 1982 race. But, when the bodywork was brought in to be mated to the chassis, it was found to be too small in key dimensions and wouldn't fit. With the new car now unavailable, Alain loaned his 3.9-litre Ford engine to the GRID team owned by Ian Dawson and Giuseppe Risi. The other driver would be Des' old Aurora sparring partner, the Spanish nobleman Emilio De Villota. This looked to be a good match as Desiré had previously driven the car with Emilio at Mid-Ohio and Pocono in 1981.

Unfortunately, the neat Graham Humphreys-designed car, while competitive on tighter tracks, was out of its depth at Le Mans, thanks to it's high downforce, high drag design. Consequently, the car struggled to get enough speed down the long straight, leading the team to run a shorter top gear ratio than normal. Despite Alain's objections and offer of suitable gears, the team persisted. Just 24 minutes into the race, with Emilio driving, the car burnt a piston when trying to slipstream a faster car down the Mulsanne straight.

The promise of Alain's new car seemed bright, until he found himself in the midst of a bizarre ownership struggle. Recognising the potential of the new car and having a financial stake in the project with Alain, Ford Motor Company decided that it wanted the car to be handed over to the Ford Germany racing division, to be developed and run by Zakspeed. Following extensive negotiations, threats of legal action, and the midnight subterfuge of the car disappearing from the designer's workshop, a settlement was reached. The result, as far as Desiré was concerned, was that another potentially competitive drive went out the window.

Incidentally, Zakspeed, having taken over development of the car, turned it into the Ford C100, a quick, but ultimately unsuccessful car, whose best-ever finish was to come at Brands Hatch, in 1982, in the hands of Desiré and Jonathan Palmer ... but that's another story.

Le Mans 1983 was to become one of Desiré s most memorable events.

A chance meeting at Riverside, in California, with former sports car racer and now the Porsche customer racing manager, Jurgen Barth, led to the opportunity to drive a new Porsche 956 for the 1983 Le Mans race. Jurgen had watched Des drive a bulky and undeveloped March to fourth place, in the early season's IMSA GTP event at Riverside, only to see the car break. While commiserating her on her bad luck, he said that he would try to see if he could arrange a drive at Le Mans as compensation for her ever-present misfortune or, as he described, he wanted to do something to stop the angels from pissing on her head!

A few weeks later, he called, telling her that if she would pay her own way to France, she could drive a new 956 for the Obermeyer team, a car owned by Jurgen Lassig.

We arrived at Le Mans and immediately made our way to the Obermeyer transporter, to a cold and

Oh Really! Alan tries selling Jurgen Barth a bridge in Brooklyn. Des remains sceptical! Jurgen has been a good friend ever since he and Des raced against each other in the World Endurance Championship, and was instrumental in setting up the Porsche drive at Le Mans. (Courtesy Ranier Hämmer)

unfriendly reception. Not from Lassig, who spoke almost no English and simply gave a quick hello, but from a dour and surly team of mechanics. Despite language difficulties, we quickly realised that the team were simply annoyed that Jurgen had given a ride in their new car to a mere woman!

With the icy atmosphere came little or no cooperation as Desiré tried to get fitted into the seat; very necessary because she was significantly smaller than both Lassig and the team's lead driver, German Formula Supervee National Champion Axel Plankenhorn. Eventually, we did the work ourselves while the mechanics silently looked on.

The unfriendliness continued through to the start of Wednesday's practice. Lassig was first to go out. He ran a few laps, at not very competitive speeds and then handed over to Axel who upped the momentum at once, putting in a few very fast, competitive laps. The mechanics were pleased and even smiled – until the time came for Desiré to get into the car, when the dour faces returned.

Her first impressions of the car gave her immediate confidence, so she quickly increased her pace until, entering the very difficult Indianapolis corner on her third lap in the car, she realised she was approaching at far too high a speed.

She prepared herself for a big impact, braked as hard as she could, and turned into the corner, waiting for the Porsche to fly off the road and into the barriers. Instead, it simply turned the corner without any histrionics, leaving Des blown away by the car's road holding and powerful ground effect; it was far better than anything she had ever experienced. With new-found confidence she increased her speed, soon realising that the car could be driven very quickly and with complete safety.

It took her just one more flying lap to get up to full speed and to match Axel's best time. Then she went quicker and on the following lap she was faster still. The team called her in and plugged in the computer to check the engine readings, convinced that she must have been revving the hell out of the engine to have gone so fast.

But the readings were perfectly normal. Axel got back into the car and promptly went faster than Des. She got back in and beat his time.

The car ended the first night of practice among the top 12, not bad considering that there were 13 brand-new 956s alone and Obermeyer was the smallest and least competitive of all the Porsche teams.

For qualifying, the next day, I decided to make myself scarce. There's nothing a professional race team hates more than an interfering father, wife, or – God forbid – husband in the pits and, as a result, I have always done my best to stay uninvolved whenever I'm at a track with Desiré.

I hitched a ride to Mulsanne Corner with the mechanic who had been given the task of signalling the lap times from the boxes at the exit of the turn. He was one of the older crew members and spoke less English than I spoke German. But he tried.

As we worked our way through the narrow lanes and farm yards that took us to Mulsanne, he began to talk.

"When we hear," he slowly and haltingly said, "that we have hausfrau in the car, we very sad."

There was a long pause as he struggled to find words.

"We have new car and we have Plankenhorn ... very fast. But hausfrau ... Nein." A long pause ...

"Plankenhorn, he drive very fast. We very happy." Another long pause ...

"Hausfrau. She drive faster. We surprised.

"Plankenhorn. He drive faster. Hausfrau, she drive more faster.

"Plankenhorn, he drive very faster – faster than Hausfrau.

Best Sports Car. Des hustles the Boss Porsche 956 through the Le Mans Esses. She rates the 956 as the best sports car she has ever raced. The Carstensen sticker on its nose reflects Des' tribute to the Johannesburg couple who surprised her with the biggest cheque she ever received. (Courtesy Wilson Collection)

Payback Time. The best part of the 1983 Le Mans race was sharing it with Norman and Heather Carstensen, whose support back in 1981 allowed Des to stay in racing at a time when she had nothing going for her. (Courtesy Wilson Collection)

"Hausfrau, she drive faster than Plankenhorn!"

There was a much longer wait while he struggled to find the right English words.

"F*****g fast hausfrau!"

The race itself was largely uneventful. New fuel economy regulations required a new racing strategy, with ultimate speed offset against the need to conserve fuel. Lassig, having qualified more than 17 seconds per lap slower than Des and Axel, decreed a lap time that all three drivers would maintain. It was a speed at which he was comfortable to race, but that was well below the capabilities of the other two drivers.

Starting from 12th on the grid, the Obermeyer car, resplendent in black bodywork and white pinstripes, as befitting its clothing sponsor Boss, cruised around for hour after hour, maintaining a good, albeit unspectacular, pace with Desiré and Axel doing the bulk of the driving. At around 2.30am they found themselves in fifth place overall, not far behind the leading cars. Then, with Des driving, the car developed a misfire that took two long pit stops, a change of electronic management computer, and much help from the Porsche factory technicians to overcome.

With the car repaired, Des got back up to speed straight away, having lost several positions and frustrated that Lassig still refused to let her or Axel increase the pace to make up lost ground.

The race wore on until the end of the twenty-four hours, the drivers working their way back up the field to seventh, when, with just over an hour to go, it became obvious that the leading cars had begun to dramatically slow their pace. All the cars in front of the Obermeyer Porsche were running low on fuel and needed to run slower to conserve their remaining stock. Yet the black Porsche still had plenty of fuel in the tanks, thanks to its steady, slower pace through the night.

The crew wanted to put Axel into the car for the final hour, believing that he could catch a few of the cars in front, but car owner Lassig chose to drive instead, wanting the glory of crossing the line at the end of the 24 Hours. He droned around, maintaining his slower, steady pace to bring the car home in seventh place.

It was a great result for the team but disappointing to Axel and Desiré; they knew they had the potential to get close to the top three, thanks to their fuel reserves.

19

THE BIG SPORTS CARS

We should have listened to John Webb! After Des failed to qualify for the 1980 British Grand Prix, John sat her down and told her to focus on a career in sports cars. But she had her sights set on the big prize and shrugged off his advice.

John was right, because when Des did race sports cars, the bigger and more powerful the better, she showed that she was among the best sports car racers in the world.

The success she enjoyed with Alain and the de Cad launched Desiré into the top ranks of the world's sports car drivers. It also led the organisers of the annual Kyalami 9 Hours race to contact her to see if she would like to drive a Porsche 935 with Derek Bell, in the November 1980 race, her first opportunity to race in South Africa since her abortive Formula Atlantic forays at the beginning of 1978.

Des was thrilled at the opportunity, but felt that she should ask Derek, first, if it would be OK with him. Even though she was now a well known driver and winner, in both the Aurora Formula One series and in World Championship endurance cars, her respect for Derek, who was already one of the world's best sports car drivers – a winner at Le Mans (which he was eventually to win five times) and a legend in English racing – was such that she wanted to make sure that he wouldn't mind having her as a co-driver.

Derek said that he would be quite happy to have her drive with him, but he cautioned her that she might find the very powerful, evil-handling, turbo-charged Porsche 935 a real handful to drive. He was very careful in the way he cautioned her about the Porsche – he was far too much of a gentlemen to suggest that, at just 135lb and a mere woman, she

might not have the sheer muscle needed to throw the heavy, hard-to-drive Porsche beast around the track at racing speeds!

Des understood Derek's warning. Concerned, she talked the problem over with Jackie Epstein and John Webb, who came up with a solution.

"We'll get you a drive in a 935 at the Brands 6 Hours."

So Des found herself in the pit lane a few weeks later, meeting a tall, scrawny American wearing a black cowboy hat, standing alongside his beautifully presented, multi-striped, 500+ horsepower, twin-turbocharged, ex-John Fitzpatrick, Kremer built Porsche 935.

Preston Henn was unique. He had made most of his wealth by buying up old disused drive-in theatres, all over Florida, that he turned into giant flea markets. He would rent small areas of paving to thousands of traders, who sold just about anything used, abused, new, or secondhand that thousands of paying customers would line up to buy. He called his flea markets the Thunderbird Swap Shops, a name that was scrawled across the top of the windshield of the 935 he had just bought from John Fitzpatrick. In the UK, flea markets are known as boot sales

Based on the road-going Porsche 911 bodyshell, the 934 and then 935, were developed into full-blooded race cars and were the dominant racing sports cars in European and American racing during the late 1970s and early 1980s. The cars were developed to extremes never intended by their designers. They eventually ended up with engines that produced over 750 horsepower; road holding that, while far more advanced than the standard car, was totally inadequate for the power available; and a reputation for being difficult to drive at the limit. They were,

Dynamite. Des was immediately at home in the big, Preston Henn-owned Porsche 935K3, lapping faster than any of the other 935s at Brands Hatch, in her first drive in a turbocharged car. (Courtesy Jeff Bloxham)

perhaps, the most outrageous production-based race cars of all time.

A Porsche 935 won Le Mans in 1979 and many other races in Germany, throughout Europe, and North America. 935s were driven by real men, like John Fitzpatrick, Rolf Stommelen, Hans Stuck, Bob Wollek, Harold Grohs, and Bobby Rahal, who, when he arrived for the 1981 Brands Hatch Flying Tigers 1000 kilometres race, had just clinched the World Sports Car Championship, driving with Bob Garretson.

Desiré's first race in the big brute Porsche was in competition with several top-level 935s, including many that raced regularly in the German championships. She was initially due to share the car with Preston, German journeyman Edgar Dören, and American Skeeter McKitterick, but Skeeter was rudely bumped from the team and Preston chose not to drive, leaving the Des and Edgar to share the driving.

Des soon learned that the top drivers in sports car racing could be less than sympathetic to their cars when Edgar ran one lap, pulled in, got out of the car, went across to the pit counter, took the heaviest hammer he could find, and smashed the driver's side window to pieces, before getting back in and returning to the track. Des had found the interior of the car to be very hot but thought was normal. Edgar, knowing that the heat would soon wear drivers out, solved the problem in his own way. Preston just watched, open jawed, as Edgar desecrated his new car.

I was obviously very interested in Desiré's reaction to driving this car, by far the biggest and most powerful she had ever handled. She was succinct, if not very ladylike: "It's like a brick shithouse blown up by dynamite!"

But then she described how great it was; to feel the full thrust of over 500 horsepower accelerating out of the slow corners; the car sliding under power and requiring handfuls of opposite lock to get it pointed down the straight. She loved the car and took to the extra power so quickly that she was immediately faster than the far more experienced Edgar, who, instead of being upset that she was quicker, became very supportive and helped her with as much guidance and information as he could. He enjoyed the fact that a woman was as fast as any of the other 935 drivers and between sessions went from garage to garage telling the other German drivers how fast she was, taunting them that they couldn't keep up with a girl.

Bad luck struck almost instantly in the race: Des ran over debris from another car's crash, damaging the oil radiator and losing many laps in the pits while repairs were made, before the car was able to return to the track.

While Des was driving I had my own job to do, running circuit operations and looking after spectator facilities, so, when I received a call on the radio from the corner workers at Stirling's Bend, to come out to the corner as soon as I could, I was concerned that something bad had happened. Apparently, it wasn't an emergency, so I ignored the request. Later, after the race in which Des and Edgar had finally finished eighth, I was accosted by the corner crew, from Stirling's, as soon as I entered the Kentagon for the post race party.

"Why didn't you come," they asked. "You really should have seen what we were watching."

They then described how, for lap after lap, they had watched Des bring the Swap Shop 935 through the fast and difficult Dingle Dell corner. In a broad, full blooded power slide, she would emerge from the right-hand corner with the car almost completely sideways across the track, it's nose pointed-in towards the spectator fence. Using the slide to slow the car for the second-gear turn, Des would quickly change direction and have the power full-on before she even reached the apex of Stirling's, again, sliding the car to the exit of the track, under full power and in complete control, before accelerating down to Clearways and the pit straight.

Even though they weren't supposed to take photos or use stopwatches (they were meant to concentrate 100 per cent on their marshalling duties), they had, nevertheless, timed her though the section: they found her to be consistently a full second per lap quicker than anyone else in the race through this 300 yard, two corner sequence. They were amazed at her car control and ability to get the most out of

the brutal Porsche and couldn't refrain from telling everyone around them in the pub how impressed they were.

I left the bar and went down to the timing and scoring office, pulling rank to get access to the race time sheets. Sure enough, Des' fastest race lap was a second a lap faster than the next quickest Porsche, the Bobby Rahal World Championship winning Garretson-built car.

I asked Des how she was able to be so quick through the Dingle Dell/Stirling's complex and she simply said that the car was so well balanced, she was able to slide it from one lock to another under total control, lap after lap. She even remembered seeing the faces of a group of spectators standing at the fence as she watched them over the nose of the car, proving that the corner workers had been correct when they claimed the car to be at 90° to the track!

The plan to share a 953 with Derek Bell at Kyalami eventually fell through. Des did drive a 953 with Dieter Schornstein, although the car lost the engine before she had her second stint. This race was, however, very important to Des because it introduced her to Norman and Heather Carstensen, who had been one of the sponsors of the car through their Carwil Plant Hire company. They soon became friends and the night before we left for England we had dinner with them. We were totally floored when they gave Des an envelope saying that they would like to help her with her racing.

Inside the envelope was a check for R50,000 – a huge amount and far more money than Des and I had ever seen in one place, at one time. Des protested, saying she couldn't accept the gift, but they insisted, telling her to spend it any anyway she liked to further her career. The first portion went to Preston Henn, to buy a ride for Des in the 935 at the next Daytona 24-Hour race.

To Americans, Daytona is the 'world center of motor racing.' It features a complex road course inside one of the biggest, meanest, steepest banked, oldest, and most feared oval race tracks in the world. While American race fans know it as the home of NASCAR and the Daytona 500, Europeans know it as the home of the fabled 24 Hours of Daytona race.

Des was due to share the driving with Preston, Preston's daughter, Bonnie, Janet Guthrie, and Floridian, Marty Hinze, while the Swap Shop team's second car, a Ferrari 512BB running in the GTO class, was to be driven by Bob Wollek, Edgar Dören, and an unknown driver named Randy Lanier. Des was listed to drive both cars. Janet Guthrie turned up at the start of practice, but chose not to race.

Derek Bell was one of the race favourites, sharing a car with Bob Aiken. John Paul Junior shared with his soon-to-be infamous father. The Whittington brothers, Bill and Don (also to later spend time in prison for drug offences), who had won the 1970 Le Mans 24 Hours race, had their 935. Danny Ongais shared another with Ted Field. It was fast and competitive company.

Des took the now even more gaily striped Swap Shop Porsche onto the track, ran four laps at relatively slow speed, and came back into the pits. Far sooner than anyone expected.

She unstrapped herself, climbed out, slammed the door, and stalked off down pit lane, leaving everyone wondering what was going on. About five minutes later she came back, climbed into the car without saying a word, and returned to the track where she immediately started lapping at competitive speeds, eventually qualifying the car in eighth position.

What had happened?

"Remember what Derek told me," she said. "He didn't think I could handle a car as heavy as the 935. Even after Brands he said to me that, while he was impressed that I could go so fast on a road course, I would still have a real problem at Daytona. When I got to the banking for the first time, I was running almost flat-out in top gear – close to 200mph – and when the car hit the banking I found that I could not turn the steering wheel because of the downforces. I thought then that Derek was right and that I could not drive the car at Daytona. So I came into the pits to talk to him, but when he said that none of the Porsche drivers could turn the steering wheel I realised that it wasn't just me, so it was OK and I went back on the track. Everything is fine now, but for a minute I thought I was finished as a driver."

In later years, Daytona authorities decided that the speeds that the cars were achieving on the East banking were too fast for their tyres and for safety, so they added a chicane in the back straight to slow the cars down. But, before then, cars simply ran straight onto the banking at the 200mph+ they built up down the long back straight. As soon as the car hit the banking, it would tilt steeply down to the left – so much so that instead of the sideways G-forces that are found on typical road courses, the centrifugal force caused by the high speed corner

would be driven straight down through the driver's spine, into their seat. This alone made it difficult to steer the car. Far worse was the weight of the car on its springs, suspensions, and tyres, that was so great that it was virtually impossible to turn the steering while on the banking. The only thing that kept the car following the race course was the shape and angle of the banking itself.

If this wasn't enough, there was an even more frightening factor. Because the car was tilted on its side and because the track continued to curve to the left, the driver could see very little of the track in front as the road curved away above the top of the windshield. Drivers in their Porsches could see no more than 100 or so yards ahead while travelling at over 200mph.

The race itself was a downer. Preston drove first, almost immediately coming into the pits with a blown turbocharger that took almost 3/4 of an hour to fix. The car returned to the track running well but many laps down, leaving the drivers, now without Bonnie Henn, to try to make up time during the following 22 hours. Bonnie had opted out of driving after running a handful of laps in practice, where she quickly realised that she didn't have the experience to compete at this level, having never even entered a race of any type before! IMSA's licensing procedures were, shall we say, not as stringent as those in Europe!

The car ran strongly for the next several hours and each driver had two or more one hour-long sessions at the wheel. During one session, Desiré found herself coming back onto the track after the pit stop, right between the two race leaders, John Paul Jnr and Derek Bell. For the next hour she ran along with them, the three cars never more than a few car lengths apart as they threaded their way through the traffic and the night. Des moved over to allow Derek through when he made a move to pass, not wanting to hold up the race leader, but was able to tuck in behind him and maintain his pace for the rest of the hour, before bringing the car in to hand over to ... Bill Whittington!

In Europe it was traditional that drivers allocated to a car stayed with that car for the whole race, but, in those days, IMSA allowed drivers to jump from one car to another, making it theoretically possible for a driver to drive cars that might come first, second, and even third in the same race. The Whittington brothers' 935 had blown-up earlier in the evening, so money passed hands and Bill moved into the Swap Shop team.

He took over from Des, drove about 20 minutes, and brought the car back with smoke billowing from the engine and oil spraying everywhere. Trying to match Desiré's pace, the much more experienced Porsche driver had turned the boost pressure up and comprehensively destroyed the engine.

With the Porsche out, Des waited to drive the team's Ferrari, that had slowly but steadily moved through the field to a remarkable second place overall, driven exclusively by Wollek and Dören. Randy Lanier, a Camaro club racer, wasn't considered experienced enough to drive in the dark, so, despite passing Preston large wads of cash before the race, he wasn't scheduled to drive until dawn on Sunday morning. Des and I watched as he got ready to take over from Bob, noting how nervous he seemed, shaking and, at the same time, making little jumps as he stood in the pit. We looked at each other and agreed that he was on something and certainly in no condition to drive a race car. He took over from Bob and on his first lap on the track ran off course and destroyed the suspension.

To say that Bob Wollek wasn't amused is to say that AJ Foyt was merely a club driver. Randy Lanier was subsequently to move up to GTP cars, win the IMSA Championship, and then flee the country in an attempt to avoid a nationwide police hunt. He was finally arrested and sentenced to an extremely long prison sentence for his role in a major marijuana smuggling operation.

A few weeks after Daytona, at Sebring, Des was to drive Preston Henn's Ferrarie 512BB, painted in Miss Budweiser colours. Bonnie Henn came into the team for this event, together with American racer Janet Guthrie. While Des and Bonnie got along really well, with Des helping Bonnie with her driving, she and Janet didn't. Des found Janet to be withdrawn and uncommunicative and thought that she might be feeling the pressure of not having driven in serious competition for some time. So Des concentrated on learning the new car and track during the practice sessions before qualifying the car 17th, quite a lot faster than her two team mates. The car ran well for the first part of the race but then suffered damage to its front suspension when Janet slipped off the track. She left the car at the edge of the track and walked back to the pits to tell the team that their race was over, and then left the paddock.

Desiré turned to team manager Dave Charlesly, saying that she had come too far not to try to finish the race, so she and a couple of mechanics loaded a golf cart with spares and tools and made their way around the track to the parked car. The rules were clear; only the driver could work on a car outside the pit lane, so Des, taking instructions from the mechanics, unbolted the front suspension, removed the broken upright, reassembled the suspension and brakes, climbed back in, and drove the car back to the pits for the team to set the alignment, bleed the brakes and finish the job. Des then returned to the track, running as hard as she could. She and Bonnie continued into the night until, eventually, the engine lost all its oil and blew up. When Janet saw that the car was back on track, she returned to the pits, expecting to carry on driving, but after a heated discussion with Charlesly did not drive and left the track.

Des went on to spend several months in America during the 1982 season, running more IMSA events, acting as a driver coach to Bonnie Henn. She drove Swap Shop 935s three more times, but mechanical problems meant that she didn't finish any of the races at Mosport (in Canada), Road America, or Road Atlanta. By then, Bonnie had decided that she didn't want to race any more, so Desiré lost her seat. But she was able to pick up a drive in the GRID GTP car, for Ian Dawson and Guiseppi Risi, the same car she would run at Le Mans the following year. She raced the car at Mid-Ohio and Pocono, but both times the race ended in accidents when the car, co-driven by Aurora Formula 1 series competitor and friend, Emilio De Villota, and American, Fred Stiff, was crashed by the Spanish nobleman.

Despite the lack of good results, the sojourn in America, racing in the burgeoning IMSA GTP series, was to become a major factor in our decision to leave England in early 1983 and move to the United States.

Desiré had one other very significant sports car ride in 1982, in the World Championship sports car race at Brands Hatch. This time, she drove for the Ford factory team. The situation was slightly weird, because the car was, in a roundabout way, the car that she should have driven with Alain de Cadenet at Le Mans earlier in the year.

After the 1980 Le Mans debacle, Alain had commissioned the design of a new car to be built to new FIA Group C rules. But the project had been taken over by Ford Motor Company, who were investors in the project, and handed over to the

Factory Ride. *Des and Jonathan Palmer with the Factory Ford C100, in the pit lane at Brands Hatch. This time it didn't catch fire when it started! (Courtesy Wilson Collection)*

Ford Europe racing department, who gave the car to Zakspeed to complete. Although quite fast on occasion, the C100 wasn't successful, despite being driven by four of Europe's best sports car drivers, Klaus Ludwig, Marc Surer, Manfred Winkelhock, and Klaus Niedzwiedz.

Late in the season, Desiré received a phone call from Ford of Britain competition manager, Peter Ashcroft. He asked her to travel with up-and-coming Formula Three star, Jonathan Palmer, to the Nürburgring to test the C100, with a view to driving the car at the final round of the World Championship, to be held at Brands Hatch in late September. Both did well in the wet and misty conditions, with the result that Zakspeed was asked to bring a third, back-up C100 to Brands. This looked as if it was going to be a great career opportunity for Des and Jonathan, as, for both, it was their first genuine factory drive. So, it was immensely disappointing to find that they were to be treated like outcasts by the German team.

When they arrived in the pit garage they found the car, but no mechanics, a few spare tyres, and no interest from anyone in the team in helping them in any way. After a while, Zakspeed gave them a junior mechanic, Andreas Leberle (who was later to move to Indy cars and become a very well-respected crew chief), to run the car, but, even then, Jonathan and

Des had to change tyres, refuel the car, and help each other with seat fittings. Then, Des had to put out a fire that flared up when Jonathan started the car for the first time!

They both drove a few laps, getting the feel of the car and then repeated the fire extinguishing exercise at the beginning of the final qualifying session. Still, both drivers ran times that were very competitive, qualifying the car a few seconds behind the other two C100s, which were on the front row. Jonathan started the race from eighth position and ran strongly just behind the leaders – until the race was stopped when the two leading C100s contrived to run each other off the track, along the straight, tearing up over 100m of guardrail and severely damaging the Winkelhock car. After a nearly two hour break while my track crew rebuilt the guardrail, the race resumed in the rain. Des soon took over from Jonathan and, when the track was at its wettest, began running lap times that were second only to Jackie Ickx in the factory Porsche 956. For the rest of the race, she and Palmer raced as hard as they could, matching laps times in the dry, with Des slightly faster in the wet, finally finishing in fourth place.

This was the best finish that Zakspeed ever achieved in the C100, a car that their drivers criticised unmercifully, although both Des and Jonathan found theirs to be a quick, reliable, effective race car that was anything but unpleasant to drive.

Soon after our move to New York, at the beginning of 1983, Desiré was contacted by Arthur Abraham, the former Castrol executive. He had arranged sponsorship for her Formula Ford Merlyn in the South African Formula 1600 Championship and offered her the chance to drive a March-Porsche GTP car with Gianpiero Moretti, founder of the Momo steering wheel company. Arthur represented a South African swimming pool equipment company whose Kreepy Krauly pool sweeper was being launched on the American market and who had decided to sponsor rally ace, Sarel van der Merwe, in a season of sports car racing in the USA. Fortunately for Desiré, Sarel's prime commitment that year was to his rally programme, so Arthur arranged for Des to drive the Momo car when Sarel was otherwise engaged.

Her first race was at Riverside, where she found the car to be very under-developed. It was basically a year-old March GTP chassis that had been designed for a Chevy V8 stock block engine, but now fitted with a twin-turbo 3.2-litre Porsche flat-six. While the

Flying! Des accelerates the Momo March Porsche over the crest of Lime Rock Park's famous hill, using a little too much turbo boost. (Courtesy Stan Clinton)

car was potentially very fast, it wasn't well sorted and its reliability was suspect. Nevertheless, she was able to drive it quite fast, lapping some four seconds per lap quicker than Moretti, before the car broke down soon after she took over the wheel. Her second race in the car was during Memorial weekend, at Lime Rock, a short, hilly track in Connecticut.

We arrived for Thursday's pre-race practice, but found that Moretti wanted to do all the testing himself, so Des first sat in the car during the Friday morning practice, when she was allowed to run a handful of laps to learn the track. Moretti then kept the car for himself throughout the rest of the practice sessions and until he had qualified the car on Saturday morning, before handing over to Desiré. He was finding it very difficult to accept that his woman co-driver was so much quicker than him.

When she took over, Desiré had a massive scare. The car was approaching the top of the very steep hill at the back of the track, when the turbo power hit. In an instant, 750+ horse power slammed the car forward, just as she reached the crest at the most critical part of the track. The front of the car rose high in the air and the car tried its damndest to loop over backwards, as the downforce along the nose turned to up-force under the chassis. Des instantly

got off the throttle and tapped the brakes and the car, thankfully, slammed down onto its front wheels without flipping over. She finished the lap, ran one more, and brought the car in, having qualified fourth. She didn't get to drive in the race, because Moretti had a large accident early in his first stint.

The final episode in the Moretti-Momo-March saga followed at Brainerd a few weeks later. Once again, Moretti refused to allow Des to drive during Thursday's open practice, but she quickly learned the track and began turning laps as much as four seconds quicker than him, qualifying the car third. During the Sunday morning warm-up, she felt a vibration in the left-front suspension and brought the car in to the pits for a check–up, but Moretti wouldn't believe there was anything wrong.

"It's the tyres," he said. "You haven't used these new Dunlops before, there is nothing wrong with the car." The March was taken back to the garage where crew chief, Alistair McNeil, immediately raised the car on stands and started to inspect the suspension. Moretti angrily told him to stop, again asserting that there wasn't anything wrong and that Desiré was imagining things. Alistair dropped the car to the ground and apologised to Des, saying that he had to listen to the car owner.

March RIP. *The remains of the Momo March-Porsche after its spectacular 140mph, 500 yard long, multiple rollover accident. The crash, in which Des broke her leg, was the result of a broken front suspension. This is what can happen when someone doesn't listen to a driver's warnings! (Courtesy Wilson Collection)*

Moretti started the race and handed over Des an hour later in fourth place. She came onto the track just as race leader Jim Trueman flashed past, putting her a lap down. Over the next few laps she chased Jim down, passing a couple of cars, before passing him and moving into second place and started to close the one lap gap.

Then, without warning, as she came out of Turn Nine, a fast right-hander that exited onto the straight leading to the final, 90° right-hander before the main straight, the car suddenly dropped its nose onto the ground and swung violently off the track, to the left. The front-left suspension had collapsed.

Desiré struggled to correct the 140mph slide, brought the car back into a straight line on the grass parallel to the track and tried to slow it down. Then, the car hit the edge of a service road that ran across the grass, dug its nose into the 9in-high asphalt, and began a series of end-over-end somersaults, before snapping sideways in mid-air and beginning a series of very quick side-over-side barrel rolls. The car finally smashed to a standstill over 500 yards from where the

suspension had broken, ending upsidedown, on fire, with all but one of the wheels torn off and the chassis and bodywork written-off.

Hanging upside down in the cockpit, with her helmet wedged between the air inlet channel and the roof, she was initially disoriented, until a corner worker dropped to his stomach alongside the car and shouted to her.

"Switch it off! Switch it off! It's on fire."

He later told me, with a mixture of amazement and amusement, that this small gloved hand had come out the remains of the driver's window clutching a switch, free of any wiring, followed by a voice saying "If you want it off so much, switch it off yourself."

The corner workers quickly extinguished the fire, then rolled the car back onto its floor, enabling Des to climb out. She stood up, walked a few feet, and collapsed on the ground in pain. Her right leg was broken and her left foot was badly strained and bruised.

Des was taken to the small track medical room, where doctors began to prepare her for the ambulance trip to hospital, but, then, they suddenly stopped working on her and ran outside.

Another accident had taken place, this time far more serious. It was fellow woman driver Kathy Rude, one of Des' good friends and a really good driver with immense potential. Driving a Porsche 935 for the first time, she slammed into the back of a car that was entering the pit lane at very slow speed. Her seat broke and she was flung around in the car as it rolled over and over and burst into flames.

Kathy was critically injured, suffering multiple bone fractures, burns, and internal injuries, and was hospitalised for many months, enduring over 180 operations as she fought to regain her health. Despite her terrible injuries, she maintained good spirits, worked through her injuries, recovery and rehabilitation and, although she quit her racing career, she eventually became a first officer, flying Boeing 727s for the US Mail. A truly remarkable woman.

Des was transported to hospital for leg X-rays and to have plaster-casts fitted and then returned to the track, only to learn that Moretti had issued a press release blaming her for the accident. This was followed by a press release issued by IMSA, in a very unusual response, which countered that the car had broken its suspension before the accident. This was subsequently proved by Alistair McNeil, who inspected the wreck and confirmed to Des in a phone call, a few days later, that the bottom suspension mounting bolt had pulled out of the upright that held the front axle and wheel.

Both she and the spectators were incredibly lucky. I visited the crash scene, following the line of fibreglass that was stuck into the grass at every point where the car had bounced. I saw that it had veered away from the track, hit the spectator fence in at least two places, and then moved back into the run-off area. The flying car must have come within a foot or two of the spectators standing at the unprotected fence!

This was the end of the association with Moretti, but not the end of Desiré's big sports car racing.

The weekend after the 1983 Le Mans event, where Des drove the Boss 956 to a seventh place finish, Desiré raced a ten-year-old twin-turbo Porsche 908/3 at the Oulton Park Gold Cup, in England, driving with car owner Siggi Brunn.

Qualifying the car on pole position early in the session, she then found that the time keepers had missed her time, so, in a bad temper, she climbed back in the car and lowered her time by over 1½ seconds! Then the car started to misfire with a fuel pump problem, so, to be safe, Siggi pulled his back-up car from the trailer.

This was a very early Porsche 908, still resplendent in the Gulf colours that it had carried when driven on the Targa Florio and other major events, by drivers like Brian Redman and Jo Siffert. Without any seat fitting or preparation she took the car onto the track and qualified it third, behind two Can-Am Lolas, despite a lack of slicks or wings.

She admitted to me that she had scared herself silly, driving it at the edge of control. We were even more shaken when the team removed the front bodywork to discover that the only material between her feet and the barriers, if she were to crash the car, was the thin fibreglass bodywork, a flimsy tubular frame that held the pedals, and the pedals themselves. To think that Redman, Siffert, et al, raced these cars on tracks like Le Mans and the Targa Florio... brave men indeed!

Des dominated the race, establishing a large lead in the turbo-charged 908 before the car was retired, with a recurrence of the fuel pump problems, when Siggi was driving.

She drove another 935 Porsche for John Fitzpatrick, at Kyalami.

This was a magic car; one of two 'Moby Dick'

models that were the ultimate examples 935 development. Named because the car looked like a whale, with its long swooping nose and tail, the Fitzpatrick car may have been the fastest 935 ever built. At Kyalami, with John driving it in qualifying trim, it became the first ever car to break the 200mph barrier down the mile-long straight.

Des and John had a great race, running in third place behind the Rothman's sponsored factory 956s for several hours. During her first session, Des enjoyed an hour-long dice with Hans Stuck, in a Group C Sauber BMW, racing nose-to-tail for lap after lap – Des passing on the straights and Hans fighting back through the twisty sections – great stuff. But, then, during her second session, she had a major religious moment when the throttle stuck wide open as she approached Crowthorne Corner, at the end of the main straight!

Des is blessed with extremely quick reflexes and an ability to avoid panic, so she was able to switch the car off and declutch the motor the moment she realised that the accelerator was stuck. She wrestled the car around the third-gear turn and brought it safely to a stop at the side of the track, where she found that the throttle cable had jammed. She jury-rigged a temporary fix and drove the car back to the pits, where the mechanics fixed the problem and sent her back on her way. John Fitzpatrick, who is one of the world's best-ever sports car drivers, was amazed at her ability to avoid a potentially horrendous accident without damaging the car or its engine; he spent the rest of the race telling everyone how impressed he was with Desiré's abilities. Unfortunately, the engine lost power while John was driving and the car retired just as night fell.

There were also a few 956/962 drives, most notably with the famous Kremer Brothers racing team at the World Championship round at Brands Hatch, in 1984, where she shared the car with David Sutherland and South African George Fouché. She qualified the car eighth on the grid, after Sutherland argued with Erwin Kremer that he should be allowed to qualify the car on the grounds that he was paying the most to drive. Kremer refused saying, that, as Desiré (or Mrs Wilson, as he insisted on calling her) was the fastest driver in the team she would go for grid position. The car finished fourth, maintaining Desiré's outstanding record of top-four finishes in World Championship events.

Her other 956 races were less successful. She drove

John Fitzpatrick's 956, at Kyalami in 1983, sharing with Thierry Boutsen and David Hobbs. This time, Thierry was the lead driver and he qualified the car fourth, but, unfortunately, David crashed the Porsche before Des got a chance to drive in the race, when he was caught out by a sudden rain shower at the very fast Sunset Bend.

She also drove Tim Lee Davey's car at the Brands Hatch World Championship round, in 1989, where they finished 14th after overheating problems, although the team was very under funded and the car not very competitive. A few months later she drove the same car at Fuji, in Japan, in what was to be one of her most stupendous race feats.

Tim had crashed the car the previous weekend and when she arrived in Japan it was still in many pieces, waiting for parts to be flown from Germany. This delay meant that the team missed the Thursday open practice, as well as the Friday morning session. Then, they were forbidden from entering the track for the last remaining qualifying session, after arriving in the paddock five minutes late, so the first time the car ran was during the warm-up session, on Saturday morning. Tim ran a handful of laps before allowing Des to take over and, within just a few laps, she was running speeds that would have qualified her in the top five. But then, it began to rain and she came straight back into the pits with the windshield wiper flailing wildly and was unable to return to the track before the end of the session.

Consequently, the car didn't officially qualify for the event, but the officials made an exception to the rules and allowed Tim to start from the back row of the grid. When he handed the car over to Des at the end of his first hour-long stint, it was a full lap down and the rain was beginning to pour.

Conditions were terrible, with pouring rain and standing water all over the track. She emerged onto the track and immediately caught up with the two fastest cars in the race, which were racing for the lead. Frank Jelinsky was in the Joest 962, running close behind one of the world's greatest ever sports car drivers, Bob Wollek in the Kremer version. She closed the gap and tucked in behind them. The spray that engulfed her meant that she could see virtually nothing of the track ahead or beside her.

Desiré was amazing. She had entered the track about a hundred metres behind the leaders but, within a lap, was right on the Joest car's tail. A few laps later, she pulled out alongside Jelinski as they flashed

Mistress of the Mist. *Des brings the Tim Lee Davey Porsche back into the pits after her remarkable wet performance at Fuji. The conditions were so bad that, a short while later, the race was abandoned.*
(Courtesy Wilson Collection)

past the pits in one large ball of spray, out-braked him into Turn One, and slotted in between him and Wollek. There she sat, for nearly an hour, never more than a few feet behind the Kremer Porsche, until Bob made a rare mistake and flew off the track. Des came into the pits the moment the yellow flags came out, to hand the car back to Tim, who ran a few more laps before the organisers waved the flag signifying that conditions were too bad to continue racing.

It was an unreal performance. The Joest and Kremer team mechanics came flooding into the pits after the race to congratulate Des, but it drew no recognition from the media. What was, perhaps, one of Desiré's greatest performances behind the wheel went virtually unnoticed.

Perhaps John Webb was right, after all, when he said that Desiré would have a better chance of a major racing career driving sports cars than driving in Formula 1 Grands Prix.

Unfortunately we were never able to capitalise on her obvious talent in the big cars. Still, her record of two wins, one third, and a fourth in World Championship Endurance races, and her seventh place at Le Mans – as well as her ability to race with and against some of the worlds best sports car drivers on even terms – is something of which she can be extremely proud.

20

TICKLED PINK AT LE MANS

ESIRÉ'S final drive at Le Mans was in 1991, in an event that proved almost too bizarre to believe; a comedy of errors and incompetence that is now one of the legends of Le Mans.

It all started when Desiré received a call from American lady Indycar driver, Lyn St James, asking her to join her and a Japanese woman in a Japanese-entered and sponsored all-woman team. Most impressively, the conversation started with "How much money do you want?"

This very unusual approach left Des floundering on the phone. Few people had ever asked her how much money she wanted to drive a race car! A call, to friend and long time pro-driver Derek Daly for advice resulted in Des asking for $15,000 – by far her largest ever up-front fee. But a value that, apparently, didn't faze either Lyn or the Japanese team, because the confirmation came through almost immediately. As it transpired, she should have asked for more ...

Des and Lyn flew to Japan several weeks before the race, ostensibly to test the car, but mainly to take part in a media function. Testing took place on a cold, damp, and misty Autopolis race track, located high in the mountains and, reputedly, built with over $100,000,000 of Japanese mafia money. It was a magnificent facility that included an art gallery, state-of-the-art pit facilities, and an impossibly long and narrow access road that made it all but impossible to hold major events. Certainly, something was funny, because the track closed soon after it opened, apparently as a result of criminal investigations into the financial dealings leading to its construction. Nevertheless, it was an impressive facility on which to test – or would have been, if it had been run with any level of professionalism.

Although Tomika Yoshikawa, the Japanese woman driver who was responsible for the entire deal, was on hand, only Lyn and Des drove the Spice-Cosworth, each running a handful of laps; far too few for either to get a feel for the track or car. The test was aborted at lunchtime and the three drivers were hustled off to Tokyo for a press conference, where the bulk of the questions from the incredulous Japanese mainstream media were along the lines of "Do women really drive race cars?" and "Aren't you all far too old?" Des was more worried by what seemed to be an inexperienced and incompetent race team than by the media's reception, however.

The drama really started when Des and I arrived at De Gaulle Airport, in Paris, on the Monday morning of race week, where Des received an urgent message to call Tomika.

It appeared that the Japanese Automobile Racing Federation had refused to give her the International Racing Licence, essential for her to compete in a major event such as Le Mans. When Des questioned her she understood why. Poor Tomika, who had put so much into finding the sponsorship and setting up the team, really didn't have the experience necessary to compete at this level. Despite Des' best efforts, she couldn't get a licence for Tomika, and so she set about finding a replacement lady driver – deciding on close friend Cathy Muller.

Cathy was certainly the best choice for the drive. Older sister of later-to-be-famous, single-seater and saloon car ace Yvan Muller, Cathy had enjoyed a very strong career, having competed successfully in the very competitive British Formula Three series, in International F3000, and in the American Indy Lights Championships. More to the point, she was very intense about her racing, hated frivolity, and

Broken. *The pink Spice hides forlornly in the garage, while the team negotiates for another car, and the rule change that would allow the wreck to be replaced. (Courtesy Wilson Collection)*

Fast Females. *The four ladies of the Women's Le Mans team pose on the car, during scrutineering for the '91 Le Mans. Left to right: Cathy Muller, Lyn St James, Tomika Yoshikawa, and Desiré. Tomika didn't get to drive. (Courtesy Wilson Collection)*

would be certain to do a good job for the team. Every bit as important, she was French.

Problem one solved.

One of the traditions of Le Mans and a major element of the event's character is the pre-event scrutineering, or technical inspection process, that traditionally takes place in the centre of the city. The four girls arrived at the square, resplendent in their startling pink and green 'Women's Le Mans' team clothing and were immediately mobbed. But the crowd's attention was quickly diverted by the arrival of the car. It was pink! God, was it ever pink? Not just pink, but completely, utterly, over-the-moon, startling, excessively, and unbelievably pink! This wasn't a car that the spectators could ever miss.

Still, it looked to be a good car. Designed by Graham Humphreys, who had penned the GRID that Des and Alain de Cadenet had hoped to drive at Le Mans in 1981, the Spice was fitted with a well proven Ford Cosworth 3.9-litre DFX engine, was relatively compact and was well built. Although not a car with any realistic chance of winning overall honours, or even of achieving a top ten finish, it

could, nevertheless, be relied on to run consistently and quickly for the full 24 hours. Or at least for the first four laps of practice – for that was how long it lasted.

The first practice session started on Wednesday afternoon in damp and dreary conditions. As nominated team leader, Lyn St James drove it out of the pits, for her first laps on a track with which she was already familiar, having raced at Le Mans for a Spice team in a similar car in 1990.

Four laps later, the brakeless car careened off the track and into the guardrail, sustaining a hard hit from which Lyn was lucky to emerge unhurt. The same could not be said of the car.

About an hour later, the wreck appeared at the back of the pit garage, riding on a flatbed truck, looking very much the worse for wear. The team unloaded the car and immediately dragged apart the broken bodywork, to discover a large hole in the carbon fibre chassis; damage that could not be repaired at the track.

More to the point, the rules of the race were very clear. The car must start and finish the practice, qualifying, and the race, using the same chassis that passed the inspection. Other parts could be replaced, but the chassis had to be the same and it was very obvious that this chassis would never make the race.

It was a major disaster, especially for the team sponsor, who was a very pleasant Japanese television executive whose entire rationale and funding for the team was based on the prime time TV documentary he was committed to make. The poor man was almost suicidal, faced now with having to refund all the sponsorship money, a wrecked car, and with no story for Japanese television.

While he and Tomika consoled themselves in unintelligible Japanese, the rest of the team stood around with harakiri looks on their faces, Desiré and I looked longingly at the car parked behind the pit next to ours. It was a bright yellow Spice of the same model as the pink wreck and it had a large 'For Sale' notice stuck to its windshield. Moreover, it was owned by Dave Prewitt, a friend who had been team manager for the Fitzpatrick Porsche team, when Des drove for John in South Africa, in 1984 and 1985.

"No problem," said Dave. "Car's for sale, we can do a deal, it's ready to race." But there was only one problem. The rules specifically stated that no team could substitute a car that hadn't been entered for one that had been scrutineered.

But wait – this was France and we had a French lady driver in our team! Not just any French lady driver. We had Cathy Muller and no one, but no one, could win an argument against this woman when she had her dander up. Cathy marched down to race control wearing her negotiating face. Twenty minutes later, she was back in the pits with a ruling from the Clerk of the Course.

"If the car that comes out of the garage tomorrow for qualifying is pink, then they won't know that there's a problem." That was their ruling; a far cry from the attitude that kept Desiré out of her drive back in 1980.

A flurry of negotiations between the Japanese sponsor and Dave Prewitt followed and a deal was struck. The team would lease the Prewitt car as-is, insure it for the race, and return it in good condition afterwards. It all made good sense, as the car was already fully prepared for the race, with a newly rebuilt engine. But this made far too much sense for the Japanese team, who insisted on removing Prewitt's engine, gearbox, and rear suspension and using the parts from their crashed car.

Within a few minutes the yellow Spice was wheeled into the Women's Le Mans pit and the bodywork removed.

This was then taken outside into the rain, where several Japanese mechanics attacked it with a box full of pink aerosol spray cans. It was a gruesome sight.

Pink paint seeped over the wet bodywork, leaving ugly streaks of yellow and pink across the previously pristine car. But miracles (and an hour or so) later, a new pink peril began to emerge. Meanwhile, work in the garage had hardly begun; the reason for which soon became very obvious.

For all the mob of Japanese in the garage, there was only one person who had ever worked on a race car before; the team manager. All the others were raw and inexperienced and, so, simply stood at attention in a line behind the car, while their leader conducted a classroom lesson in car mechanics, he alone doing all the work.

It was preposterous, especially when the whole team packed up when qualifying ended at midnight, closed the doors on a very unfinished car, and headed back to the hotel for a good night's sleep. No all-nighter for this inexperienced squad.

Desiré and I arrived back at the track at seven o'clock the following morning, expecting to see frantic work in progress. But, instead, we had to stand around outside the locked garage until after eight, when the team dragged themselves in.

Work was slow and amateur. The decision to change engine and rear end proved to be a major problem because the Prewitt car and engine combo used a completely different wiring harness to the Japanese unit, necessitating hours of detailed work by Prewitt's mechanics, working under the feet of the inexperienced Japanese crew. Worse still, help in setting up the car, that was offered by Graham Humphreys and his factory team, was flatly rejected. The team's incompetence was epitomised when the three girls tried to get them to replace the rear wing, which was creased down the middle and which would obviously fail the first time the car got up to speed. Again, Cathy took the initiative and, miraculously, a French official appeared to instruct the team to make the change.

As the clock wound around to the start of qualifying, it became more and more obvious that, while the car might get onto the track, it would by no means be a fit race car. Finally, late in the afternoon, the now pink Prewitt chassis appeared on pit lane and Desiré prepared herself to take the wheel.

Danger has always been an intrinsic and inevitable part of racing and one which both Desiré and I have always acknowledged and accepted, even if it had never been the subject of soul searching discussions. Now, as the hastily re-built car was being pushed out of the garage onto pit lane, something occurred which was to touch the core of Desiré's commitment to her sport.

The possibility of her dying in a race car is something we had never discussed. Even the presence of death at a track was something which had been more my focus as track manager at Brands Hatch and the other MCD circuits, rather than a subject of discussion with regard to her racing activities. It was something we both acknowledged, but chose not talk about. Not that the possibility of her being gravely injured or killed in a race had never occurred to me – it was just something we didn't wish to discuss openly. Consequently, although I believed that I knew my wife very well, I had never really known how she would react should the possibility of her death stare her in the face.

The 1980 Brands Hatch World Championship Endurance event, where she drove the de Cadenet DFV with Alain to third place behind the factory Lancias, had given me a clue as to her approach to disaster.

Soon after she had taken over the car after the half-way mark, a red flag brought the race to a halt as the result of an horrific accident between the very fast Westfied and Dingle Dell corners.

I happened to be in race control at the time and as soon as the corner reports came in over the telephones, we all realized that a major catastrophe had taken place. In the immediate confusion, it was impossible to determine which cars and drivers had been involved, so it was with considerable relief that I saw that the first car to be brought into pit lane, by the workers holding the red flags at Clearways, was the green de Cadenet.

For the next hour or so, while the race was halted, I was completely immersed in my role as Circuit Director, working with the rescue and clean up crews and with the local police, whose presence was unfortunately required by the fatality incurred by British race driver, Martin Raymond. It was only when the race was able to resume that I made my way down to the pit lane to tell Des to get ready to climb back into her car.

I found her standing outside her pit garage with an expression on her face that was difficult to read.

"We're going to restart in five," I told her.

She just stood there, at first saying nothing, just looking into my eyes. Then she quietly said.

"He's dead, isn't he?"

This was a surprising question: the policy of the race organisation is never to announce a fatality at the track, if at all possible, because of such needs as notifying family. There was no way Desiré could have known of Raymond's death unless she had been directly involved in the accident.

Without further comment Des went back into the race, driving superbly to finish third overall and win her class, leaving the rest of the discussion until we arrived home that evening.

"How did you know he was dead?" I asked. "I was involved in the accident," she replied and went on to describe what had happened.

Martin Raymond's Chevron had broken down, several laps previously, at the entrance to Dingle Dell corner and was parked on the side of the track, where Raymond was trying to make repairs. He was bending over the cockpit when a Porsche and an Osella touched as they exited Westfield, and spun violently down the track. The Porsche struck the Chevron, sending Raymond flying into the air where his body was caught in the branches of a large overhanging tree. The Porsche then bounced high in the air, before crashing down into the middle of the track, where its entire fuel tank broke free. Desiré had been right behind the Osella and she drove the open de Cad underneath the flying Porsche, saw Raymond's flying body, and witnessed the whole horror of the incident.

In the hour delay that followed, Desiré said nothing to anyone about the accident, although the images must have been terrifying, and when the time came to continue the race, she didn't allow the experience to effect her driving to even the minutest extent.

This incident and her reaction to team-mate and friend Gordon Smiley's terrifying death at Indianapolis, in 1982, had given me a whole new appreciation of my wife's psyche and her inner strength. So it was with considerable surprise and concern that I listened to her as she prepared to get into the re-built Spice in the Le Mans pit lane.

For the first and only time in her racing career, Desiré said to me, "Alan, just understand that this is what I want to do. It is my job. If something happens to me, just remember, I know what I am doing."

Then, she climbed into the worst prepared car she was ever to drive and drove the hell out of it.

The car was completely unstable down the 200mph-plus Mulsanne Straight; the brakes were

Focused. *A very pensive Desiré gets ready to return to the track as the re-painted bodywork is finally fitted to the Spice after its botched rebuild. She was very aware of the extreme danger that the incompetence of her crew was placing her in at this dauntingly fast track. (Courtesy Joseph Emonts-Pohl)*

terrible, the gears were wrong; the windshield wiper simply flopped its way around the screen, and so on. The car was a disaster, yet all three drivers had to qualify within a specified lap percentage of the class leaders. They also all had to run at least three laps during the night session.

By late evening both Des and Lyn had completed their mandatory night laps and, with only fifteen minutes left in which to qualify, it was now Cathy's turn. Then, as she approached the car to replace Lyn in the cockpit one of the Japanese crew tried to stop her.

We looked at the team manager, wanting to know what was up, but he simply pointed at another driver in overalls and helmet standing by the car – the Japanese driver of another Spice car that had broken down and had not been able to qualify.

"He must drive," he said.

A fierce argument immediately followed, during which Des, myself, and Cathy's fiancé, a former French professional soccer star, quickly helped Lyn from the car, strapped Cathy in, and sent her on her way.

While she made her way on her out lap, we tried to make sense of what was happening, realising that the other Japanese team had asked for their lead driver to get into our car so that he could qualify for the race; something completely forbidden by the rules. Not that this worried the Japanese.

We also saw a look of abject fear, then pleading, on the face of our team manager, who stood by as Yves punched and wrestled to the ground one of the second team's mechanics who had come to the pit wall with a signal board calling for Cathy to return to the pits. Something which, if she had responded, would have automatically disqualified her from the race for not completing her mandatory quotient of three timed night laps. Later, we learned that the second Japanese car was funded by a Japanese mafia group and that our team manager had been made the traditional 'offer he could not refuse' to put their driver in the pink car!

The official timed results were soon available, and we saw with horror that, although Des had run times that put the car somewhere in the mid-thirties in the field, neither Lyn nor Cathy had lapped within the prescribed cut-off percentages and, as a consequence, the car wouldn't be allowed to start.

Cathy immediately put her negotiating face back on and marched down the pit lane to race control, returning with the ruling that the car could start at the back if Des was the starting driver.

This was a great relief, but all three drivers understood that the car was far from ready to race, far from safe, and could easily prove to be a danger to other cars in the race. However, with the rest of the night available for work and a further 24 hours until the nine o'clock morning warm-up, the team could work on the car to address the long list of problems the girls had identified. After some media work, the girls returned to the pit garage to see how work was progressing.

The doors were locked and the lights were off. The entire team had gone back to the hotel!

Work resumed sometime after eight o'clock on Friday morning, but it soon became obvious that nothing was going to be achieved: the Japanese didn't want to take any advice from the Spice's designer or the five Englishman on car owner Prewitt's crew, who all knew Des from her UK days and were, like many in the pit lane, both frustrated and bemused by the goings-on in the pink car's garage. Yet, despite their skills and their enthusiastic offers of help, their assistance was also rejected.

Finally, at six that evening, the Japanese team packed their tools, locked the garage, and left the unfinished, ill-prepared car and the circuit, to get another full night's sleep. We, too, then left the track, with no enthusiasm for the upcoming race and with the understanding that Des would run a few laps at the back of the field before parking the car to avoid becoming a slow moving hazard. That is, unless, it broke before she could even complete her first session.

We arrived back at the circuit at around seven thirty on race morning, determined to put a good face on what had become a very unpleasant situation, to find the Japanese mechanics in the garage polishing the car.

One of the English mechanics walked up to Des with the cryptic remark "I think you'll like the car today." Leaving a bemused Des to wonder what he meant, he rejoined the rest of his group as they waited in pit lane, watching the teams prepare for the warm-up session.

At nine o'clock the track opened for the half-hour warm-up session. Des drove the, now sparkling clean, pink Spice onto the track, passed the pits on her first completed lap, and then again and again, the Spice absolutely flying, with times that would have put the car in the top 15 places on the grid!

As the session ended, one the Prewitt boys walked over and told us an incredible story. With their car unqualified and nothing to do, the boys had picked the locks of the Women's Le Mans' team garage after the Japanese crew had left for the night. They'd then worked on the pink beast throughout the night, completely rebuilding the suspension, brakes, gearbox, and windshield wipers. They had sorted out the electrical problem that had caused the misfire and then performed a complete suspension and aerodynamic setup, before re-locking the doors shortly before the Japanese crew arrived.

The Japanese mechanics remained totally unaware of what had happened, completely self assured that their work was responsible for the transformation.

The final dramas came in the race. Des started from the back of the grid and quickly carved her way up to 18th of the 55 cars – a drive that caused Graham Humphreys to come over to our pit signalling stand and laughingly relate his team driver, Cor Euser's, radio call when the pink Spice blasted past him.

"Who the f**k's driving that thing?" Cor had demanded in amazement.

But with Cathy at the wheel the underbody started to drag on the track, the subsequent repairs causing a delay, and she later came back in to hand over to Desiré.

For the first part of Des' second session, things went well, until, as she raced through the Porsche Curves, approaching pit-in, the car suddenly lurched off the edge of the track. Immediately suspecting a punctured tyre, she dived for the pit entrance, bringing the car to a stop in front of the garage.

The interpreter leant into the cockpit.

Brits to the Rescue. *Once the race started Des was able to race the revitalized car, flying now that it had surreptitiously been rebuilt by a group of English mechanics, from the back row of the grid into the top fifteen. What a difference. (Courtesy Wilson Collection)*

"The rear end, something is wrong at the back," she shouted above the noise of the engine. The crew swarmed over the car, jacked up the front end, pulled off the front wheels and started working on the front brakes! It took a few minutes of frantic shouting and gesticulating, both from Desiré and from all of us along the pit wall, for the Japanese crew to understand that the problem lay at the rear of the car!

By now, the whole saga had become common knowledge along pit lane and every pit stop brought a large number of mechanics, media, and hangers-on to watch the shambles. This pit stop was no exception. A hapless mechanic tightened up a wheel he was trying to remove, panicking as he couldn't remove the nut. One of the Prewitt crewmen, who'd been standing behind him, calmly leant over and flicked the switch on the top of the air wrench. It fired up, unwinding the nut and, then, when the mechanic failed to take his finger off the trigger, flung it several feet into the air, before it landed at the feet of the watching onlookers. The nut then slowly rolled down pit lane, through the crowd who, as if rehearsed, each raised their

feet, one at a time, to allow the nut to wend its way unimpeded across the concrete. Mel Brooks couldn't have choreographed the scene to be any funnier.

After a few more minutes of this farce, Prewitt's English crewmen, together with a watching engineer from the USA IMSA GTP Nissan team, could take no more. As a group, they descended on the car, literally pulling Japanese crewmen from under the chassis by their legs. They opened up the rear bodywork and started to search for the problem.

They worked on the car for another 20 minutes or so, but could find nothing wrong, so one leant into the cockpit where Des sat, patiently waiting. "We can't find the problem, so go out and see if you can work out what it is," he said to her, "but be bloody careful!"

Des left pit lane, driving well below normal racing speed, but as she entered the Esses, just after the pit exit road joined the track, the right rear suspension collapsed, causing the car to spin around wildly and plunge backwards into the tyre barrier. The accident didn't seem to be too severe, but Des knew that she

Elegance Personified! *There was nothing elegant about the pink Spice pit stops. (Courtesy Joseph Emonts-Pohl)*

had come to a standstill in a very dangerous position, so she signalled to a corner worker, asking for permission to drive to a safer place, where she could evaluate the damage.

We all stood and watched the final scene of the Pink Peril saga play out on the TV in the pit garage.

The Spice's bodywork was damaged and we could see the rear wheel pointing outwards, but, otherwise, the car didn't look too bad. We watched as Desiré gesticulated to the corner crew, looking for the OK to cross the track. The marshal signaled for her to move, but a second stopped her. The pair started to argue, with arms waving. The waving turned into shouting, then into pushing, shoving, and, then, into a fully-fledged fist fight!

Des calmly ignored the fracas, saw a gap in the traffic, and drove the car across the track to a safe overlap in the guardrails. She climbed out, took one look at the damage, and saw that the collapsed suspension was the result of a major structural failure in the chassis of the car, a part that had most probably been damaged in Lyn's practice accident and that had been transferred from the wreck to the new car. The race was over. We have no idea what kind of programme appeared on Japanese TV.

Desiré had gone to Le Mans in 1980 with hopes of winning, but was rudely stripped of that chance by race officials. Her return in 1983, to finish seventh in the Porsche 956, was, in some ways, a consolation. The 1991 Women's Le Mans experience was simply bizarre and almost unbelievable. We certainly weren't tickled pink – but at least the cheque didn't bounce!

21

"Slow down and let Parnelli catch you!"

IN the past thirty years of racing, Desiré has driven more than 100 different race cars, on almost as many tracks, in 13 different countries. By far the majority of these were one-off drives, where she never had the benefit of any testing or pre-event practice. They included a wide variety of type, shape, size, and category of car.

As a consequence, Desiré became one of the most versatile race drivers in the world, quickly developing the ability to drive a variety of unfamiliar race cars on unfamiliar tracks and attain competitive lap times in a very short period of time. For instance, in 1992, driving a Mustang GTO car for Tom Gloy, at Daytona, on a track that she hadn't seen for 11 years, it took her just five laps to match the times of regular driver and Trans-Am champion Ron Fellows. At Fuji, her speed in the wet in the 962 caused the entire Kremer and Joest teams to show their respect. This ability was an important factor in her being able to justify the many varied drives that she was offered. And there were many different cars and different tracks.

One of the more memorable experiences took place at Macau: she qualified eighth and finished sixth, with no pre-event seat time, in Teddy Yip's a brand-new, unsorted, Ralt Formula Atlantic car – again beating many, much more experienced Macau and Formula 3 stars. This race ended in the agony of severe foot cramp, caused by the team failing to adjust the accelerator cable as requested. She spent the next few hours in hospital, having the muscles in her severely contorted right foot medically relaxed.

Desiré's had many drives in saloon cars, even though this wasn't something she particularly wanted. For her, single-seater and sports cars were, by far, more challenging and satisfying, but she always recognised the need to accept these offers. Some of these were quite fun. She even shared a car with Stirling Moss at the Snetterton Willhire 24, in 1980. Also in 1980, while driving a March Formula Atlantic car in the Tasman Series, in New Zealand, she drove a Ford Escort in support events for Auckland Ford Dealer, Masport Motors. With two Escort and two Formula Atlantic races at each event, together with their respective practice and qualifying sessions, she was kept very busy. After the first weekend, Des decided that it would be best to run as few laps in practice and qualifying in the Escort as possible, to conserve her energies for the more important Formula Atlantic races.

The problem, however, was that the Escort Championship was extremely competitive and featured many of New Zealand's most experienced and most aggressive drivers. She discovered this during the first race at Pukekhoe, outside Auckland. She qualified on the front row and led the race from the start, but was closely followed by several cars, in particular, two driven by the Fava brothers. They ganged up on her, driving in unison, to close the gap she had opened. When they were close, they began to get physical, hitting and bumping the Masport car so much that, by the end of the race, they had not only bounced her back to third place, but left the car with only the roof panel undamaged. But that was the last time they, or anyone else, beat her.

She went on to Manfield and won both heats. By the third weekend, she had become so dominant that she ran just two or three laps in qualifying and then sat in the car in pit lane, waiting to see if anyone could out-qualify her. Her dominance clearly annoyed these macho New Zealanders and they tried everything they could to get her thrown out of the series. At Pukekhoe they protested against the legality of the engine. It was legal. At Manfield they protested the gearbox. It, too, was found legal. At Wigram they protested that, as a professional, she shouldn't be allowed to race in their series! They lost that one too.

In 1988, the Sports Car Club of America set up a race series for Chevrolet Corvettes, which became an immediate hit. Or should I say hits ... many hits! With Chevrolet factory support and promotion, the series immediately attracted large numbers of top-line production car drivers and teams, including many of the best showroom stock drivers in Canada and the USA. Des was asked to drive in a multi-car team for Doug Rippie.

The first event was held on a temporary circuit in Fair Park, Dallas, a track which, coincidently, I had designed. Des was fastest after the first session, but hit the wall in the second. The race, like all the ones to follow, proved to be fraught with multiple car-to-car incidents, off-track incursions, and extremely close racing. Future ChampCar stars, like Jimmy Vasser and Paul Tracy, also raced the series. On the first lap at Portland, she was rammed in the door by Jimmy Vasser and had to wait for the entire 36-car field to pass before she could regain the track. Then, she charged through the field, reaching 12th, and came up behind Paul Tracy. She pulled alongside to pass him on the fast, curving back straight – where Paul looked across at her, turned his steering wheel, and drove his car into hers, sending her off the track into a series of long fast spins that, again, dropped her near the back of the field. Once again she carved her way back to the front, eventually catching Paul at the same point on the track where he'd taken her out. This time, he saw her coming and prepared himself to be taken off in return. Des, however, wasn't interested in playing games with someone as stupid as Paul, so she simply gave him a finger and drove past. At the end of the race, she drove into the paddock, waited for him to come off the track, and then walked straight over to where he was talking with his father, who was a real firebrand. She stretched up on her toes, pushed her finger hard against the end of his nose, and let him know what she thought of his immature and dangerous tactics, leaving Tracy's father and son speechless.

But there was better to come when she joined the Mustang team run by Steve 'Gas' Saleen. Steve was one of the real characters of American racing, a respectable Formula Atlantic driver who became prominent by modifying Ford Mustangs and selling them through Ford Dealers. The Saleen Mustangs were significantly quicker than the standard product and sold quite well, thanks to the racing image he created with his Saleen Endurance Team.

This multi-car team raced very competitively in the SCCA Escort Endurance Series, from 1986 to 1988, with Steve himself leading the driver line-up that included Indycar driver Pete Halsmer and Rick Titus. A third car was entered for Desiré and fellow lady driver, Lisa Caceras.

Desiré joined the team for a 24-Hour Enduro, at Mosport and won the race overall. In 1987, she and Lisa won outright at Sears Point, after Des had put the car on pole at her first visit to the track. Then, two new drivers joined the team at Mid-Ohio, in 1988.

Des had gone up to track, which was an hour from our home in Columbus, while I stayed in the office, working on the street race event that we were promoting later that year. When she arrived home that evening she seemed very frustrated. I asked her why.

"Steve's doing it again," she said, "He's losing focus."

Des was constantly frustrated that Steve would see such things as mere promotion and publicity as being more important than winning the race. "He's brought another car and got two old guys driving. I wish he would just focus on winning." The 'old guys' were Indy legend Parnelli Jones and former Shadow Formula 1 and Can-Am winner George Follmer!

Des hadn't a clue that Parnelli and George were two of the all-time greatest American race drivers, whose exploits in Trans-Am, Indy cars, Can-Am, and F5000 were legendary. To her, they were just older guys who would detract from Steve's concentration on winning the race. To Steve they were the best promotional and publicity boost he was ever to pull off. Bringing these two back into racing after many years in retirement was a very big deal.

Des out-qualified Parnelli by more than a 1½ seconds and by the time the race came, she and the two 'old guys' were getting on extremely well. She'd learned to respect them, both as drivers and as gentlemen, and they her, for her speed and commitment.

The 24 hour Mid-Ohio race was dominated by the championship leading Porsche 944. But the Saleen's held second, third, and fourth places during the night and into the final hour, with Des leading the team, running just under a lap behind the Porsche, whiled the Parnelli Jones/ George Follmer car was third, a lap or so back. Pushing the now race-worn car to the limit, she started to close the gap and put pressure on the Porsche.

Her pit-to-car radio called. "Desiré, slow down, stop chasing him." She ignored the call, confident that she was looking after the car and might – just might – catch the Porsche. "Desiré, slow down!" The call was more insistent. "We want you to slow down."

A few laps later it was an insistent Steve on the radio. "Slow down and let Parnelli catch you."

How many drivers have ever been told to slow down so that Parnelli Jones could catch them?

Des finally got the message – and slowed, allowing Parnelli to draw alongside – when Steve explained that he wanted a photo taken of his three cars crossing the finish line abreast. A great promo shot, even if it was only for second position.

The final round of the 1988 championship was a six-hour enduro at Sebring. The manufacturer's championship was very close, with the Porsche 944 entering the race in the lead, but with a point advantage so small that it could lose the championship, even if it finished second, should one of the Saleens win. In addition, an overall win by any Mustang would secure the driver's title for Steve.

Ford Motor Company made its star Trans-Am driver, Scott Pruett, available and he joined Des in her car, Lisa choosing to step aside to let the two faster drivers take the race to the Porsche.

There was a full day of open practice before the event and the Saleen team took advantage, running plenty of laps. It was all very relaxed and no one noticed that Des and Parnelli seemed to run many more laps than anyone else, passing the pits time-and-again, running nose-to-tail. When they eventually stopped, both drivers climbed from their cars laughing, making their way to the motorhome that was the team driver's base for the weekend. They'd really enjoyed nudging each other, each trusting the other's ability.

Team Orders. It took strong words from team owner Steve Saleen to get Des to stop chasing the race-leading Porsche and slow down to let the rest of the team, including Parnelli Jones, catch her for this staged photo finish at Mid-Ohio. (Courtesy Wilson Collection)

Des and Scott matched qualifying times and Scott was chosen to start the race. Conditions were terrible, with incessant rain and by the time Des took over for her last stint, over a lap behind the Porsche, the Mustang was in second place. The track was soaked and covered in dense spray and mist, but I could sense that she was having one of her magic drives and started comparing her lap times to that of the Porsche. Sure enough, she was reeling it in.

I asked Steve to let her know, by radio, that she could win if she could maintain her pace, but he declined, saying that she might crash if she felt any pressure. I tried to convince him that Des performed best under pressure, but he was insistent.

"Leave her alone," he said, which to me meant that he was admitting defeat.

Des continued to reel-off lap after lap around the long 5.2 mile circuit, taking huge chunks out of the lead time, until, with just a few laps remaining, everyone in the team could see that victory just might be possible. Finally, the message went over the radio. "Go for it."

Des responded, running even faster. At the

Rush Hour. The 1990 Indycar event on the streets of Denver provided Des with her only opportunity to compete in a Trans-Am race. With a deal to run the one-year-old Beretta V6 struck just days before the event, there was no opportunity to test, so Des had to race through the field from a lowly 18th grid position to challenge Lyn St James' factory Roush Mustang for fourth place. A brush with the wall in the closing laps dropped her back to a tenth place finish, but her drive impressed champion driver Tommy Kendall so much that he pushed for her to be taken into the factory Chevrolet team. To no avail. (Courtesy Linda McQueeney Tipton)

beginning of the last lap the Porsche was some eight seconds ahead of the Saleen Mustang, being urgently waved on by its worried pit crew. Des continued to close the lap until the very last corner, where she stormed past the Carlssen Racing Porsche, crossing the line to take the win, clinch the manufacturer's championship, and giving Steve Saleen the driver's title.

Just as Des had faced Divina, in the Sports 2000 at Snetterton and again in Formula 1 cars at Thruxton, it was inevitable that she would have to race against Lyn St James to establish her record against America's then fastest lady racer. The opportunity came at the first Denver Indycar race, on a track that I built. Lyn was already an established Trans-Am

driver, racing for the multi-championship Roush team. With sponsorship from local supporters, Des rented a one-year-old Chevy Beretta, from Tom Gloy. Again without the benefit of any pre-event seat time, she qualified well down the pack in 18th place, but stormed through the field to catch Lyn, who was running strongly in fourth. The two raced nose-to-tail for many laps, until Des slammed the wall, bending her steering and had to drop off the pace. Although Lyn won that race, Des confirmed her prominence, racing faster than the American star had when they shared the pink Spice at Le Mans.

The list of cars that Des raced in her career goes on and on. We stopped counting when the number exceeded 100.

22

A NEW TANK OF GAS

ESIRÉ'S career hit the buffers in the early 1990s, at a time when we were working long hours to establish our track operating and design business in America. The difficulties we faced in this, our need to adapt to an American way of life, and Desiré's frustration at not racing made things somewhat tense around the house. It wasn't an easy time for the Wilsons. This period was difficult for other reasons, too. We had sacrificed any idea of having a family for Des' career and we both worked many jobs and projects, often at the same time. Des was traveling almost every weekend of the season, working at Indycar events for the PPG Pace Car team, while I traveled very little.

She did very few pro races in the nineties. The Women's Le Mans race in the pink Spice showed that she could still race as quickly as ever and that the intensity was there, and the same happened later, at Daytona, with the Tom Gloy entered Mustang. Then she made the colossal mistake of trying to compete in the short-lived United States Touring Car Championship, driving a three-year-old Mazda that hadn't even been competitive when it was raced by a factory-backed professional team in the British Touring Car championship. The car was, quite simply, awful, and even though the team tried hard, a lack of funding and experience relegated the car and Des to the back of the grid. Although she tried her best, she was unable to overcome the deficiencies in the car and, when she was driven off the track by a back marker at the Toronto street race, forcing her into a hard impact with the wall, she decided that she had had enough.

Although she now acknowledged that her serious race career was finally over, she still had an urge to drive fast and began to take out her frustrations by driving a 125cc shifter kart that we'd purchased, mainly, for me to race. This kept her adrenalin going for a while, but she soon found that racing it did nothing for her, even though she enjoyed the ability to drive it at near lap record speeds in practice.

Then she received an invitation to Goodwood.

Desiré has always enjoyed her racing, but never had much fun. She certainly liked what she did; she enjoyed being good at her profession and she reveled in the recognition that her achievements brought. Her racing gave her confidence and a reason for living, but it was never fun. She was far too intense for that.

Now, for the first time in her racing life, Des was drawn into the fun side of racing.

Goodwood has become a byword in the world of racing. The Festival of Speed and the Revival represent the two most extraordinary and wonderful race events of their kind, anywhere in the world.

Both are run by Lord March, the Earl of March and Kinrara, who is one of England's leading aristocrats and the heir to a family that owns large tracts of lands in the South of England, between Portsmouth and Brighton. Included in this land is an airfield that, in the Second World War, was on the front line in the Battle of Britain and a stately mansion with a long, private driveway. The airfield, which is still active, is surrounded by the Goodwood race circuit, a track which, from 1948 to 1965, was England's most important and spectacular race course, but which dropped out of racing when newer, safer tracks like Silverstone and Brands Hatch began to emerge. For years, Goodwood remained a racing legend and a part of English racing history, but Lord March, grandson of the Earl who had fostered racing on his lands in the postwar years, always harboured a desire to bring the sport back to his property.

Neighborhood concerns and the reality that modern cars could not compete safely on the old circuit, meant that he was unable to promote modern championship level races, but that wasn't his goal. March wanted nothing more than to recreate the glory days of the old Goodwood.

Initially, he was unable to get permission from local authorities to revive the track, but was able to get permission to run a hillclimb for a few old cars, up his private driveway. Some hillclimb! Some old cars! Some driveway!

Lord March's hillclimb became, within just a few years, the largest single crowd attracting motorsport event in England, bigger, even, than Silverstone's British Formula 1 Grand Prix, until he voluntarily restricted the number of tickets on sale.

The Festival of Speed has since become the world's largest and most spectacular gathering of famous and important old race cars, and of famous and important old (and not so old) drivers. Every car and every driver at the event are personally selected and invited to attend by Charles March and his team, and an invitation to the 'hillclimb' has become one of the most prestigious invites in the world of racing.

In 1999, Lord March invited Desiré to drive her old de Cadenet Le Mans car up the hill.

For the first time in her life, Desiré saw a side of motor racing that wasn't only sheer fun, but that showed the respect that fans had for her. Out of almost 100,000 spectators, there were hundreds who came up to her, wanted to talk with her, wanted to tell her that they had seen her race, that they respected her and, most importantly, that she and her racing had played an important part in their lives. She had never signed so many autographs in her life; she was handed race programmes from events back in the 1970s that she hardly remembered and listened to fans tell her the lap times she had achieved; heard them recount seeing her race, overtake, crash, and win. And they all did so with total respect for the girl from Brakpan.

She was overwhelmed.

And she was also bloody fast.

Martin Birrane, owner of Lola Cars and an excellent driver in some of the long distance races in which Des had raced, now owned the de Cad, having bought it to set an Irish land speed record. Although the car was no longer in its British Racing Green livery

(instead, painted in the red and white Belga colours in which it made its final Le Mans appearance, in 1981) and the last time she had climbed out of the car was when it was lying upside down on the tarmac at Le Mans, she was immediately familiar and at home with it.

She drove the car twice on each of the three days of the event, running up the 1.2 mile hill in a little under a minute, each day getting faster and faster. On her final run, in the dusk of a beautiful English summer evening, she and the de Cad found their stride and she poured on a climb that, once again, showed not only her latent talent, but also the sheer intensity of her competitive spirit.

Although the car was on old tyres, had sat in a museum for many years, and had very little preparation, she won her class (for 1980s Le Mans cars) and a special award for the fastest lady driver of the day. Forget the ladies, she was even faster than World Sports Car champion and five times Le Mans winner Derek Bell, in the much more modern Le Mans-winning Porsche 956; faster than Grand Prix driver Marc Surer in a Formula 1 Arrows, and much faster than a host of other famous names in very quick cars. She was, in fact, 11th fastest overall, after less than five minutes in the car (the total of her previous five runs).

It was a very impressive run and it earned her an invitation to Lord March's other famous event. The Goodwood Revival takes place on the old race course, which is exactly as it was in the 1960s. The event, again by invitation only, is a full-blooded road race meeting, which features races for the classes and types of cars that actually raced at Goodwood during its heyday. It also features England's fastest historic race drivers, many of whom are out-and-out professionals who have been – and are still rated – amongst Britain's best racers. Competition is fierce and the top drivers show no mercy for the hugely valuable and historic old cars they race.

The Revival is famous for its atmosphere. Lord March has decreed that the entire setting, not just the cars, should bring back memories of the old 'Glorious Goodwood' days, so everyone in the paddock is asked to wear period clothing. Only cars made before 1965 are allowed in the infield. Spectators come in their thousands, dressed as if they were attending a 1950s race and Lord March adds an incredible range of supporting features. There are air displays featuring Spitfire and Hurricane fighters, like those which flew

History and Tradition. Des shared this magnificent Aston Martin DB4GT with Gillian Goldsmith, during her first visit to the Goodwood Revival.
(Courtesy Jeff Bloxham)

Epiphany. Her Cooper Jaguar drive in 'the zone' made Des re-think her need for total commitment to her driving, and signalled the beginning of a new, fun approach to racing at the Revival.
(Courtesy Jeff Bloxham)

from the site during the Battle of Britain, to which he adds P51 Mustangs, an occasional Messerschmitt ME 109, sometimes a Lancaster bomber, and many other priceless mementos of the Second World War. While racing is the prime activity, the event is full of social occasions; starting with a cricket match (played on the exact site of the first ever recorded match in the history of the game) and including cocktail parties and an amazing gala ball that takes place in one of the old hangars.

It is an extraordinary event that has come to mean a tremendous amount to Des in the twilight of her driving career.

Each year, since 1999, Lord March has invited Des to compete, arranging cars for her to drive that she would never otherwise have the opportunity to race. In 1999 it was a 1962 Aston Martin DB4GT Zagato, just like the one driven by Jimmy Clark on this same track. The next year it was a near priceless Ferrari 250 GTO. The following year she was due to drive a 1962 Ford Galaxie, but couldn't attend because her flights were cancelled as a consequence of the 9/11 terrorist attacks on the World Trade Center, in New York. But she was back the following year to drive a Lotus Elite and a 1953 Cooper Jaguar.

Des had been fast in all of these cars, running the same lap times as the highly rated and very fast Gary Pearson in the Ferrari, for example, but her

performance in the Cooper Jag was one of the best drives of her life.

Only three Cooper Jaguars were ever made. This one was owned and prepared by Gary Pearson and was to be driven by his father, John, and Desiré, in a recreation of the old Goodwood 9 Hours race. The car is as old-fashioned as a 1953 car can be. A big and powerful engine in a very rudimentary frame, with suspension and brakes that were adequate for their time but hardly comparable to modern equipment. The open cockpit was cut low on one side, allowing spectators to see the driver working hard to control the car. It had only a lap belt and no roll over bar. It was also very very fast.

Des first drove it during practice, on a wet and very slippery track and found it a real beast to handle. Struggling to get used to the car, she saw Stirling Moss in a light green C-type Jag closing behind her, so she waved him past and set out to follow him, knowing that, even though he was long retired from professional racing, she could learn from one of the world's best-ever drivers and a specialist in these older cars. Sure enough, she soon saw that these old, front-engine racers needed to be driven extremely smoothly and she instantly increased her pace, eventually qualifying the car eighth on the grid.

John Pearson drove the first part of the two-hour-long race, handing over to Des after refueling with the car almost two full laps behind the leader (John had been caught behind a pace car). Straight away she set out to reduce the gap and, before she knew it, was in 'the zone.'

Race drivers know about the 'zone.' It's a state where they're at complete harmony with the car, the track, and the conditions. Where they can drive at a limit far beyond the ordinary, where everything comes easy, where sheer talent rises. Where they drive way faster than anyone can ever reasonably expect.

Driving several seconds per lap faster than anyone else in the race, she soon caught up with the leaders, Willie Green and Mark Hales, although she was still a full lap behind. Despite some dirty driving by one and hard defensive driving by the other, she quickly found her way past and set out to make up the lost lap. The car had misfired from the moment she took over and it was rapidly getting worse, but, despite this, she drove her way back into contention, until, with about 15 minutes left in the race, she could see the two leaders ahead of her. Then it all came to an end. Without any warning the engine cut out just as she entered the treacherous Copse corner. She nearly lost control, but gathered the car and allowed it to run onto the infield safety area to quit the race.

It seems funny that an unimportant race in an historic event, near the end of her career, should hold such a valuable place in her memory, but the race and her off-the-wall drive in an unheralded old car, brought with it the realisation that she no longer wanted to have to race at that level and intensity.

For several months after the 2003 Goodwood race, Des seemed, to me, to be very quiet and reserved until, one day, we sat down and she described what she had felt. For the first and only time in her career, Des said that she had been driving beyond her ability. She had done things with the old Cooper Jag that had, quite literally, scared her. Not scared in the sense of being frightened to carry on, but scared to the extent that she now realised, that, although she still had the inborn talent to drive a car – any car – to the limit of its performance envelope and had the experience to keep it on the track at the very limit of its road holding capabilities, she no longer wanted to extend herself that far. The intensity that made her perform near miracles in the old Cooper Jag had flared for the last time and, while she knew that she still wanted to drive at events such as the Goodwood Revival, she would never again allow herself to enter the 'zone' and put her life at stake for the sake of a fast lap time.

In the previous years at Goodwood, she had driven well, certainly as fast as, or faster than, her team-mates and had felt totally competitive and totally confident. However, each year she had arrived at the track with more concerns and less confidence in her abilities. She put this down to the fact that Goodwood was almost the only race event at which she has competed since 1997 – so, when she found herself racing against some of Britain's best historic racers, she did so knowing that they still competed almost every weekend, while she raced only once a year.

At the same time, she had now discovered that racing could be fun, even without winning. She now really enjoyed the atmosphere and social side of the Goodwood events. She enjoyed spending time with old friends and rivals from her days in the UK and she liked driving the old historic cars. She knows that she can drive them fast, but that she doesn't have to drive them to the nth degree.

Desiré's race career is now winding down, but she wants to continue to drive neat cars at charismatic events. Since driving the Cooper Jag, she has driven two different Cobras; a magnificent Shelby Daytona Coupe; the famous Willment Cobra Coupe; a humble Ford Anglia; a Lotus Elite (the famous Les Leston DAD10); a 1953 Lincoln Cosmopolitan (talk about going from the sublime to the ridiculous); two beautiful E-type Jaguars; and a heavy and unwieldy

Fierce Competition. Racing at the Goodwood Revival is fierce and very competitive. In 2009, Des qualified the famous Willment Cobra Coupe fifth on the grid and had a great race, sharing the car with Lyn St James. (Courtesy Jeff Bloxham)

Corvette. She has raced some very unusual cars, too, especially the 1948, V8-engined Gordini and a NOTA Formula Junior. She has been very quick in all. In 2009 she raced a Mini for the first time and was spectacularly quick, finishing fifth in a field that included former Grand Prix, Indycar, and sports car stars, as well as several past British Touring car champions. In 2009 she also renewed her acquaintance with Herb and Rose Wysard, driving their 1952 Glockler Porsche at both the Goodwood Hillclimb and American Monterey Historic events. She looks foward each year to an invitation from Lord March to return to Goodwood, and would like to drive at the historic events at Le Mans, Laguna Seca, Spa, and the Nürburgring.

Ultimately, if she could win the lottery, Desiré would buy the Wolf, return it to its red Aurora series colour scheme, and enter it for the historic event at Monaco. Then she would buy the old de Cad from Martin Birrane, repaint it in British Racing Green, and drive it at the Le Mans historic weekend. The cars would then retire to our garage, to remind her that she was, once, the best woman racer in the world ...

Thank You. Lord March has made Desiré's final years in racing the most pleasant of her career. Here, he recognises her great performance in the de Cadenet at the 1999 Festival of Speed. Lady March, the Countess of March, looks on. Great cars, great track, great atmosphere, and great friends.
(Courtesy Wilson Collection)

Back up to Speed. Des hustles Larry Miller's amazing Daytona Coupe through Goodwood's Madgwick corner. From museum to track ... a bit like her new racing life after being put out to pasture! (Courtesy Jeff Bloxham)

THE CARS OF GOODWOOD

HOW MUCH FUN CAN ONE GIRL HAVE

(Courtesy Linzi Smart (1), Wilson Collection (15), and Jeff Bloxham (all others)

23

SPONSORSHIP, POLITICS, MONEY, AND SEX

ORGET Shell, BP, Gulf, or Mobil. Racing is fuelled by money, not petroleum, and every driver needs to have access to an awful lot of it, if they're to progress to the top. In almost all forms of racing, other than the top levels of Formula 1 and NASCAR, race teams rely heavily on their drivers as their main source of income. This doesn't mean that there aren't professional, or paid, drivers, but that the money that teams pay a good driver to race often comes from the sponsorship raised by the driver himself, or (as is often the case in endurance racing) by money brought to the team by a second, less skilled, but well paying driver.

Other than when we ran our own teams in FF1600 and, of course, the South African Formula Atlantic disaster, we have only paid for one drive for Des. That $5000 (for Le Mans, in 1983) came from the Carstensens. The only fees Des received for driving came from Nick Challis, at £80 per race, for his Sports 2000 and FF2000 cars, from Saleen for the Mustang drives, and from the Womens Le Mans team who paid her $15,000 at Le Mans, in 1991. She did, however, receive a percentage of the money the car earned in her Indycar and Britsh Formula 1 races (40 per cent), although getting her Brands Hatch winners' share from Sid Taylor proved to be hard work.

Sponsorship Comes in all Sizes. The tiny blue and yellow Cartsensen decal, above the rear wheel, is almost lost amongst the Boss clothing company colour scheme on the Porsche 956 at Le Mans, but was probably more important to Heather and Norman Carstensen than the large-scale visibility was to the cars' major sponsor. This small gesture thanked the South African couple for their unsolicited, but immensely valuable support, which came at a time when Des' career seemed to have come to a standstill. (Courtesy Wilson Collection)

I have been very candid about the sponsorship amounts we received – from the £1500 or so we received for our South Africa Formula Ford campaign; our unusual sponsorship of ƒ30,000 from F&S Properties; our free ferry rides from Olau Lines, and the significant support she received from Norman and Heather Carstensen – to show that racing wasn't a money making career for Desiré. She raced because she wanted to race. It was just the way things happened back then and she has no regrets or envy of any woman driver who can now make money from racing.

 Des paid for her racing by enticing teams to run her for her skills and for the publicity she brought to them. Many of these arrangements were made by patrons who never disclosed how much it cost them. The John Webb arrangements epitomised this. He supported Des because she generated publicity; was a great image for Brands Hatch; because he believed in her and because she was very, very quick. We never knew the financial arrangements he made for her racing.

By far her most valuable selling point was the publicity she generated. In the UK, this was all very carefully planned and extremely well executed, thanks, in large part, to the exceptional skills of Brands Hatch's publicity manager, Juliette Brindley. Juliette was a very competent race driver in her own right, but she never resented Des' abilities or success and instead worked extremely hard to push Desiré's name into the British media. Her success can be gauged by the racing media's nickname for the 1979 Aurora British Formula 1 Championship – Formula Desiré!

A significant level of support came from an extraordinary character called Teddy Yip. Teddy was an exceptionally wealthy Hong Kong businessman, of Chinese/Indonesian extraction, who started his business life working in the mailroom for NCR and ended up one of its largest shareholders. Among the multiple businesses and properties he eventually owned were several casinos and hotels in Macau and the ferry line connecting Hong Kong to Macau. He was rich enough to personally pay the entire electricity bill for the former Portuguese colony close to Hong Kong. Teddy wasn't just rich; he was extremely eccentric. Although a wizened little man, he had a never ending stream of lady friends in every port or city he visited. It wasn't unusual, for example, for him to hold business or team meetings, during

the month of Indianapolis, while sitting propped-up in his motel room bed, with his lady lying alongside. But Teddy was an out-and-out racing enthusiast who raced in the Macau Grand Prix in its early days and was largely responsible for bringing that amazing event into world prominence.

Over the years, Teddy became a benefactor for many drivers and teams, most notably Morris Nunn's Ensign Formula 1 team and drivers such as Vern Schuppan, Alan Jones, Brian Redman, Derek Daly, Marc Surer, Geoff Lees, and even Ayrton Senna, who all drove cars sponsored by Teddy. He started his own Theodore Racing Formula 1 team with drivers like Irishman Tommy Byrne, Patrick Tambay, Eddie Cheever, Johnny Cecotto, and Jan Lammers. He even won the Silverstone International Trophy, a non-championship Formula 1 race, with Keke Rosberg driving one of his Theodore cars. During the period 1978 to 1983, Teddy Yip's teams were to Formula 1 what Minardi came to be in the early 2000s; a back-marker team whose drivers could never be competitive, but were, at least, being given the opportunity to showcase their abilities to the better teams.

Teddy loved Formula 1, but loved Indianapolis even more and, even though he achieved very little direct success at the Speedway, he was an important part of the personal backing that supported Bobby Unser and other drivers. Teddy's support for Desiré came through her British Formula 1 drive with Jack Kallay, in the Ensign, in 1977, thanks to Kallay's association with Sid Taylor.

Taylor is another of those characters who played a role in Desiré's career, albeit one that had as many bad points as good.

Sid 'Bejeezus' Taylor was Teddy's 'racing manager' and was the essential link between Teddy's money and the cars that carried his name. An Irishman, who lived in Birmingham and some of whose other business interests are, perhaps, best described as 'interesting,' Sid had previously run his own sports cars for drivers like Denny Hulme, Trevor Taylor, and Brian Redman, in the UK, with great success. His contact with Teddy was the key to Teddy's involvement in British and, subsequently, international racing.

Although Kallay's Ensign carried Theodore Racing Chinese signage, there was little or no direct Yip/Taylor involvement in the team, or with Desiré, until the beginning of 1980, when John Webb arranged for her be placed in the Theodore Wolf at the beginning of the season's Aurora series. This led to Des' historic win at Brands Hatch and, almost immediately after, to her being dropped from the team, because Sid believed American, Kevin Cogan, was the next big Grand Prix star. Des, who was working for an annual salary of around £4500 a year at her Brands Hatch racing job, had to wait several years to get her share of the prize money for that Brands win, which she received only after informing Teddy that she'd never been paid the £2500 we desperately needed. We never understood why Sid constantly undermined the relationship between Des and Teddy. Despite the Aurora saga, Teddy still went on to sponsor Des at Indianapolis.

Significant support also came from Herb and Rose Wysard, who were great enthusiasts. They owned one of the last of the small, unsponsored teams to compete in the CART Indycar series. They put everything they could into providing Des with a drive throughout 1983, but the days of the small team had passed and they could no longer compete against the likes of the Penske, Newman-Haas, and Patrick teams that dominated the series.

Most of the remaining sponsorship in Desiré's career came because she had established herself as a professional driver with a record of generating media interest. Companies (like South Africa's Kreepy-Krauly swimming pool cleaning equipment manufacturer) supported her IMSA and Indycar activities in 1983 primarily because of the publicity she provided back in South Africa.

There is no doubt that Desiré generated an enormous amount of media coverage wherever she raced. It was common to see as much written about her as about the race winner, especially during the pre-event lead-up promotional coverage. This was particularly true in England and, later, in South Africa, but surprisingly, not such a big deal in the USA, where, one might think, track promoters would have jumped at the chance to get free editorial publicity for their events, capitalising on the presence of a competitive woman driver in their race.

We've often been asked why Desiré, with all the publicity she generated in England, was never able to attract a major sponsor that could have taken her all the way into World Championship Formula 1. First, John Webb certainly didn't have the money to take her there on a full time basis and, even if he had, there would have been little benefit to him because he was very much focused on promoting his UK tracks.

Second, even during her peak promotional years when she was winning with the Wolf and the de Cadenet, neither Des nor I tried to capitalise by seeking major additional sponsorship, because Des felt a huge obligation to John and didn't want to do anything that might have upset him, or the deals he had arranged. He was her unofficial racing manager and he handled all her drives and sponsorship. By the time we realised that John may well have agreed to Des setting up a sponsor-finding relationship with someone else (Barrie Gill's CSS company, for example) it was too late. Her chance to get into Formula 1 was gone.

Third, Teddy Yip's support for her Formula 1 aspirations never progressed past the Aurora win, thanks to Sid Taylor's conviction that Kevin Cogan had greater potential and to an incident involving Morris Nunn. In 1980, Mo was running his Ensign cars in Formula 1 Grand Prix, but, despite Teddy Yip's financial support, could only afford to race with paying or well sponsored drivers. Halfway through the season, he had need to replace his current driver with one with greater funds, so, Mo attended an Aurora Formula 1 round, at Mallory Park, to watch up-and-coming drivers like Cogan, Tiff Needell, and Desiré. When Des handily outperformed all of the 'hopefuls,' Morris made a statement to the media along the lines that he couldn't hire any of the drivers that he had seen because they'd all been beaten by a woman! His lack of interest in putting Des in his vacant seat drove another nail into the coffin of her Formula 1 aspirations. Ironically, many years later, Morris' second wife played a strong role in the success of one of the few current British professional lady drivers, Audi DTM racer Katherine Legge.

Then there was the question of Des' nationality. The fact that she was a South African was, certainly, well known in the UK and had absolutely no effect on the support that John was able to pull together through the Brands Hatch link. In fact, despite the rising prominence of the anti-apartheid movement, England, as a whole, was still very supportive of South Africans, tending to treat them as 'welcome back to the motherland' colonials, like their Australian, Canadian, and New Zealand counterparts. But, her nationality certainly was a factor with large multinational companies.

It wasn't just Des who suffered. Fellow countryman Rad Dougal formed a strong link with the Toleman company and won a major FF2000 championship for them. As a result, it commissioned fellow South African Rory Byrne to design and build a Formula Two car, with which Rad was immediately very competitive, winning an early season race at Thruxton. Then, all of a sudden, Rad was out of the car, replaced by Englishman Brian Henton. As Rad was a proven winner and a long time driver for Toleman, it appeared that he had been let go because of their sponsor's concerns about having a South African in the team.

Like Rad, Des also found doors closed the moment her nationality came up. Her inability to get any major company even vaguely interested in supporting her move to Grand Prix with Ken Tyrrell, in 1981, can be related directly to her nationality. Later, the same issue killed at least two separate million-dollar sponsorship deals, in America. In both cases, the recommendations of senior marketing management was rejected by the President or Chairman of these Fortune 500 companies as soon as they learned her nationality. Another cancelled an agreement because he believed that no woman could ever beat Mario Andretti, so there was no point in backing her!

At the same time, no South African company would, back then, contemplate sponsoring Desiré on the international scene, because of the possible adverse publicity from anti-apartheid movements. We even made approaches to SA government agencies, that seemed only too happy to use Des as a figurehead in their diplomatic activities in London, but showed zero interest in helping her acquire financial support.

All these deals and setbacks took place behind closed doors and never became public. Which is more than can be said of her experience in New Zealand, when Des flew there, in 1980, to compete in a Nashua copiers-sponsored March Formula Atlantic car. The promotional wheel began to turn as soon as we arrived and by the second day her face was on the front page of the Auckland papers and on the TV news. By the third day, it was an even bigger story, but, this time, she was the subject of vociferous anti-apartheid activism.

The protests were engineered by a political group called HART (Halt All Racist Tours), a group that had just achieved major success by forcing the abandonment of a tour by the Springboks, the South African national rugby team. In a country that loved rugby and that had long standing, friendly sporting relations with South Africa, this success was huge.

Now, HART turned their attention on Des,

demanding that she be immediately deported from the country. We were, obviously, both very upset and extremely concerned. Des called the Nashua president, offering to walk away from his sponsorship, but his response was, we were to find, far more the sentiment of the average New Zealander than the headline-seeking HART activists.

"No way," he said. "We've never had as much publicity. We're with you all the way!"

The HART people carried their protests to the country's parliament, where a special session was called to discuss Desiré's participation in the races and her sojourn in New Zealand. The arguments didn't get far and were shut down completely when the Prime Minister, who had the splendid nickname of 'Piggy' Muldoon, made a statement welcoming Des to New Zealand and wishing her well in the races, ending with an emphatic, "I hope she wins."

HART then threatened to hold protests at the gates of the track but, eventually, their protest fizzled out – which was just as well for them, as many of the Formula Atlantic mechanics planned to welcome them with bags of rotten fruit! The silly thing about the whole issue was that, had HART asked Des for her feelings about apartheid, it would have found her supporting much of its position. But activists such as HART never concern themselves with facts in their search for publicity.

Once Des moved to the USA, the whole South African thing seemed to die out. Except for the fact that no major company would sponsor her, for the average race fan was more interested in her racing than her nationality. She and I went on to earn a green card in 1985 and eventually had the honour of becoming American citizens in 1993.

On several other occasions she did, however, face situations where her South African nationality threatened her driving opportunities.

Prior to racing at Le Mans, in 1980, Des had to apply for a visa from the French Consulate in London, because France, then, had an official policy of not allowing South Africans to take part in sport in its country. Her first application was turned down by front desk officials, but, after protesting, we were ushered into a large, stately office where the very attractive and well dressed lady French consul asked Des to provide her rationale for wanting to go to France. Des explained that she had just won the previous two rounds of the World Sports Car Championship and was hoping to win Le Mans.

Without hesitation she stamped the passport and told Des to "Go and beat the men."

Years later, when we were living in the USA, Des was asked to race a Porsche 962 at Fuji, in Japan. Once again, Japanese policies forbade sporting contact with South Africa, so, her application for a visa was rejected. Des talked with a lady official in the Japanese consulate in San Francisco, who suggested a way around the problem. She would be admitted if she had an American 'Stateless' or Refugee passport. Des would have to rescind her South African citizenship and formally apply for Stateless classification, which would result in the USA issuing a document that would act as a passport. We were already in the process of applying for American citizenship, so, with the help of a Colorado State Senator, who opened doors at the immigration office, and some very fancy and fast footwork through the administrative jungle, Des appeared in the Japanese Embassy just three days after her application had been rejected, with her Stateless documents in hand. She raced in Japan that weekend.

Des was also to find that being a woman in professional racing was a double edged sword.

The fact that she was a woman undoubtedly opened many doors, led to invitations to drive cars that might not otherwise have been made and helped with her passage through British national racing. It also helped her get into Indy cars and a few other drives in America. But it also had its disadvantages.

The Bruce Leven situation, for example.

Bruce owned a huge garbage disposal business and a very successful IMSA GTP team, running Porsche 962s for himself and, in 1987, for Bob Wollek, at the time perhaps the world's best sports car driver. Wollek, as part of his deal, had the right to choose his own co-driver. At the end of 1986, Des and I went to Daytona, to the season-ending IMSA race and bumped into Bob, who'd become a good friend and whom Des had raced against on many occasions. He immediately asked her if she would like to be his team-mate in the Leven car the following year, even asking how much money she wanted.

He then went off to tell Bruce that Des was his choice for co-driver as "... she's almost as fast as me, never bends the car, and is completely committed." What a complement! But he quickly returned with Bruce's response: "No f*****g woman is going to drive his car." The ride went to Italian Mauro Baldi.

There was an amusing postscript to this story. I was running the Columbus 500 IMSA street race at this time and, the following year, Bruce brought two cars, including one for hometown favourite Bobby Rahal. During Saturday's final qualifying, where Bobby put the car on pole, Bruce got into a pushing match with a city policeman who had asked him to show his credentials. Bruce – whose ego wouldn't allow him to carry a credential – pushed the cop aside and, then, quickly found himself lying on the ground with his hands cuffed behind his back. When the police threatened him with a charge of assault, he said he would withdraw his front running cars from the event.

I was notified and went to the scene, where Bruce was standing against the wall, looking sheepish now that there was a chance he could spend the rest of the weekend in jail. I asked the officers to move him to a place where he wouldn't be seen by all the other competitors and race fans and then went to see the Mayor and Chief of Police, managing to persuade them to drop charges. The thought did pass through my head that I could get our revenge and let him spend a night locked up!

Another rejection came from Nissan. Des heard that it was looking for drivers for its new IMSA GTP team and that it intended to hold an evaluation test session. She called its team manager, Kas Kastner, and asked to be able to join the test. His answer was that Nissan was not looking for a woman driver. Forget that Des had a better international sports car record than any of the drivers he did test.

Des never went to the media with these, or any other, stories of discrimination, although, in this case, we seriously considered doing so. But, we chose not to because, for all her racing life, Des recognised that being a woman in racing brought with it advantages and disadvantages and she had long ago decided that she would never play the 'women's lib' card that some female drivers have used. She was a race driver in the car and a lady outside.

I have already shown some of the reasons, including male chauvinism and an honest, if misguided, belief amongst male decision maker's that women cannot do the job, despite the facts proving otherwise. There are, however, two other overriding reasons that, we believe, will ensure that no woman ever gets the chance to be successful at the highest levels of racing, by which we mean Formula 1 Grand Prix.

The first reason is that working with sponsors often includes socialising with their top brass – nearly all men – and this often takes the form of a game of golf or a social occasion, and, in America, outings such as fishing and hunting trips. In Corporate America, it could involve travelling around the country with the CEO, perhaps in his executive jet, visiting company outlets, suppliers, or customers. To do so in the company of a woman who is not his wife, especially a high profile woman like a professional race driver, raises the potential for unfounded rumour and insinuations. Even the exec's wife must be taken into account: will she allow her husband to go off for golfing weekends, or into the bushes to hunt deer with another woman? It's much easier to say no to sponsoring the lady and yes to sponsoring the man.

The second reason overrides even this and it's related to the amount of money being spent. To get into Formula 1 today, companies must spend many millions of dollars sponsoring a team, and even more to provide enough money to influence the choice of drivers, especially in the better teams. Very few, if any, corporate decision makers are going to take the risk of funding a woman driver in a sport as expensive and competitive as Formula 1, when the chances of any driver, even the best, being successful are very difficult to guarantee. While a decision to sponsor a male driver who fails might be justified at Board level, it's highly unlikely that any executive who sticks his neck out to support a woman would survive in his position were she to fail.

In the sports car chapter, I mentioned Des' success in 1981 with the Zakspeed run Ford C100, alongside future Formula 1 driver and Brands Hatch owner, Jonathan Palmer. Des' performance impressed Ford competitions manager, Peter Ashcroft, so much, that, he told her that she would be driving the C100 for the company in the 1982 race season. More importantly, he told her that, because her input on the handling and setup of the car had been so much better than that of the regular drivers, she would be doing most of the testing of their new car.

Des spent the winter off-season looking forward to her first true factory ride, only to be disappointed when Ashcroft, having held meetings with Ford executives in Detroit, called her to say he would lose his job if he continued with the plan. The American 'suits' simply didn't think a woman could do the job. Not that it mattered because, a few days later, Ford brought in Stuart Turner to run the competitions department and he promptly cancelled the entire C100 racing programme.

Des has often been asked how much money she has made from her racing. Impolite, certainly, but a reasonable question given how much money flows through and around the sport.

The answer, in Desiré's case, is a big zero. She certainly received some prize money, was paid to race on a very few occasions, and received the patronage support from the Carstensen's, – but, in overall terms, her racing has cost far more than she earned.

In today's highly commercial racing world, it would be unthinkable that a driver of Desiré's capability and promotional potential wouldn't earn a fair income from racing, but times were different in the late seventies and early eighties, when she was at her prime. Then, it was a case of just trying to put the next race together and to find a way to stay in racing. The money wasn't important – and wasn't there anyway. Today, a new Desiré would have a business manager with the responsibility for securing and servicing a sponsor, for negotiating regular drives, and for handling her income. She would be marketed as a 'brand' and her image would be subject to the demands of marketing, and not always in the most tasteful way.

Finally, there is the question of sex.

Throughout history, there have been women in politics, the theatre and motion pictures, in sport, and in business who have used the bed to get ahead. This is equally true in racing.

Desiré, however has always maintained her standards and never lowered herself to these levels. Not for want of opportunity, but because she has never been the type to demean herself in that way. It's quite possible that, had she been single, she might have attracted sponsorship because she may have been seen to be available, or at least unencumbered by a husband. But, Des entered pro-racing as a married woman, so she was never faced with such situations – at least, not to any serious extent.

Most importantly, however, Des, while welcoming the advantages that being a woman has given her, has never considered herself to be an icon for women's movements. Nor has she ever sought advantage or consideration on the track from her male competitors. Quite simply, when the flag dropped, Desiré was always just another race driver.

A very good race driver, a fierce competitor, perhaps a star … but, ultimately, just another driver.

24

WOMEN DRIVERS

DESIRÉ'S story wouldn't be so unusual if she were just another male driver, who had risen through the ranks of club racing to reach the fringes of Formula 1. The reality is that she is a lady racer, by no means the only woman in the sport, and it's important to recognize the exploits of some other leading woman racers.

Although Desiré has always compared herself to her male competitors, wanting to be judged as a racing driver and not as a woman driver, it's inevitable that she has been judged against other women who have tried to make their mark in the sport. The difference, in Des' case, is that she managed to elevate herself to a level where her talents and ability are most fairly compared to that of her male counterparts. Many believe that she is the best-ever woman racing driver; I agree but I am, of course, biased!

But how did she achieve this status? Perhaps it was her unusual career path. The start, at the tender age of five, the competitive South African single-seater scene, and the rough and tumble of European racing, all helped build the tough and competitive professional she became.

But what made a slip-of-a-girl from a small town in South Africa such a fast driver? I am sure Des inherited her natural talent to go fast from her motorcycle champion father, Charlie Randall, but speed is only one element in the makeup of a successful racing driver. Des has an unusual level of intensity and an ability to focus which embraces so much more than just driving the car. It includes understanding the nuances of the car, working with her team, and sensing the nature of the track.

Then there's her determination. Anyone who's worked with Des knows that she doesn't give up. She has a massive will to win for everything she does,

whether it's video games, golf, or even a game of Scrabble.

As far as her driving is concerned, she's incredibly smooth, which shows particularly strongly in the wet, but she can still wrestle an ill-handling car when needed. Her smooth braking and steering style allow her to carry speed through the apex of a corner. Her ability to brake extremely late has been mentioned several times in this book. She has an uncanny ability to bring a car back after a race with minimum brake, clutch, and tyre wear. The fierce competition she faced in her early days; the necessity to get up to speed quickly, and her ability to learn tracks within just a few laps have helped add to the package that is Desiré Wilson. Despite being a relatively small, 5ft 6in, 9 stone woman, she has always been extremely strong, with the endurance to drive big, heavy sports cars quickly, for long periods of time.

Desiré learned racing the way a man does; through hard work, by driving in the toughest possible races, and from sheer miles behind the wheel. Consequently, when the time came for her to drive faster and more complex cars, she was able to call on her hard-earned experience and skills. Few other women drivers have come into meaningful racing with this type of background.

Today, most lady racers start as schoolgirl karters. If they win races in serious championships, they stand out in exactly the same way as, say, Lewis Hamilton did, and are quickly recognised. Family money, or even sponsorship, can then catapult the talented lady racer into categories like Formula Ford or Renault. At this level, the talented girl racer is probably at an advantage over her male counterpart, for she has become more visible and is, therefore, more likely to receive the support necessary to move forward in her career.

This is where she begins to need much more than her basic talent. She needs experience and knowledge. Unfortunately, she may well have moved through the lower ranks of racing at a quicker pace than the typical male driver, stepping into ever faster cars for short periods of time, but without gaining the basic experience needed to race them at their limits. Ultimately, she reaches a level where, despite good equipment, experienced teams, and sufficient funds, she just cannot compete for race wins against the best of her competitors; men who have had a longer, harder climb to prominence, but who have been able to gain more meaningful experience on the way.

This is where the advantage of being a woman in racing can turn negative.

A woman driver who is heavily supported or publicised, but who is not immediately successful, is nearly always judged to have failed. Failure results in immediate scepticism from fans; criticism from the media; loss of credibility within the industry; loss of sponsorship, and lack of interest by race teams.

Her career loses momentum and, typically, comes to a screeching halt. A result certainly not exclusive to the woman driver, but made more vicious because of her gender.

No matter how talented the driver, there's no progress in racing without experience. The simple fact is that the vast majority of talented women drivers are encouraged to move too quickly through the early, learning stages of the sport – so when they really need to call on a base of experience, it's not available.

For these and other reasons, only a small number of women drivers have risen out of club racing to national and then international prominence.

I have previously discussed how difficult it is for a woman to earn the commercial support necessary to finance the next steps to Formula 1. Most women drivers drop out because they cannot sustain the momentum of their junior careers and the reason is nearly always lack of ongoing support within the industry and of the support necessary to find them places in good teams and the top race series. Are things getting better? It would seem that, at last, America is opening doors to lady racers, now that Danica Patrick has reached beyond the race track into the national celebrity spotlight. It's likely that the Indy 500 will continue to see five or more ladies competing into the future, too. Indycar racing has come a long way since Janet Guthrie walked into Gasoline Alley. Formula 1? There's still a long way to go.

It might be difficult to comprehend in this age of so-called equality that more women raced regularly at Le Mans in the 1930s than today, and before the Second World War there were a number of women – including Glenda Hawkes, Doreen Evans, Kay Petre, and the Australian, Joan Richmond – who were very competitive at Brooklands. In Europe, the controversial French driver, Helle Nice, was very competitive; she raced for Bugatti and was invited to race in America.

As fast as these and other prewar lady driver's may have been, their skill is extremely difficult to

The Tigress of Turin. Lella Lombardi was given the Tigress name by John Webb, when she raced in his Shellsport F5000 series in the UK. She went on to become the only woman driver to earn points in a Grand Prix race. (Courtesy Joseph Emonts-Pohl)

compare to postwar drivers, simply because the technology and format of racing is so different. Let's just say that, when they beat men, they beat some of the best, so we should recognise their achievements.

Postwar, however, there are several lady drivers who have made their mark. Maria Teresa De Filippis, an Italian, who was very quick in sports cars and who performed brilliantly against the best drivers in the world at the challenging Targa Florio, became the first woman to race in the Formula 1 World Championship. In the 1950s, she raced eight Grand Prix events, driving a Maserati 250F. While she never ran very competitively at this level, she still scored some good finishes, including tenth in the Belgian Grand Prix. Now a feisty woman in her 80s, she still attends the occasional Grand Prix and runs a club for former Formula 1 drivers. How good she was is difficult to judge, given her privately entered car and the level of her competition.

The first and, so far, only woman to race consistently in Formula 1 was Italian Lella Lombardi. Lella started 12 Grands Prix between 1974 and 1976 and earned half a point for finishing sixth in a crash-shortened Spanish Grand Prix, in 1975, driving a factory March. While never a contender for serious front-of-the-field finishes, Lella was certainly no less a qualified racer than any number of men who have filled the back of Formula 1 grids in rent-a-drives over the years and was treated with respect by her competitors and by the media. Sadly, Lella died of cancer in 1992.

Divina Galica raced in F5000 and Formula 1 cars in the British Championships and tried to qualify for three Grand Prix events in 1978, driving a factory entered Hesketh. In Desiré's opinion, Divina Galica is the fastest woman driver she has raced against. One wonders how Divi would have fared if she had enjoyed the same background in racing as Des; if she had started in her teens, rather than when she had completed her stellar skiing career; if she had managed to retain her sponsorship through1979 and been able to compete with Des in equal equipment? Regardless, Divina was a hard and fair competitor and a great racer. She has since carved out a successful business career in American motorsport. She and Des have become good friends.

Most recently, in1992, the well funded Giovanna Amati started the season as a Brabham driver, but failed to qualify in the first three races and withdrew from the team.

Divi. Desiré rates Divina Galica as the best woman she ever raced against. Divi started her career after competing in the Olympics, on skis, and raced F1 in the Aurora series against Des.
(Courtesy Joseph Emonts-Pohl)

There have been several other really good European women drivers, including Germany's Ellen Lohr, who ran competitively in F3 and in German Touring Car races for Mercedes Benz, and Cathy Muller, the French girl who shone in British F3 and ran a season in each of F3000 and Indy Lights. The aggressive and always competitive Cathy shared the pink peril Spice with Des and Lyn St James, at Le Mans in 1991. Sabine Schmitz was one of the team that won the Nürburgring 24 Hours in 1996 and 1997 and is still one of the quickest drivers around the Nürburgring Nordschleife, but rarely races elsewhere. Lillian Bryner had sports cars successes,

Janet. Janet was the true Indycar pioneer, who breached the male-only wall to establish herself at Indianapolis. Her legacy can be seen in the growing number of women drivers now racing in the IRL and at Indianapolis each year. (Courtesy IMS Photo)

Lyn and Cathy. Lyn St James (centre), is seen here with Desiré and Cathy Muller at Le Mans in 1991. Lyn was the first woman to win Rookie of the Year honours at Indianapolis and had a strong career in North American Trans-Am and IMSA racing. (Courtesy Wilson Collection)

in the late 1990s and early 2000s, with Ferraris and Porsches, usually racing with her partner, Enzo Calderari. Vannina Ickx tried, but never emulated the successes of her famous father.

Then there are the ladies who have raced at Indianapolis and in the Indycar series in America.

The first serious woman Indycar driver was the American, Janet Guthrie, who, from a background in SCCA club racing, found instant fame when she became the first woman ever to race both the Indianapolis 500 and the Daytona 500.

Again, it's quite difficult to determine the level of Janet's skill, partly because the whole Indianapolis racing world was more interested in finding fault or failure than in encouraging a woman's talent or success. After all, she was the first lady to break the exclusively male domain of Indianapolis racing – a world so macho that there weren't even any women's toilets in the paddock! Yet Janet persevered and

was able to finish ninth at Indy, in 1978, in a car she owned and managed herself. She qualified fourth at Pocono, in 1979, and finished fifth at Milwaukee in the same year. Janet also made a mark in NASCAR, finishing sixth at Bristol, in 1977.

Desiré only came across Janet once on the race track, when both shared the Miss Budweiser Ferrari 512 IMSA GTO car at Sebring, in 1981. Desiré handily out-qualified Janet and ran a lot faster in the race.

Lyn St James was the most prominent American road race and Indycar oval driver of her time. She came to prominence as a Ford-supported driver, in IMSA and Trans-Am racing, driving for the powerful Roush team for several years. She also drove Ford's Probe IMSA GTP car, surviving at least one horrifying crash, when she and Doc Bundy tangled at Riverside. Lyn's main recognition came from her Indianapolis drives, where she became the first woman to win

Rookie of the Year Honors for her 11th place finish, in 1992. While never a strong contender for a top-end finish, Lyn was, nevertheless, a quick and steady driver at Indy and in her 15 CART Indycar starts.

Des may well have been a faster, more aggressive, and ultimately more successful road racer than Lyn, but Lyn was far better in the vitally important area of sponsor relations. Where Des was reticent, Lyn was confident and aggressive and was able to establish a longstanding successful relationship with Ford Motor Company, finding significant amounts of sponsorship money for her Indy 500 races. Since retiring, she has continued to promote women racers through a series of foundations and activist programs and remains a leading figure in American racing, while Des has slipped into a quiet retirement, working with me in our track design business.

A combination of Lyn's business acumen and promotional ability and Desiré's driving skills, might well have propelled Des into the top ranks of American Indycar racing, but such a concept was never considered and, anyway, their careers ran simultaneously, so such a partnership could never have transpired.

When comparisons are made between Des and the best of her contemporary women drivers, there's little doubt that she stands out as the most versatile, accomplished, and fastest. While Lella Lombardi has the undeniable accolade of earning a coveted Grand Prix point (or, at least, half a point), her overall accomplishments don't compare and, in any case, on their single head-to-head encounter Des clearly out-performed the Italian girl, whose Williams was undoubtedly a better car than Des' (two-years-older) Ensign.

In American racing, there's been a surge of interest in women racers, thanks to Danica Patrick's rise to prominence.

Danica has become a media magnet, fuelled as much by her on-track exploits as by her celebrity status exploitation by some of her sponsors on TV and in magazines. On the track, she's now a veteran of over 100 Indycar races. She won at the Japanese Motegi track, in 2008, was third in the Indianapolis 500, in 2009, and finished her 2010 season with second place at Homestead, which shows how competitive she is on the ovals. Her attempts to make the grade in NASCAR's Sprint Cup have yet to be successful, but there's no doubt that Danica is the most marketable and recognised racing driver in the States. She is most

Danica. *Danica Patrick has raced very competitively in Indy cars, winning at Montegi, in Japan. She has become a major celebrity and marketing brand in the USA. (Courtesy IMS Photo)*

certainly the woman who has earned, by far, the most money in motorsport.

But Danica isn't the lone lady in the IndyCar Championship. Sarah Fisher, an engineer by training, pre-dated Danica in the series and has raced Indy cars off-and-on for some ten years. She now runs her own team and only recently announced her retirement from driving to start a family. While her results were patchy, she did put her car on the pole at Kentucky, back in 2000 and scored a third there; her best result. Katherine Legge entered ChampCar racing with a winning reputation in Formula Atlantic, ran several races, and moved back to Europe to race Audi's in the DTM. She has now moved back to the USA to try to restart her career in Indy cars.

Two other women made their Indycar debuts in 2010; the talented Swiss, Simona De Silvestro, who has won races in US Formula BMW and Formula Atlantic; and the Brazilian, Ana Beatriz.

Simona. Simona De Silvestro could be the lady to challenge Danica. The Swiss Indycar driver is extremely fast and determined, and may be the next top lady racer. (Courtesy IMS Photo)

Michelle. Possibly the best woman ever to compete in a car. Michelle Mouton was a star rally driver for Audi, but never made an impact on circuit racing. (Courtesy Press Release)

Desiré particularly rates Simone who, she feels, has the makings of a strong career. Venezuelan, Milka Duno had some success in sports car racing, but her Indycar speed has been lacking. In the 2010 junior Indy Lights series, English girl Pippa Mann scored several poles and one victory.

Other lady racers with undoubted talent include Susie Stoddard, who performed extremely well in lower level British single-seater races, attracting accolades that include two consecutive Autosport up-and-coming Driver of the Year finalist awards. She's currently a factory driver for Mercedes Benz in the in the German DTM series and, in 2010, had two points scoring finishes – better than DTM rookie David Coulthard. Katherine Legge raced for two seasons in Indy Cars and looked to have the talent to continue but, instead, moved back to Europe for a career with Audi in the DTM.

Comparing Des to other women drivers in other classes of racing is unfair to both. There have been many woman who have been extremely quick in less well known classes of racing, some of whom may have been able to beat her in their chosen cars – although the number of women who have beaten her head-to-head can be counted on one hand.

Comparisons with drivers in other motorsport disciplines is also difficult. Lady rally drivers, such as Pat Moss and Rosemary Smith, had major European success 60 years ago and, in the 1980s, Michel Mouton was certainly in the top handful of rally drivers, winning a World Championship round for Audi. Amazingly, there are currently no successful lady rally drivers, nor are there any top tier lady motorcycle racers. Only in drag racing do woman compete on equal terms.

Desiré watches the careers of all the women who show talent in the top forms of racing and wonders if any of these girls, or perhaps some future Michelle Schumacher, will ever make it to Formula 1.

Des very nearly did make it. Not just as a lady driver, but as one of the fastest and most competitive drivers of her time. But she was just one of many talented drivers who went unrewarded with a Formula career. Racing at the top of the sport is tough, competitive, and cruel to those who don't succeed. A few of those that she raced against did make it– but many more didn't.

Desiré is, by no means, the only outstanding driver not to earn a full time career in Formula 1, but she is one of a mere handful of women to get so close.

25

LIVING IN THE REAL WORLD

I N the middle of 1982, with her Formula 1 career over and few drives available in the UK, Des and I decided that we wanted to move to America to see what we could achieve there. So, after July's British Grand Prix meeting, we let John Webb know that we would be leaving Brands. We worked there for the rest of the year and left Brands on good terms with John and Angela and the whole staff, who gave Desiré a magnificent Graham Turner original painting of her winning the 1980 Aurora race. John also recognised her by naming the grandstand at the entrance to Paddock Bend the 'Desiré Wilson Stand,' a real honour, as other track elements featured famous racing personalities such as Graham Hill, Sir Jackie Stewart, Sir John Surtees, and Sir Jack Brabham.

Soon after we announced that we were leaving, I received a message from Bernie Ecclestone, asking if I would be interested in helping start-up a Formula 1 Grand Prix street event in New York City. As a result, we arrived in New York at the beginning of January 1983 to start a new life.

We moved to Manhattan and, then, quickly out to Forest Hills, in Queens, where we rented a small house, choosing to commute into Manhattan each day rather than put up with the incessant noise and hassle of big city life. For the next six months we both worked on the New York Grand Prix, a Formula 1 World Championship event that was planned to be held in September 1983, on a temporary track that would have run around the lake in Flushing Meadows

Grand Gesture. *John Webb commemorated Desiré's F1 win at Brands by naming a grandstand after her. 27 years later, the owners of Miller Motorsports Park, in Utah, did the same for me. (Courtesy Wilson Collection)*

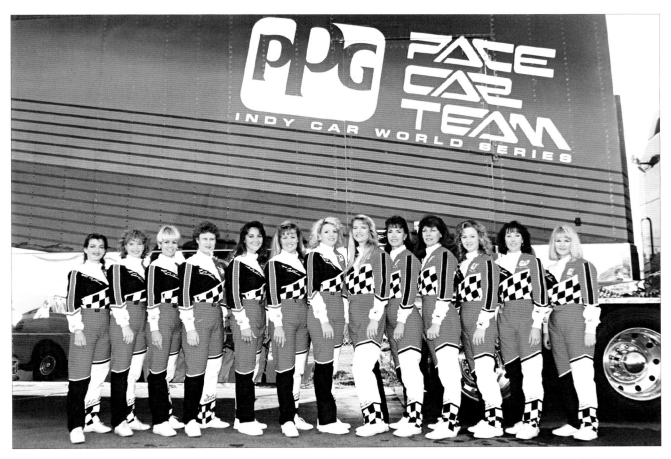

PPG Girls. *Des was a member of the PPG Pace Car team for 14 years. This programme supported the CART Indycar World Series, where the girls drove PPG clients around the tracks at high speed in a fleet of beautifully painted custom cars. (Courtesy Wilson Collection)*

Park, the site of the 1949 World Fair. Unfortunately, on the very day construction was due to start, we had a major problem. Although we finally had all the necessary permits, having endured several months of bitter political infighting between Queens politicians and anti-race activists, a conservationist group filed a law suit against the city, with the potential for several years of very expensive court activity. This led to the event being abandoned and the loss of my New York Grand Prix job. Fortunately, Des had just started her Indycar career, driving for the Wysards, which was very fortuitous because the income was very welcome.

From mid 1984 onwards, Des became a member of the PPG Pace Car Team that helped CART Indycar World Series sponsor, PPG Industries, promote

its paint products at Indycar events. The team, consisting of 15 or so lady race drivers, took prime customers around the various tracks at race speeds, driving highly modified show cars, each presented in vivid PPG paint schemes. The team was extremely professional and very well presented, providing Des with a 14 year part-time career in addition to her other full time jobs and race driving activities.

After a short period where we both worked for Desiré's South African Toyota dealer-owning boss, Dan Perkins, who had opened a Chevy dealership in Milford, Connecticut, we moved west to Columbus, Ohio. The purpose of the move was to establish, build, and run an IMSA GTP street race event for Jim Trueman, owner of the Truesport Indycar team, Mid Ohio Race track, and the Red Roof Inn chain of motels. Unfortunately, Jim, who was an exceptional person who we respected and liked very much, died of cancer within 18 months of our arrival in Columbus. Des and I then ran the event – myself as Executive Director and Des as office manager and accountant – for another four years. During this time, even while having to work exceptionally hard to turn the beleaguered street race into a profit making company, Desiré still worked with the Pace Car team, at some 15 or so Indycar races a year and raced as often as she could.

We moved to Denver at the end of 1989 and built our first house. I took up the position of VP of Operations for the new Indycar street race, to be run through the streets of Denver and when the CEO lost his position after the first race, I took over the company and ran a second and final event. While the Denver event was widely acclaimed as a great race and an exceptional city event, it was also founded on very badly drawn-up contracts with the city and nearly 250 property owners, so the event lost an immense sum of money. In fact, when asked by the company's Chairman, Roger Werner (who subsequently founded and ran the Speedvision television company), what my first task would be as the new President, I replied that it would be to shut the event down!

After closing the Denver Grand Prix Company, Roger Werner and Fred McCallister (whom I had brought in as my replacement as operations chief and whose daughter, Lauren, was to become Desiré and my godchild) started up a new company, Prime Racing Ventures, that set out to build a permanent race facility in the Denver market. This didn't work out; even though we found a location and secured permits, we couldn't wait the several years that it would take to secure NASCAR sanctions for the oval course. Instead, we concentrated on developing the basic groundwork for a major oval facility in Southern California, for what was to become the California Motor Speedway, in Fontana. Unfortunately, we were beaten in the final contract negotiations to build and operate the site by race industry legend, Roger Penske, who subsequently sold the giant facility to the International Speedway Corporation, owners of the Daytona, Talledega, and several other major ovals. Prime Racing Ventures closed after a failed attempt to buy Road Atlanta and Desiré (who had worked for PRV as office manager and accountant throughout its existence) and I decided that it was

time to establish our own business designing race tracks – Wilson Motorsport Inc.

Des has played an essential and valuable role in our company, handling all its administrative and accounting needs, as well as developing her skills working the CAD computer and assisting in track detail design. Her input, particularly in ensuring that tracks flow well and meet the racing needs of their users, has been an essential ingredient in the acclaim that our designs have received. Our company was also instrumental in working with Roger Werner's Speedvision cable TV company and the Sports Car Club of America, to redevelop their production car based professional race series, the World Challenge, into one of the USA's most prominent and successful racing series.

In 2005, we moved from Denver to Salt Lake City, Utah, to build and manage Miller Motor Sports Park, a track I designed for car dealer Larry Miller. Larry gave me the goal of building the very best track facility that I could and put up far more money that anyone ever expected in order to achieve his dream. Just 11 months after breaking ground, we opened the $100,000,000 super track and embarked on our first full season of professional and club racing. At the end of 2006, Larry's dream was recognised by the

Race Facility of the Year. In 2006, Miller Motorsports Park, the Wilson Motorsports-designed track in Utah, was declared Race Facility of the Year by the Professional World Motorsports Expo, in Cologne. (Courtesy Jeremy Henrie)

Mardi Gras. *New Orleans' Motorsport Park is under construction, just minutes from the famous French Quarter. It promises to become one of America's most spectacular club race track venues.*
(Courtesy Wilson Collection)

Mountain Magic. *The Wilsons' design for the new Inje Autopia track near Seoul, in Korea, was a real challenge due to the extreme elevation of this mountain setting. The track is due to open in 2012.*
(Courtesy Wilson Collection)

Professional World Motor Sports Expo, in Cologne, as its 'Race Facility of the Year,' as judged against every other track in the world. The following year we added an American round of the World Superbike Championship and were awarded the series' 'Race Organiser of the Year' trophy.

I left Miller at the end of 2008, to 'retire,' but, instead, Des and I set up a new business in conjunction with Tom Mabey's Sahara construction management company. Sahara had managed the construction of Miller Motorsports Park and we immediately found ourselves overwhelmed with design and development work.

In 2010, we focused our efforts on designing and helping with the construction of the new NOLA Motorsports Park, in New Orleans. This is a spectacular project that will surely become one of the country's most prominent race facilities.

Since 1994, Wilson Motorsport has become one of the most prolific race track design companies in the world, had opened 30 race facilities by the end of 2010, with a further seven or eight under design or construction and at least another 70 for which we have presented designs, but which, for one reason or another, have not been built. The finished tracks include Barber Motorsports Park, which is acclaimed as much for it beautiful surroundings as

for its challenging track; Autobahn Country Club, a private membership twin track facility near Chicago, and others such as GingerMan Raceway, Carolina Motorsports Park, Mid-America Motorplex, and the very successful Motorsports Park Hastings, in Nebraska. Inje Autopia, an FIA 2 level track under construction near Seoul, in Korea, is due to open in 2012.

While Wilson Motorsport is the center of our business lives, Desiré continues to work outside the company. Her skills and experience as a race driver have enabled her to become an excellent driver coach and she undertakes this role with the same levels of intensity and commitment that characterized her racing career.

Although Desiré's main focus in life has been driving a race car as fast as possible, she has always maintained a parallel life in the 'real world.' It would have been great to have earned a large income from her racing, but her time in the limelight didn't offer those opportunities, so she was forced to work extremely hard, all her life, to allow her racing career to prosper.

The girl from Brakpan has enjoyed an unusual, exciting, and fulfilling career. It's amazing to realize that she has raced for more than 50 years.

And she's still bloody fast!

153

FROM FIVE …

… TO FIFTY-FIVE

INDEX

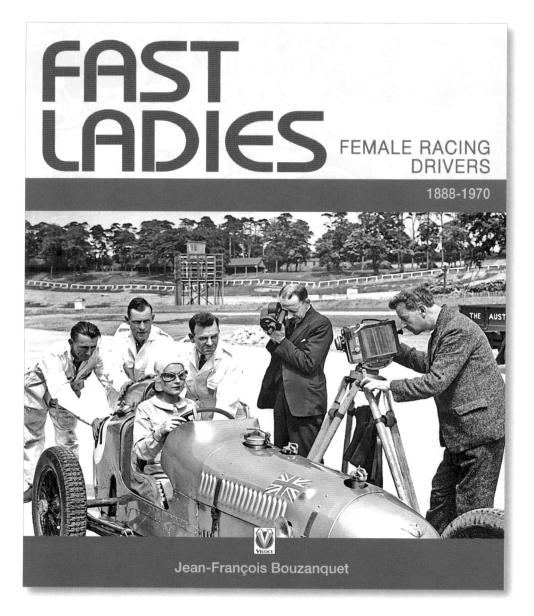

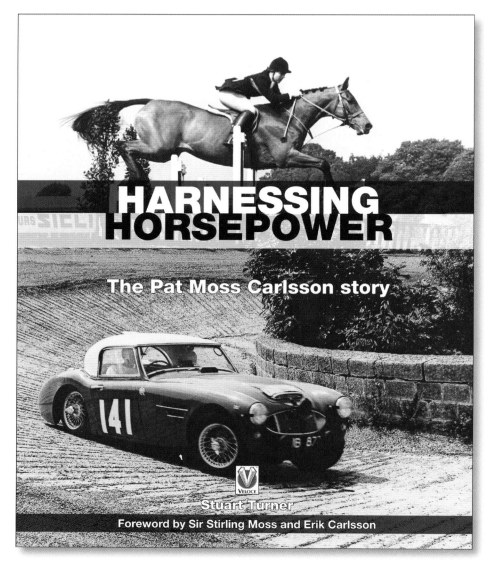